Additional Praise for *Teaching Is f...*

Hey, teachers, this one is for you! Whether you are a long-time
Daniel Bergman has filled this book with accessible ideas to imp
By reading this book, I know that Bergman's classroom is meaningful, purposeful, respectful, relevant,
and fun. Yours will be, too.

—**Joan Wink, Ph.D.,** Professor Emerita, California State University, Stanislaus

"*Teaching Is for Superheroes!* captured my attention from the first page. The connection to pop culture
is creative, innovative, and will engage future educators. As an educator and early childhood ally,
|I applaud the strong research foundation blended with stories from the field, sense of humor, and
real-life solutions essential for today's educators."

—**Jane Ann Benson,** Grand Rapids Community College

"Every teacher has those days when everything clicks and they feel superhuman, and every teacher has
those days when everything goes sideways, and they feel like a heel. Veteran teachers, pre-service
educators, novice teachers, and anyone serving in a mentor capacity for those in education will appreciate *Teaching Is for Superheroes!* A sagacious field guide for every educator and the teacher walking into
school for their first day alike, this resource covers all those "teacher life" moments through references
to the superheroes of comics and film so beloved today. You know—that other group of people who
attempt to accomplish the impossible daily."

—**James Bucky Carter, Ph.D.**

"In this book, Bergman draws upon his own experiences as a former secondary educator, providing
realistic examples of best teacher practices within the classroom, school district, and community. This
book is witty and clever and utilizes popular culture comic icons that many future educators can relate
to as they navigate the dispositions and traits of becoming successful classroom teachers and developing their own superhero powers of introspection, reflection, and growth mindset."

—**Cathie English, Ph.D.,** Associate Professor of English, Missouri State University

"Daniel Bergman's fantastic book shows teachers how to superpower their educational practices and
empower wonder, yearning, and learning within young minds captivated by the capes and cowls of
superheroes."

—**E. Paul Zehr, Ph.D.,** Author of *Becoming Batman, Chasing Captain America,* and more

"This is one of the most beneficial—and enjoyable—educator books I've read."

—**Maria Smith,** Maryland school educator

TEACHING IS FOR SUPERHEROES!

TEACHING IS FOR SUPERHEROES!

INSIGHT *AND* INSPIRATION *FOR* YOUR CLASSROOM

(TIGHTS AND CAPE OPTIONAL)

DANIEL J. BERGMAN

JB JOSSEY-BASS™

A Wiley Brand

Library of Congress Control Number:

2022059644 (print), LCCN 2022059645 (ebook)

Cover Design & Illustration: Paul McCarthy

Illustrations by Kevin H. Yancey

SKY10045494_041023

Dedicated to my teachers at O'Neill Public Schools, including Miss Evans, Mrs. Carroll, Mrs. Hansen, Mrs. Devall, Mrs. Tompkins, Mr. Hayes, Mr. Walters, Mrs. Tummins, Mr. Hrbek, Mr. Hostert, Mrs. Appleby, Mr. Larson, Miss Ball, Mr. Johnson, Mr. Davis, Mr. Kruse, Mr. Musson, Mr. Osenbaugh, Mr. and Mrs. Mueller, Miss Myers, Mr. Brosz, Mr. Hiebner, Mrs. Henderson, Mr. and Mrs. Scott, and everyone else who taught and inspired me—and countless others.

Contents

I have been reading comic books since I was around 6 years old. I was first introduced to superheroes with the 1966 *Batman* TV show, and then the *Super Friends* cartoon and the 1960s Spider-Man cartoon. These cartoons captured my imagination! My cousin, who was in high school at the time, would visit my house a few times a week after football practice and he would bring comic books. But more importantly, *he would leave them behind*. The adventures in these comics went way beyond the world I knew from the TV shows. My young mind was blown! Exploding with creativity and wonder, I knew immediately what I wanted to do with the rest of my life. I wanted to tell stories. I wanted to be a cartoonist.

I carried this dream to high school. On the first day of freshman year English, my teacher asked the class what we wanted to be when we grew up. She went around the room asking the same question to all the students. Most kids answered . . . fireman, doctor, lawyer. I said, "I want to be a cartoonist." My teacher seemed a bit confused when she asked me, "I think you misheard the question. What do you want to do for a living? To pay your bills? To support your family? I said again, "I want to be a cartoonist." I didn't care for that teacher too much. It wasn't her I didn't like. *It was the fact that she didn't* **believe in me**.

My junior year was a bit different. My first day in U.S. history class, we had to learn the Constitution in order to graduate. I sat there along with 30 other students ready for the most boring class ever to begin. In walks our teacher. She made it to her chair and sat down with an exhausting thud. Of course, us kids chuckled, but she looked at us with a scary glance, eyes above the glasses, and we all immediately quieted down. "Oh no, what have I gotten myself into? Why do we need this class to graduate? Is there a way I can get out of this?"

But then, Mrs. Ibom stood up and began to speak.

She talked about the current times. How the things happening now are a result of the things that happened years ago. How stories in the past plant seeds for stories in the future. How it's all connected. When she spoke, it was magic. She told *stories*. *We listened*. I don't even remember opening up my textbook. We didn't need to. Her stories were so amazing, I looked forward to her class every day. I didn't want the class to end. There was even a slight groan when the bell rang. She was a bit strict, didn't want talking in class, hated when students were late. But she was cool, and she cared about her students enjoying learning. She even had her own catchphrases.

You remember certain teachers for the rest of your life. They can give you knowledge that prepares you for the future. For life itself. I understand American history and am still fascinated by it because of my junior year U.S. history teacher. She walked around the room flaring out her arms, gesturing madly at times, and told these adventures. These stories. There were good guys. There were bad guys. There were people in struggle. Stories that unfolded. Main characters with dramatic endings. Just like in the comics.

Mrs. Ibom was a character unto herself. Her wig, her stature, her voice, her persona were her superpowers. Besides many art teachers, I think she taught me the most.

I don't remember if I ever showed her my drawings. I don't know if she knew I wanted to be a cartoonist. But one thing is for sure. She was super.

Superheroes are everywhere. They may be difficult to notice at first, but when you find them, you'll soon realize how super they are.

– Art Baltazar
Famous Cartoonist

Acknowledgments

Thanks to the entire team of superheroes at Jossey-Bass/Wiley for making this book possible: to Natalie Muñoz and Pete Gaughan for their leadership and expertise; to Kezia Endsley for her thorough edits and thoughtful comments; to Maria Smith and Brian Behrman for precise and positive feedback; to Julie Kerr for her pinpoint copyediting; to Prem Narayanan for putting it all together; to Mary Beth Rosswurm for keeping everyone connected; and to the design team who made everything look fantastic!

Kudos to Kevin Yancey for his amazing interior artwork plopping superheroes into the teaching world. Even I was unsure how to make this mash-up work, but he did so brilliantly with the perfect touch of fun.

Art Baltazar is a kind and generous creator, and a terrific ambassador for comics and children's literature. I'm humbled and honored to have his uplifting words in this book. Every teacher should have Art's books on their classroom shelves, and also catch a dose of his enthusiasm!

Andrea Braker is a brilliant, creative force for helping share the love of teaching and superheroes. Her work with Community Creative Services found all kinds of savvy avenues to spread the word.

Thanks to my teaching colleagues, friends, and family for their encouragement and examples in the classroom and beyond.

And of course, endless appreciation to—and for—my fabulous family: Jaunty Jonathan, Mighty Molly, Daring David, Magnificent May, Lively Lily, Busy Bea, and especially Lovely Laura!

About the Author

Daniel J. Bergman, Ph.D., is a Professor and Program Chair of Science Education at Wichita State University in Wichita, Kansas. Like Superman, he considers the Sunflower State his adoptive home. Unlike Superman, Dr. Bergman cannot leap tall buildings in a single bound.

Dr. Bergman previously taught middle and high school science in Nebraska and Iowa, and currently works with students and teachers from kindergarten to graduate school and every grade in between. As a fan of science, teaching, and superheroes, he is the ultimate SuperNerd. He writes about these passions at `www.teachlikeasuperhero.blog` and elsewhere.

Find out more at `www.danieljbergman.com`!

"This looks like a job for ..."

- Clark Kent,
Superman,
"The Mad Scientist" (1941)

Introduction

These days, you can't swing an enchanted hammer without hitting a caped crusader or masked vigilante. *Superheroes are everywhere,* jumping from comic books to store shelves, novelty socks and shirts, streaming series, and—of course—the silver screen.

Few film franchises have enjoyed the level of success as the Marvel Cinematic Universe (MCU), starring Iron Man, Captain America, Thor, Black Panther, Black Widow, Avengers, Guardians of the Galaxy, and many more. Over the past decade and a half, nearly 30 MCU movies have combined to make more than $25 billion worldwide (Clark 2022). According to Box Office Mojo (2022), almost one-fourth of the top 100 all-time earning films (worldwide) star superheroes from Marvel, DC Comics, and other sources.

Teachers are everywhere. In the United States alone, there are 3.2 million public school teachers, along with another half million private school teachers (NCES 2021). And don't forget the parents and guardians who teach 3.2 million homeschool students—over 5% of all school-age children in the United States (Ray 2021). New teachers mostly come from the 2,300 U.S. colleges or universities that award degrees and certificates in education (AACTE 2018). These teacher education programs prepare new teachers for initial licensure and support veteran teachers with postbaccalaureate degrees and professional development.

Such efforts are essential because *teachers need help*. Even before COVID-19, the annual teacher attrition rate was 8%, with higher numbers for low-income communities and high-demand subjects (Carver-Thomas and Darling-Hammond 2019). During the successive pandemic school years, teachers have reported twice as much stress and three times more depression than adults in other professions (Steiner and Woo 2021). It's no surprise, then, that more teachers are thinking of quitting; as many as half say they are "very likely" or "somewhat likely" to leave the profession in the next two years (Will 2021).

"We need new heroes. Ones suited for the times we're in."

– Sam Wilson,
The Falcon and the Winter Soldier,
"New World Order" (2021)

Teachers Are Superheroes

Both groups have *superpowers and specialties*. Strength. Speed. Does whatever a spider can. Can leap tall buildings in a single bound. Can get a class of first graders to sit still and listen to a story. Can inspire teenagers to apply algebra to their personal budgets. Possesses the stamina to grade a hundred essay exams in one weekend.

Both also have *hidden weaknesses*. Kryptonite. The color yellow. PowerPoint poisoning. Eighth period on Fridays. Chocolate.

Both groups have *super-cool names*. Mr. Incredible. Ms. Marvel. Doctor Strange. (Personally, I've had teachers named Mr. Little, Miss Ball, and Professor Snow.)

Both endure *never-ending trials and tribulations for the cause of good and the greater benefit of others*. Teachers may not save the world on a daily basis. But they do make a difference with individual lives, one day at a time.

Teaching Is for Superheroes! can make a difference in the lives of teachers. It is not a textbook, although it could be used in college classrooms and professional learning communities. It is not a self-help book, but teachers can review chapters to reflect on their practice and sharpen their skills. It is not a gift book or coffee table tome, even if it is the perfect present for celebrations, inspiration, and decoration.

Teaching Is for Superheroes! supports teachers and schools in all of these ways and more. With a dynamic format and visual style, it uses superhero archetypes and tropes to engage readers in a reflective examination of educational topics. Whether new or veteran, educators will find both practical information and meaningful motivation.

Admittedly, *Teaching Is for Superheroes!* is not a comprehensive compendium of every school issue. Teaching is context-sensitive and complex. Still, there are common issues and applications to explore. And given the ever-expanding multiverse of superhero media, it may feel like I barely scratch the surface. Examples will mostly stick to well-known characters and stories. Even so, I'll sneak in a few deep cuts and Easter eggs for all of you true believers and superfans to enjoy.

The "teachers are superheroes" metaphor is not just a pandering slogan riding atop a pop culture wave. Rather, this analogy provides a rich venue through which teachers can thoughtfully analyze their purpose and pedagogy: origin stories, secret identities, costumes and gadgets, powers, weaknesses, archvillains, allies, and more. Each of these superhero themes is an inspirational springboard for practical insight and application in the classroom.

Although there is a general sequence to the chapters, readers can skip around and go in any order. Start with the items that interest you most. Or seek out your favorite superheroes. (There's a nifty index in the back that lists teaching topics, educational leaders, and all the featured characters—super neat!)

Look for additional features in *Teaching Is for Superheroes!* such as

- Heroic quotes from an array of eras and media.
- "Thought Bubbles" for private contemplation.
- "Caption Captures" for quick-write reactions.
- "$uper $avers" for cost-effective habits.
- Recommended resources for "To Be Continued" reading, viewing, and learning.

Plus, each chapter provides questions for reflection and discussion, along with other elements linking teacher quality and superhero phenomena. The school setting may not be as glamorous as futurist skyscrapers, alien planets, or alternate universes. But the adventure is just as exciting—and *real*!

Questions for Reflection and Discussion

1. Who is your favorite superhero from film, comic books, or elsewhere? What about them inspires you as a teacher?
2. How have your heroes changed from childhood to now? In what ways have they stayed the same?
3. Who is an inspirational classroom teacher? How have they inspired and informed your teaching?

4. What is your honest reaction to the phrase "teachers are superheroes!"?

5. What about teaching makes it unique with respect to other professions or callings in life?

References

American Association of Colleges for Teacher Education. (2018). Colleges of education: a national portrait. https://secure.aacte.org/apps/rl/res_get.php?fid=4178&ref=rl.

Box Office Mojo. (2022). Top lifetime grosses, worldwide. https://www.boxofficemojo.com/chart/top_lifetime_gross/?area=XWW.

Carver-Thomas, D., and Darling-Hammond, L. (2019). The trouble with teacher turnover: How teacher attrition affects students and schools. *Education Policy Analysis Archives* 27 (36). http://dx.doi.org/10.14507/epaa.27.3699.

Clark, T. (2022). All 27 Marvel Cinematic Universe movies, ranked by how much money they made at the global box office. *Business Insider* (16 May). https://www.businessinsider.com/marvel-movies-ranked-how-much-money-at-global-box-office-2021-11.

National Center for Education Statistics. (2021). Back-to-school statistics. https://nces.ed.gov/fastfacts/display.asp?id=372#PK12-teachers.

Ray, B.D. (2021). How many homeschool students are there in the United States? Pre-COVID-19 and Post-COVID-19: new data. National Home Education Research Institute. https://www.nheri.org/how-many-homeschool-students-are-there-in-the-united-states-pre-covid-19-and-post-covid-19/.

Steiner, E.D., and Woo, A. (2021). Job-related stress threatens the teacher supply: key findings from the 2021 state of the U.S. teacher survey. RAND Corporation. https://www.rand.org/pubs/research_reports/RRA1108-1.html.

Will, M. (2021). The teaching profession in 2021 (in charts). *Education Week* (20 December). https://www.edweek.org/teaching-learning/the-teaching-profession-in-2021-in-charts/2021/12.

> ## "I'm just a kid from Brooklyn."

– Steve Rogers,
Captain America: The First Avenger
(2011)

Origin Stories

An alien baby lands on Earth, grows up in Kansas, and uses superhuman strength to champion truth, justice, and a better tomorrow.

After witnessing the death of his parents as a child, a billionaire swears to fight criminals–a superstitious and cowardly lot.

An ordinary teenager bitten by a radioactive spider discovers that with great power comes great responsibility.

Every superhero has one. So does every teacher.

What is *your* "origin story"?

Tales of Passion!

If you've read Spider-Man's origin story (or seen it depicted on film), you know that Peter Parker initially exploited his newly gained spider abilities to earn quick money. In fact, he was sort of a selfish spider-jerk. It took tragic consequences for Peter to eschew apathy, accept responsibility, and, ultimately, use his powers to help others.

Like superheroes, teachers' endeavors arise from a passion to make a difference. Often, this passion was ignited through life-changing experiences. Such experiences might occur at a single, memorable "flashbulb" moment in time. Perhaps more frequently, there is a slower, gradual development peppered with key steps. These events can be good, bad, and anywhere in between.

Spider-Man's life-changing experience was tragic and traumatic, a common trend among superheroes' backstories. Murder. Abuse. Crime. Exploding planets. Hopefully your teaching origins are absent of too much death and drama. But in all honesty, some teachers did choose this profession following an unfortunate or negative experience in their own youth. To right a wrong, if you will.

My Tragic Backstory

I'll never forget my kindergarten gym class, and it's all because of the wrong reasons. Instead of fun activities like scooter soccer, rope climbing, or parachute canopy, the only memory I have is getting in trouble with the P.E. teacher. It happened one day as we lined up following obligatory stretches.

I don't remember what I did, but I know it wasn't on purpose. Mr. Clench—that's not his real name, but it sounds like a supervillain—must have thought I was misbehaving. He stormed over and yanked my five-year-old frame out of the student line. Grabbing me by both my biceps, Mr. Clench lifted me up to his eye level and began yelling. I don't recall his particular words, but they were loud and full of spittle. After returning my fragile, quivering body to the padded floor, Mr. Clench ordered me to sit out in the hall for the rest of gym class. For the next 30 minutes, I listened to the delighted squeals of my classmates through the closed door. Even worse, I received shameful glances from the hallway traffic. Everyone who passed by knew why I was sitting out there. I was the "bad kid."

The entire experience still makes me shiver. But thankfully, that's about as traumatic as my childhood ever got. And the experience became a good enough excuse for my subpar pull-up performance.

I don't remember getting in much trouble throughout the rest of my K-12 education. So maybe Mr. Clench's aggressive model of discipline did the trick. Like the Punisher's methods of cleaning crime off the streets . . . permanently. Actually, a healthy upbringing by my parents and other caring adults had more impact. At least, I like to think so.

Mr. Clench didn't kill me, but I believe his aggressive intervention did significantly impact my pathway toward adulthood, as well as my teaching. I tell myself and my students that I will never yell at them in class. Safety issues aside, there are other ways to communicate clearly and directly. Whenever I do feel irritated with my students (or children at home), a recollection of Mr. Clench's vice grip and bulging neck veins comes to mind, helping me keep perspective.

That's just one example. How about you? Do you have negative educational experiences motivating you to be a better teacher? It doesn't have to be flashy or theatrical. Maybe you were just bored in school for so long, and now you've sworn to fight such stagnation as a teacher. That's a good motivator right there. And a noble cause, if I've ever seen one.

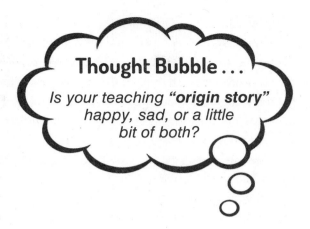

Thought Bubble . . .

Is your teaching "origin story" happy, sad, or a little bit of both?

Happier Thoughts

While tragedy makes for a good backstory, some superheroes find their passion from more positive experiences. Although Superman lost his parents (and entire home planet), he benefited from a wholesome upbringing by adoptive parents Pa and Ma Kent. After growing up in literal "paradise," Wonder Woman chose to leave her secret island home to help war-torn humanity. Tim Drake—the third Robin—was a smart kid who figured out Batman's identity and convinced the Dark Knight to accept him as his sidekick.

One of my favorite "cheerful" origin stories is that of teen superhero Mark Grayson, aka Invincible (Kirkman and Walker 2003/2021). Although the storyline of *Invincible* takes all kinds of twists and turns, its beginning is rather quaint. At the outset, Mark thought he was an ordinary half-human son of a superpowered alien hero. But when his own super strength manifested while throwing out the garbage (launching a trash bag into orbit), Mark simply smiled and said, "It's about time."

What do you remember about the time you decided to be a teacher?

I'd bet most teachers entered the profession due to positive educational experiences. They can name a teacher, or several, who inspired them to be where they are today. My personal list of caring, dynamic teachers impacting me outnumbers Mr. Clench by at least 10 to 1. (See the dedication at the front of this book.)

One of those individuals—Miss Evans, which is her real name—was my homeroom kindergarten teacher. The only other event I remember from my devastating P.E. discipline experience happened during recess later in the morning that very same day. Miserable and still shell-shocked, I stood alone on the playground, underneath the shadow of the broken tetherball pole. That's when Miss Evans came over and asked me what was wrong.

I shook my head and said, "Nuthin'."

She asked if I wanted to tell her anything, and my response was the same. Without another word, Miss Evans waited beside me on the playground, until we all returned to her classroom to finish the day. I'm pretty sure she heard what happened and wanted to get the facts straight. But Miss Evans said no more about it the rest of the year. She was a first-year teacher that fall, brand new to the building just like me.

Last I checked, Miss Evans still teaches at the same school, four decades and counting. She was one of the first people who received my graduation announcements—for high school, college, and my Ph.D.

If you haven't done so, make a point to send your influential teachers a letter or card. Write kind words expressing your appreciation for their positive impact in your life. If that person is still teaching, your thoughtful gesture alone could inspire them to teach for another 10 years.

In addition to positive role models, many teachers have positive memories of school. There are plenty of social and extracurricular activities to remember fondly, but teachers also frequently recall classroom experiences. These could be vivid lessons that evoked "Aha!" moments in one's mind. They could be enjoyable activities involving collaboration or competition. We were engaged in meaningful, memorable lessons—including some we may even use in our own classrooms today.

Catchy Catchphrases and Super Slogans

Along with activities and strategies, some of us even use exact phrases and mottos borrowed from influential teachers. Sort of like repeating our parents' patterns when raising our own kids, teachers often reuse or rebrand favorite classroom mantras.

"There's no such thing as a stupid question."

"Fair does not mean equal."

"I do not give grades; my students earn them."

"You can disagree without being disagreeable."

If you find yourself lacking in catchphrases, look no further than your favorite superheroes for inspiration. Many of these can translate to the classroom with minor (or zero) modifications:

"Up, up and awaayyyyy!"

"Here I come to save the day!"

"Your friendly neighborhood Spider-Man."

"SHAZAM!" (Educators should like this one, since it's an acronym.)

"Don't make me angry. You wouldn't like me when I'm angry."

Again, these are mere suggestions for inspiration, not direct duplication. I'd be careful using the previous quote by Dr. Bruce Banner, and advise avoiding the following two favorites from his angry alter ego:

"Hulk SMASH!"

"Puny humans!"

Legendary Marvel creator Stan Lee hatched the catchphrase "Excelsior!" to use as his standard sign-off. At first, this word seems like nonsense. But it's actually the state motto for New York, a Latin term for "to the highest," or "ever upward" (Lee, David, and Doran 2015; Thomas 2006). That's a terrific sentiment for schools and students, too.

Caption Capture: Write down your **favorite** catchphrases, mantras, or mottos for the classroom.

Catchphrases are also useful for encapsulating one's mission in life. Consider these superhero slogans:

- "Sworn to protect a world that hates and fears them." (X-Men)
- "With great power comes great responsibility." (Spider-Man)
- "Wakanda Forever!" (Black Panther)
- "Higher. Further. Faster." (Captain Marvel)
- "I am vengeance, I am the night, I am Batman!"

Without getting into all of the details, these phrases get at the heart of the characters. There's obviously more complexity when you dig deeper, but a simple sentence can still convey the general idea. It's concise and memorable, ready to share when the opportunity arises.

When was the last time someone asked you, "Why do you want to be a teacher?"

It could have been a friend or family member who asked about your career decision. Or maybe a student in class yesterday. Or during one of your job interviews. Every teacher hears the question at least once. Or a hundred times.

Do you have an answer? A good answer?

I don't have the best answer to the question. But here's how I respond when someone asks me why I teach: "I love to learn and I want to share that love with others."

There are other reasons, sure, but that sums it up nice and clean. A heroic catchphrase, so to speak, like those of the heroes above. The late teacher and astronaut (and hero) Christa McAuliffe shared one of the better slogans teachers can use: "I touch the future. I teach."

Here are a few other statements with their attributed origins. You often find these words in front of gorgeous landscape photographs on inspirational classroom posters:

- "Education is not the filling of a pail but the lighting of a fire." – William Butler Yeats
- "The highest result of education is tolerance." – Helen Keller
- "Education is not preparation for life; education is life itself." – John Dewey
- "Education must not simply teach work; it must teach life." – W.E.B. DuBois
- "The future is worth it. All the pain. All the tears. The future is worth the fight." – Martian Manhunter

Okay, so that last one actually has comic book origins; but it's still applicable to why we teach, isn't it? Look back at your past experiences—both good and bad—and try to summarize your passion for teaching in just a few words. You don't have to divulge your entire life story, but a few powerful words can make a lasting impact.

One of my colleagues shares the following motto with her classes of future teachers: "Go be brilliant." It's a simple phrase, but I find it particularly "brilliant" because of the numerous meanings of that word—intelligent, illuminating, amazing. And it works. This short phrase is so memorable that her students write it on their graduation caps during commencement ceremonies. And I'm sure they remember to be brilliant in their classrooms, too, for years to come.

"Every great superhero origin story starts with a grappling hook."

– Fred,
Big Hero 6 (2014)

Finding Purpose

Whether you became a teacher due to positive or negative influences, or, more likely, a mixture of both, your motivation to teach does not rest on past experiences alone. There is something in the present that drives you. Or maybe it's a focus toward the future, like Christa McAuliffe's famous quote. You not only need passion for teaching; you need a purpose. Like a grappling hook, your purpose anchors your teaching.

Purpose is intricately linked to heroes' origins. Batman hunts down criminals to avenge his murdered parents. Spider-Man fights crime due to an undying responsibility he learned from his fallen Uncle Ben. The Fantastic Four use their powers and inventions to explore unknown worlds. The X-Men protect fellow mutants and humans alike in an effort to create a safe world for both species. Likewise, many teachers may refer to past experiences as they explain their current reasons for teaching.

Regardless of prior influences, teachers still work in the "here and now" as they shape students' lives for the "there and then" future. I encourage every teacher to consider this convergence of past, present, and future in their classroom. It is a key foundation to the work I share with teachers.

Near the start of every school year, every teacher should envision the final day of classes. Consider your students as they leave your classroom one last time. Imagine what those kids will be like. In an ideal world, what talents, skills, attitudes, and attributes will they exhibit?

You may never see some of these students ever again. What lasting legacy do you want to make on those kids? What do you want them to be like as a result of spending nine months together in your classroom?

Brainstorm the qualities you believe all citizens should possess to promote a productive society. Write down any thoughts that come to mind—ideas like compassion, critical thinking, and creativity. Create an all-encompassing wish list for education and humankind. Do not worry about potential duplicates. As fast as you can, start writing your ideas. (Hint: use pencil or erasable ink.)

Caption Capture: What are your **long-term goals** for students? Describe the traits and skills you want them to exhibit by the end of the school year.

After working your mind and scraping down to the bottom of your brain's barrel, take a break. Wait an hour or a day. During this time off, think of items you want to add. Include them when you return to your master list.

Did you take a break? Good!

Are you back now? Great!

Now you will want to examine your exhaustive recipe for utopia's residents. Scrutinize your list and simplify it. What traits are common? Where do you see synergy? Merge these two, three, or more similar phrases into one category. For example, the following three items—a) students will show respect to teachers, b) students will appreciate diversity, and c) students will have a sense of self-worth—may be combined to the following goal: "Students will possess respect for themselves, other students, and teachers."

Ultimately, work your visionary list down to about 10 items, give or take one or two. You don't want too many, or you will not be able to remember all of your goals. You don't want too few, however, which may become too broad and difficult to articulate. If you think of another goal during this process, add it or merge it with an existing item. Always feel free to imagine and include new goals you deem important.

Once you have trimmed your list into a manageable size, clean it up. Compose sentences beginning with the words "Students will . . ." or something similar. Avoid unnecessary or repetitive words. Focus on the end product. Use action verbs for straightforward goals. Convert "develop," "have," and "become," into overt actions such as "demonstrate," "show," and "exhibit." The example goal used here could become "Students will exhibit respect for others and themselves."

The following image shows a sample list of visionary goals for students in a science classroom (middle or high school), which is my professional background. You'll notice, however, that most of these student goals are not exclusive to science or any particular subject. Use this example to jumpstart a vision-casting exercise for your own classroom context.

Sample goals list for a science classroom.

What goals do you have for your students?

Students will . . .

1. Demonstrate a robust understanding of science concepts and practices.

2. Use critical thinking skills to investigate and solve problems.

3. Exhibit effective communication and cooperative skills.

4. Exercise creativity and curiosity.

5. Set goals, make informed decisions, and self-evaluate.

6. Convey an appreciation for science as a human endeavor.

7. Apply scientific knowledge and skills in other enterprises.

8. Participate as productive citizens in their communities and beyond.

This is not the only list of educational goals, nor is it the best list. That's because it's mine. What's your vision for students? Make your goals list personal, professional, and passionate. Although similar in format, your goals list is *not* the same as what you use for lesson or unit objectives. Whereas objectives deal with specific outcomes or curriculum context, these goals apply to the *entire* year of teaching. Moreover, they should permeate every lesson. If it helps, you also can think of this goals list as an itemized mission statement.

Determine your inner beliefs for learning and life. Then develop your agenda accordingly. Starting today, how will you shape tomorrow's teachers, leaders, voters, and parents?

Your list should be a living entity. It will change with time. Over the course of a school year, reflect on your list and update your goals. And you must promote them. Your goals for students will thrive only when you give them appropriate attention.

Promotion of visionary goals is not an extra burden on your classroom teaching. All teachers promote certain student goals in their classrooms. The challenge is to bypass passive, disconnected, rote memorization in favor of active, interconnected mastery of concepts and skills. Your list of goals will guide intentional teaching. Remember the quotable advice of Hall of Fame baseball player Yogi Berra: "If you don't know where you are going, you might wind up someplace else."

Always keep your list of goals accessible. Slip copies inside your lesson planner and teaching guides. Refer to your goals daily as you plan, teach, and evaluate your lessons. Some teachers have posted their goals on door-sized signs in their classrooms. Such prominence not only motivates you, but also addresses occasional inquiries posed by your students. When they question a particular lesson's purpose (e.g., "Why are we doing this?"), you can simply point and smile.

Interestingly, many of the skills and characteristics teachers frequently identify in their list of long-term goals align with what people want from their schools. Not only should students gain content knowledge, they should acquire the dispositions necessary for succeeding in a dynamic society and challenging workforce. This includes 21st century skills, abilities designated necessary to succeed in our "information age"– communication, collaboration, analytical thinking, problem-solving, creating, innovating, researching, and evaluating information (NEA 2012; P21 2008). Another popular initiative is "career and college ready" students, who possess not only academic knowledge, but also higher-order thinking strategies, social and emotional intelligence, self-directedness, adaptability, civic engagement, and other life skills (ACT 2022; NPTA 2022).

More than alignment with a set of standards or initiatives, your classroom goals list (your vision) has merit because it instills your professional purpose with personal passion. Intentional planning and inclusion of these goals in your instruction can create timeless memories for your students.

Born or Made?

Most of us were not bitten by a radioactive teacher. Or injected with a super-teacher serum. Does that mean good teachers are born? Or are they made?

This fundamental dichotomy is better known as "nature vs. nurture." Are we born with built-in capacities? Or do we have to learn them?

We all know individuals who appear naturally gifted as teachers. They seem to effortlessly exhibit the abilities and attitudes of effective classroom instruction. They're personable and perceptive, quick-thinking and charismatic, able to build rapport with all kinds of students.

Most of us did not acquire all of these skills naturally. We have to learn fundamental principles and practice necessary competencies. But the truth is that everyone has strengths and weaknesses (more on that in Chapters 5 and 7). And we can all get better. Even those teachers who are inherently talented still have to improve and refine their skills.

A useful analogy is the X-Men. Back in the early 1960s, Stan "The Man" Lee, Jack "The King" Kirby, and other creators were churning out new characters every month, including the Fantastic Four (November 1961), the Incredible Hulk (May 1962), Doctor Doom (July 1962), Spider-Man (August 1962), Thor (August 1962), Iron Man (March 1963), and the Avengers (September 1963).

Each Marvel hero (and villain) had their own origin story and unique super-power pathway. In 1963, writer Stan Lee envisioned a new team of teen superheroes, but struggled with how they got their powers. He admits he took the easy route and just decided, "They were born that way. They were mutants!" (quoted in Hiatt 2014). Thus arose Cyclops, Marvel Girl, Beast, Iceman, Angel, their mentor Professor X, and—eventually—a hundred different X-Men.

Even though Marvel's merry mutants possess inborn superpowers, they still have much to learn. Attending Xavier's School for Gifted Youngsters (isn't that a great name?), the X-Men work to harness their abilities, collaborate as a team, and serve those they have sworn to protect.

Sounds a little like teachers, doesn't it?

You may not be a mutant, but perhaps you do have a genetic disposition for classroom prowess. And like the X-Men, you must learn and "evolve" with enhanced abilities and expanding applications.

Year One

Many teachers will tell you they remember learning the most during their first year of teaching. "First" rhymes with "worst," and many veteran educators will admit their toughest and least successful year of teaching was Year One.

Several critically acclaimed comic book issues and movies feature "Year One" stories. These tales explore commonly known origin stories, expanding on the narrative and reexamining the mythos. *Batman: Year One* was a miniseries written by Frank Miller and illustrated by David Mazzucchelli (1987). While Miller is more famous for his take on an older, grizzled Batman in *The Dark Knight Returns* (1986), his *Year One* tale is often copied and considered the definitive origin story of DC's Caped Crusader. *Year One* starts with a pre-caped, pre-Batman Bruce Wayne struggling with grief and finding his way. Through successes and failures, Bruce develops his skills, dons his Batman identity, and acquires a few allies (and enemies) along the way. If that sounds familiar, the story is pretty much the basis for film director Christopher Nolan's lauded Dark Knight trilogy, starting with *Batman Begins* (2005). More recently, a slate of superhero television series have taken their time exploring the ups and downs of a well-known hero's infancy (*Ms. Marvel, Green Arrow, The Flash, Supergirl, Gotham,* etc.).

Year One stories are quite popular. DC Comics has published over a dozen miniseries with this first-year focus, featuring all kinds of characters–Robin, Batgirl, Huntress, Black Lightning, even Metamorpho (look him up). They even spent an entire year's annual issues on the topic back in 1995.

DC doesn't own the exclusive copyright on Year One stories. Marvel Comics has produced some of these first-year tales about heroes (including Spider-Man, the X-Men, the Punisher, and more). One of the most beloved Year One Marvel tales is *Daredevil: The Man Without Fear* (1993), which coincidentally was also written by Frank Miller (with art by John Romita Jr.). Miller builds off of Daredevil's original origin story—created by Stan Lee, Bill Everett, and Jack Kirby—and adds more nuanced intricacies and dramatic elements.

Teachers with current or recent Year One experiences assuredly understand that teaching is not just born. You have to work at it.

If you're a veteran of many years (or decades), you can hopefully remember the trials of managing through that first year. For some of us, Year One is shrouded in a fog of fatigue, confused student faces (and our own in the mirror), wobbly classroom management, late nights of preparing lessons and materials, figuring out how to fill every single day with meaningful instruction (*Just do something!*), and grading papers. (As one of my colleagues says, every teacher wants to apologize to their first year of students.)

Fortunately, a lot of that first-year grit eventually transforms into pearls of wisdom you use to guide students and encourage colleagues, especially those deer-in-the-headlights new teachers down the hall. (See Chapter 10 for more on mentoring others.) You learn so much that first year—indeed maybe more than all of the semesters you spend studying and practicing in preparation. Use those awkward and challenging experiences as a springboard for ongoing growth and development.

How you taught your first year of teaching should be much different than how you teach your second year, your fifth, tenth, twentieth, and so on. You hone your craft, try new techniques, and refresh your content knowledge year by year, day by day, minute by minute. That's what keeps it interesting!

$uper $aver!
Advice is FREE. Ask trusted veterans how they survived (and thrived) during their early years. Learn about your current students by talking with teachers who taught them the previous year.

Year One stories are not all grim and actually can be quite fun. Consider the adventure of stretching your muscles and trying new things. This often results in soaring high as well as failing miserably moments later, just like it is with new superheroes. But the best part is you keep that optimism and keep on going.

Maybe that's why we enjoy origin stories so much.

To Be Continued!

Further Reading

Kirkman, R. and Walker, C. (2003/2021). *Invincible Volume 1: Family Matters*. Portland, OR: Image Comics.

Miller, F. and Mazzucchelli, D. (1987/2007). *Batman: Year One*. New York: DC Comics.

Miller, F. and Romita Jr., J. (1993/2010). *Daredevil: The Man Without Fear*. New York: Marvel Comics.

Waid, M., Augustyn, B., and Kitson, B. (1998/2017). *JLA: Year One*. New York: DC Comics.

Further Viewing

Ali, B.K. and Feige, K. (producers), El Arbi, A. and Fallah, B. (directors). (2022). *Ms. Marvel* [Television series]. Marvel Studios.

Arad, A., Pascal, A., Lord, P., Miller, C., and Steinberg, C. (producers), Persichetti, B., Ramsey, P., and Rothman, R. (directors). (2018). *Spider-Man: Into the Spider-Verse*. [Motion picture]. Marvel/Sony Pictures.

Feige, K. (producer) and Johnston, J. (director). (2011). *Captain America: The First Avenger* [Motion picture]. Marvel Studios/Paramount Pictures.

History Channel. (2018). Superheroes decoded playlist. History. https://www.youtube.com/watch?v=C7pZRfMmNxM&list=PLob1mZcVWOaj613Br1bq3VNqNT_3Mn9sQ.

Roven, C., Thomas, E., and Franco, L. (producers), and Nolan, C. (director). (2005). *Batman Begins* [Motion picture]. Warner Bros. Pictures.

Questions for Reflection and Discussion

1. How do you respond to "Why are you a teacher?" What might change depending on who asked you?
2. What about your origin story is "tragic" like Batman's or Spider-Man's?
3. Why do you suppose so many superheroes' origin stories are tragic? Is it more important for teachers to have happy or tragic origin stories?

4. Without sounding superficial, how can you share your catchphrase or slogan as a teacher? (Here are some resources for finding inspirational quotes or mottos for the classroom: https://parade.com/1034814/marynliles/education-quotes/. Or sign up to receive a "Quote of the Day" from websites such as https://wisdomquotes .com/quote-of-the-day/ or https://www.brainyquote.com/quote_of_the_day.)

5. To what extent are good teachers born? Made?

6. What are your Top 10 visionary goals for your students? If possible, make a list with colleagues. If you are daring, try this exercise with your students.

7. How would you respond to someone who said, "You don't have time to include long-term goals in your teaching. Just stick to the curriculum pacing guide."?

8. Near the end of each year, ask your students what advice they'd give the next year of students following them. Use their ideas as inspirational words to display in the classroom, as well as insight to revise your long-term goals.

9. What sort of memories do you have from your Year One teaching experience?

10. If you are in your Year One of teaching or will begin soon, what main accomplishments do you hope to achieve?

11. How much of your origin story do you feel comfortable sharing with your students? Colleagues? In what ways?

12. How much of your students' origin stories do you want to know?

References

ACT. (2022). ACT College and Career Readiness Standards. https://www.act.org/content/act/en/college-and-career-readiness/standards.html.

Hiatt, B. (2014). The true origins of "X-Men." *Rolling Stone* (26 May). https://www.rollingstone.com/tv-movies/tv-movie-news/the-true-origins-of-x-men-77108/.

Kirkman, R. and Walker, C. (2003/2021). *Invincible Volume 1: Family Matters*. Portland, OR: Image Comics.

Lee, S., David, P., and Doran, C. (2015). *Amazing Fantastic Incredible: A Marvelous Memoir*. New York: Gallery Books/Simon & Schuster.

Miller, F. (1986/2016). *Batman: The Dark Knight Returns 30th Anniversary Edition*. New York: DC Comics.

Miller, F. and Mazzucchelli, D. (1987/2007). *Batman: Year One*. New York: DC Comics.

Miller, F. and Romita, Jr., J. (1993/2010). *Daredevil: The Man Without Fear*. New York: Marvel Comics.

National Education Association. (2012). Preparing 21st century students for a global society: an educator's guide to the four Cs.

National Parent Teacher Association. (2022). Is your student college or career ready? Components of CCR. https://www.pta.org/home/family-resources/college-and-career-readiness/College-and-Career-Readiness-Components.

Partnership for 21st Century Skills. (2008). 21st century skills, education & competitiveness: a resource and policy guide. Battelle for Kids. http://www.p21.org/storage/documents/21st_century_skills_education_and_competitiveness_guide.pdf.

Roven, C., Thomas, E., and Franco, L. (producers), and Nolan, C. (director). (2005). *Batman Begins* [Motion picture]. Warner Bros. Pictures.

Thomas, R. (2006). *Stan Lee's Amazing Marvel Universe*. New York: Sterling Publishing Co., Inc.

> "I promise loyalty.
> I promise secrecy.
> And I promise courage."

— Batgirl,
Batgirl: Year One #9 (2003)

Secret Identities

How much of your origin story should you share?

During my first year of teaching on the very first day of school, I presented to my students a carefully crafted PowerPoint slideshow. It was all about me: my hometown, my family, my hobbies, my school and college experiences, and so on. As an added treat, I embellished this autobiographical exposition with pictures and bullet-listed highlights.

Big mistake.

Not because I divulged secrets that would come back to haunt me. On the contrary, most of these high school students—I'm guessing 95%—could *not* have cared less about my personal history. I had committed one of the cardinal sins of teaching: too much information (TMI).

Besides wasting nearly an entire class period, all my info dump accomplished was annoying and boring the students. They didn't give one fig how many football halftime shows I performed with the University of Nebraska's Cornhusker Marching Band during my college career (it was 37, by the way, each home game a sellout crowd).

My students were most interested in why they should care about coming to my science class. And secretly, they wanted to know if I cared about them and *their* personal highlights and histories.

Q&A FYI (No TMI)

In subsequent years, I've spent my first days of school inviting students to do more talking. They have the freedom and responsibility to choose conversational topics. It's basically a brief Q&A session, but all questions come from the students.

Specifically, the students have to ask me questions about myself or the class. The challenge is to get the teacher to give informative and useful answers. If you need to encourage student participation—especially with older grades—you can post a lengthy book reading/writing assignment on the board and tell them if there is ever more than 30 seconds between questions, the class must complete this homework. You'll probably never need to use this book assignment, but it's there for motivation. After the first few questions get the ball rolling, students typically have no problem coming up with more. Students can ask anything they like. There are only two rules:

- Questions must be in good taste.
- The teacher has the right to refuse answering any question.

Caption Capture: What questions do you want students to **ask you**? Write down examples.

Compare this interactive Q&A session with the PowerPoint info dump from my first year. Students still get to know me as an individual, but they get to listen and learn about things *they* find interesting. Rather than how many of my relatives are teachers, maybe they want to know where I bought my shoes. They may not care that I marched in two Orange Bowl Parades; but they do want to know if I'm coming to their next volleyball game. Instead of me telling them why my class is so great, they can ask me about specific projects, content, and procedures. The students decide what is important to discuss.

The most powerful outcome of this Q&A is not what the students learn, but what they practice. It goes back to my long-term goals, my visionary purpose for teaching. Starting with this first-day activity, the students develop skills and habits that go beyond the school experience. From this one simple exercise:

- They consider how to respectfully ask questions and foster appropriate discussion.
- They think and talk at higher levels of reasoning—application, analysis, synthesis, and evaluation (Anderson et al. 2001; Bloom 1956).
- They listen to each other and the teacher, working to continue a conversation and evaluate information.
- They use critical thinking skills and grow in their awareness of others and the world.

Through this single Q&A activity, I promote several of my long-term goals for students (see Finding Purpose in the previous chapter). Moreover, I can build off this experience and continue practicing these skills and habits for the rest of the school year.

During those 180+ days of class, you can also continue to build your relationships with students. Like monthly comic book issues or weekly TV episodes, you slowly reveal new information and insight over time. And you don't ever need to share all of your deepest, darkest secrets. Take a look at some of the coolest superheroes as examples.

The Best at What I Do . . . Forget

Marvel Comics' Wolverine has been a favorite superhero for decades, and there are so many reasons why:

1. Adamantium-laced claws (and skeleton).
2. Healing factor.
3. Canadian.
4. Short.
5. The best there is at what he does. (Which isn't very nice.)
6. "Bub."
7. Hugh Jackman.

I've always thought Wolverine's past has been one of his coolest features—namely, that he had no memory of his past. Over countless issues of *X-Men* and related titles, comic book readers saw only snippets of these lost years through sporadic flashbacks. Partnering with Captain America during World War II. Secret scientific tests. Tragic romances and plenty of trauma. Wolverine only went by Logan, and we didn't even know if that was his first or last name.

After teasing readers with piecemeal glimpses (and maybe deciding they'd better beat the movie studios to the punch), Marvel Comics finally revealed Wolverine's true origin with the aptly titled miniseries *Origin* (Jenkins et al. 2001/2009). Readers soon learned that the man known only as Logan was actually a sickly boy named James Howlett who wore a knee-length nightshirt and cried a lot. (A little disappointing, to say the least.) A few years later, at the end of the *House of M* crossover (Bendis and Coipel 2005/2006), Logan/Wolverine/James Howlett eventually does regain all of his memories. He remembers everything. This sudden wave of memories also weakens Wolverine's coolness factor.

Or take another example from the X-Men corner of the Marvel Universe: Cable—the gun-toting telekinetic cybernetic mutant (and 1990s comic book stereotype, complete with shoulder pads and exorbitant pouches). When Cable first appeared, he was a mysterious freedom fighter from the future (Simonson and Liefeld 1990). He took a team of scrawny New Mutants and toughened them into the brazen X-Force squad (adorning them with additional pouches and shoulder pads, to boot).

Readers didn't know much about Cable aside from his stoic machismo. But over the course of a few years and crossovers, it's revealed that this battle-hardened soldier is actually Nathan Summers, the future-flung baby son of X-Man Cyclops and then-wife Madelyn Summers, clone of Jean Grey—it's all rather complicated (Nicieza and Turner 1993). Envision a hybrid of Clint Eastwood/Arnold Schwarzenegger as a drooly infant in diapers, and you'll understand how Cable's future/past was a lot cooler as a mystery. Still, the continuity and family tree connections are admirable, and the gradual revelations pay off nicely.

This slow reveal of personal history is not limited to mutants. Even Spider-Man (and readers) had to wait years before learning the truth about his parents' deaths (Lee and Lieber 1968). The secret circumstances surrounding Richard and Mary Parker have been sparse—with particular details about their S.H.I.E.L.D. spy activities revealed decades later (Stern and Romita 1997). Such "top secret" confidentiality creates anticipation and appreciation from readers.

Consider the connection to your classroom teaching. You don't have to divulge every tidbit of personal trivia to students during the first week of school. They'll come to know you better—as you will know them, too—over months of multiple experiences and activities. Wait until the second quarter, at least, before you share your secret future freedom fighter history.

Thought Bubble . . .
*What are you okay with your students knowing about you? What do you prefer to keep **private**?*

But teachers don't have to share all of their secrets. Take one middle school teacher I know. She goes to great extremes to ensure none of her students know her first name (spoiler alert: it's Darla). Favoring formality over familiarity, ~~Darla~~ she hides her first name by strategically placing a sticker on her lanyard-attached school ID badge.

How about you? Is it a big deal if your students know your first name?

What's in a Name?

During my first semester teaching in small-town Nebraska (Aurora), a group of students approached me before school one day with conspiratorial grins. Over the weekend, the Aurora High School band had marched in a festival parade and just so happened to march right behind the band from my hometown, also in Nebraska (O'Neill). I knew some of these O'Neill kids from church or summer jobs, and others as younger siblings of my friends and classmates. And these hometown kids knew me, including where I currently taught. Before the parade, students from these two schools struck up conversations, and I became a common topic.

"Guess, what Mr. Bergman?" the Aurora kids told me that Monday morning after the parade. I had just entered the school's front lobby, ready to start a week of teaching and learning. My students had other plans. They could hardly wait to reveal their big secret. "We talked to people from your hometown, and now we know your first name."

They ended this sentence in a sing-song tone, which got the attention of my building principal standing nearby. With little time to think, I did my best to play it cool and stay professional. I responded by saying, "My first name? Sure, it's 'Mister,' right?"

I said it with a smile and I got a laugh from the students as well as my principal. And I never heard about it again. Since I made it no big deal, it became no big deal.

Your school band may never encounter your hometown's school band, but students can easily figure out your name if they really want to know. My students could've found my name in numerous places—the Internet, a phone book, the school directory, or even the diplomas I hung on my classroom wall (read more on this in Chapter 4).

Bottom line: Don't act surprised or offended on the day your students talk about your first name. The novelty of it will fizzle out fast, if you take it in stride and focus on teaching. And if some students need a reminder, you can teach them how and why they should address you in a respectful manner.

"My very name speaks of higher truths, higher goals. That is my identity. How can I deny it?"

- Shang-Chi,
Master of Kung Fu #76 (1979)

That's *Mister* Fantastic to You

I recall two experiences from my very first back-to-school in-service staff meeting. One memory is a litany of details regarding medical insurance and employee benefits. (This information made zero sense to a fresh-faced first-year teacher, relatively healthy and completely clueless about retirement plans.) The second memory is our assistant principal reminding us all that we are "Mr. Smith," not "Smith" or "Mr. S."

His point was to start the school year maintaining a professional identity and requiring our students to address us as such. It may seem like no big deal for a student to abbreviate your name ("Mr. B.") or leave off your honorific ("Bergman"). Some teachers may even welcome such nicknames to foster a more relaxed classroom environment. But we must always be careful to not get too comfortable with our students. Stop and consider the range of impacts this lackadaisical habit could impart.

I'm sure I've allowed my students to call me all sorts of things and get away with it. But it does help to maintain a level of courtesy among everyone—teacher to student, student to teacher, teacher to teacher, student to student, and more. Appropriate use of names is a step toward proper respect and positive relationships.

Proper names matter among superheroes, too, and not just with maintaining secret identities. Personally, I cringe whenever I read or see heroes call each other playful nicknames.

Of course, nicknames have long been a staple in comics. Witty banter and clever monikers keep the "funny" in funny books, after all. And it helps convey some characters' personalities. Wolverine, for example, has a nickname for nearly everyone:

- Professor X = "Chuck"
- Cyclops = "Cyke"
- Jean Grey/Marvel Girl = "Red," "Darlin'"
- Colossus = "Tin Man"
- Nightcrawler = "Fuzzy Elf"

Unfortunately, widespread use of nicknames can undermine the job of life-risking heroics. Take a look at other heroes and their less-dignified labels:

- Batman = "Bats"
- Superman = "Supes"
- Green Lantern = "GL"

Apparently, DC Comics has a thing for abridging names. Marvel nicknames, though more colorful, can still cheapen a heroic legacy.

- The Mighty Thor = "Goldilocks"
- The Incredible Hulk = "Ol' Greenskin," "Jade Jaws"
- Iron Man = "Shellhead"
- Captain America = "Cap," "Winghead," "Star-Spangled Avenger," "Steve"

Captain America's various monikers are especially egregious, the clearest example of a noble hero whose legendary status is downgraded by casual familiarity.

Call me old-fashioned ("Bromidic Bergman"), but superheroes deserve more formality. The same goes for teachers. Although it may seem cool for kids to use teacher nicknames, be wary of letting things get too capricious or contemptuous.

So, whenever you hear a student or colleague refer to you as "Mrs. T" or "Thompson" or "Yo, Teach," gently inform them how they should address you more properly.

Remember, it's not "Mr. I." It's Mr. Incredible.

It's not just "Fantastic" or "Fanny." It's Mr. Fantastic.

It's not "Bruh." It's Brother Voodoo.

And it's not "Marv." It's Ms. Marvel.

(Actually, the original Ms. Marvel goes by Captain Marvel now. But never "Cap.")

They Know Where You Live!

Students can figure out much more than teachers' first names. Like where you live, for example. Even so, I wouldn't broadcast residential information freely in front of the student body. Not even my ZIP code, if possible.

During my first five years of teaching, I rented an apartment two blocks from the school building. Any kid who paid attention knew where I lived. But the only memorable time anyone came knocking on my door was during one Halloween, and no, it wasn't egg-throwing hooligans. It actually was a group of high school boys dressed as old grannies, trick-or-treating at all the teachers' houses.

Like my first name, I didn't try to hide where I lived. Had I exhibited any paranoia or desire for extreme secrecy, I'm sure that attention would have made things worse, heightening my students' interests and tendencies to toss eggs, toilet paper, or otherwise.

$uper $aver!
Want more privacy? Contact your local phone company to request the "unlist" your information. Also, go to DoNotCall.gov and register your phone number(s). Both resources are FREE!

Dial H for ~~Hero~~ Help

What about your phone number? I know a lot of teachers who maintain unlisted phone numbers. They prefer privacy and a lack of prank calls. But I also know some teachers who list their home or cell phone numbers on their classroom syllabi or handouts. They make this contact information available so students (and parents) can reach them with questions or concerns. I wasn't that forthcoming with my phone number (like my address), but I didn't try to hide it. I've only had one challenging episode due to this accessibility.

One year I had a student I'll call Joe. Joe was a quiet kid during class, and pretty bright. The only time Joe spoke openly in class was to ask me to review instructions or repeat answers, which I had often posted visually as well. This wasn't too big of a deal at first. Most students didn't mind, and I do tend to quicken my pace as I teach—I just get so excited, I love what I do! But despite my repeated answers and rehashed information, Joe still didn't always keep up. I learned he had no individualized plan or exceptional needs; he just operated at a slower pace than most students. For a while, Joe would stop by after school to ask me to go over that day's information. No big deal. That's what I'm here for, and sometimes I was helping other students at the same time.

But then Joe started calling me at home. I didn't have one of those fancy caller ID functions on my landline phone, so I found myself picking up the receiver and answering Joe's questions during the evenings. This began to occur two or three times a week. Again, it wasn't because Joe was cognitively in need of extra help; he just wanted extra attention and reassurance that he had the correct homework assignment written down.

I probably should have given Joe better help by sharing some strategies for follow-ing along and organizing information, as well as getting him connected to classmates who could provide additional support. And I probably should have given him some parameters on when it was appropriate to call me. Instead, I started avoiding the phone, letting the answering machine pick up the call. With no caller ID, this was my only way to protect myself and my time, providing a way to sift through calls from Joe and calls from my mother.

I thought my unanswered calls would give Joe the hint he should stop phoning me at night. Instead, he just called back multiple times. One evening, I had returned late after an exercise session. I noticed my answering machine beeping and ignored it. I'd see Joe in less than 10 hours. He could ask me his question the next morning, if it was really that important. But as I got out of my post-workout shower, my phone rang *again*. This was at least 11 p.m. I absolutely refused to answer, resisting the urge to lash out when I heard Joe's voice while my answering machine recorded his message.

The next morning, Joe showed up first thing at my classroom. This was his ques-tion, asked in an exasperated, parental tone:

"Mr. Bergman, what time do you get home at night?"

Joe's query about class was replaced by a question about how I spend my late-night hours. Finally, I took the opportunity to explain to Joe how I don't answer the phone after 10 p.m. Also, unless it's an emergency, it's often considered discourteous to call some-one's home phone at such a late hour. That might have been Joe's biggest light bulb moment the entire year, having absolutely nothing to do with chemistry.

I'm pretty sure Joe called me a few more times after that, but they became less frequent. Eventually the phone calls stopped altogether. If they hadn't, I probably would have changed my home number and kept it out of the phone book.

My cautionary tale does give merit to the thought of "unlisting" your phone number. There is utility in maintaining a secret teacher identity. So, let's tackle the issue of why have a secret identify in the first place.

I Am . . . Teacher Man!

Spider-Man would gladly welcome a kid's late-night phone calls about homework as opposed to keeping Aunt May safe from the Green Goblin. Superman hides his connection to Clark Kent to protect Ma Kent, his Smallville friends, and coworkers at *The Daily Planet*. Superman's hidden secrets—including his Fortress of Solitude—also serve to protect himself. The more Lex Luthor knows about Superman's alien heritage, the more ways he could exploit possible weaknesses (e.g., kryptonite, reliance on the sun's rays, vulnerable to magic, etc.).

Lately it's been trendy to have superheroes reveal their secrets or not have a secret identity at all. The first *Iron Man* movie (2008) is notable for reigniting the star power of Robert Downey Jr., whose performance as the cool, cocky Tony Stark culminates in his nonchalant reveal, "I am Iron Man," at the end of the film. Before the movies, Tony Stark spent decades in comic books maintaining a separate identity from Iron Man. In fact, he explained away the armored Avenger's recurring appearances due to Iron Man being his personal bodyguard. (And everyone bought it.)

The Fantastic Four have always done the superhero thing with their personal identities in the public eye. Even with code names—Mr. Fantastic, Invisible Woman, Human Torch, the Thing—this quartet of heroes was just as comfortable out in public and in the news using their regular names—Reed Richards, Susan Storm-Richards, Johnny Storm, Ben Grimm.

There are other superheroes who have recently or always been open about their personal identity—the Atom/Dr. Ray Palmer, the Beast/Dr. Henry McCoy, Giant Man/Dr. Henry Pym, Doctor Strange/Dr. Stephen Strange (strangely not that secret to begin with, eh Doc?). But most of these heroes typically have two things in common: 1) they are super rich, and 2) they are super smart. Thanks to these two traits, these heroes often live "openly" in giant mansions or skyscrapers filled with the latest gadgetry for security and protection. Sort of like how celebrities keep the paparazzi at bay.

I know many teachers who are super smart. Super rich? Not so much.

Either way, I still recommend maintaining a moderate degree of confidentiality as a teacher—to protect yourself, your family, your friends, and your students (even if they *do* know your first name, your phone number, and/or where you live).

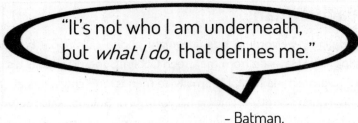

"It's not who I am underneath,
but *what I do*, that defines me."

– Batman,
Batman Begins (2005)

Hero vs. Civilian

Maintaining a distinct line between your hero identity and civilian identity is not just something in name, but also in person. More than your title, your behavior and attitude can help to maintain a personal/professional dual identity.

Superman has always been an interesting study with regard to secret identity. His heroic persona doesn't wear a mask at all. Nor does his costume have gloves. Debate and discussion among superfans highlight possible reasons for this apparent openness (Witnessing101 2012). No mask conveys a sense of camaraderie between Superman and the public, which he is committed to protecting. No gloves reinforces this same belief, although some argue Superman's alien skin doesn't emit oils like that of humans, thus leaving no prints from his fingers (Jung 2020). All of this openness instills trust from the public, so they don't even care to try learning his identity. That's a nice theory.

Another fan idea is that Superman's true mask is his Clark Kent persona, complete with glasses, slouching, and timid affectations. This act actually works pretty well, as even archnemesis Lex Luthor once used a computer to figure out Superman's identity and refused to believe the correct answer (Byrne 1987). Why would such a powerful individual choose to live in relative anonymity among the dredges of humanity? (Many non-teachers have the same blind spot with respect to those in the education profession. Why would an intelligent, hard-working, personable individual choose to "waste their talents" working with scores of juveniles from all sorts of challenging situations?)

We could discuss that matter at another time (holiday dinners with extended relatives, for example). But for now, let's consider the idea of portraying different personas in different contexts—home vs. school. Many teachers have to transform into their classroom character every day before the students show up. It's more than just wearing nice clothes and answering to Mr. or Mrs. It's turning on the optimism, alertness, and energy to guide and inspire children eight hours a day, five days a week (at the bare minimum).

This transformation is especially common among introverts who teach. The sub-population of introverted educators is essential in every school, but also potentially more susceptible to burnout (Godsey 2016; Walker 2016). Do you know a teacher who conveys dynamic energy in the classroom, but comes across as aloof or withdrawn in other contexts? Don't assume the individual is two-faced. They simply know how to "turn it on" and "turn it off" depending on the situation. Much like Superman/Clark Kent, Wonder Woman/Diana Prince, Batman/Bruce Wayne, and any other number of superheroes, such teachers manage dual identities to survive—and thrive—in both professional and personal settings.

Buffers for Blurred Boundaries

One challenge in our current age is boundaries weakening between personal and professional arenas. Over the course of time, most cultures have become more casual and less formal. And given the state of constant connectivity in today's society, it's nearly impossible to be totally anonymous. Although if you want to try, you can strengthen privacy settings on sites such as Facebook (Antonelli 2022), Instagram (Germain 2022), Twitter (Johnson 2022), TikTok (Kelly 2022), and elsewhere.

Appropriate boundaries protect teachers and students alike. Given the unique nature of teaching—different expectations for behavior, more visible in the community—teachers can't share the same information, experiences, and opinions that others may be free to do. An age-old axiom is that teachers should "be friendly with students, but never friends." Shuffelton (2011) points out several reasons to reject the notion of a teacher being friends with their students: 1) the fundamental conflict between friendship and authority, 2) an obligation to impartiality, and 3) interference with student learning.

Teacher-student friendships with unchecked boundaries can lead to ethical dilemmas, local news headlines, and worse. The same truth transfers to the realm of social media, where the term "friend" takes on new meaning and ubiquity (Grisham 2014). For your personal accounts, don't be friends with current students or their families. Wait until after students graduate to befriend them and "like" their posts about pets, food, and travel photos.

Moreover, be judicious in choosing what details to share on your own social media accounts. Teachers have lost their jobs because of photos, jokes, or strong opinions they posted online (Simpson 2008). Americans certainly have a freedom of speech, but teachers need to consider who is watching and listening to what they broadcast on the Internet. Consider what impressions you leave through your digital footprints, and the impressionable young minds who may be observing. As with your overall identity, maintain healthy boundaries and a professional/personal dynamic that is safe for everyone and conducive to learning.

 ## To Be Continued!

Further Reading

Busiek, K. and Immonen, S. (2005). *Superman: Secret Identity*. New York: DC Comics.

Jenkins, P., Quesada, J., Jemas, B., and Kubert, A. (2001/2009). *Wolverine: Origin*. New York: Marvel.

Waid, M. and Samnee, C. (2014/2016). *Daredevil: Volume 4* [Collecting issues of *Daredevil (Vol. 4), #1-10, 1.50, 0.1*]. New York: Marvel.

Further Viewing

Arad, A. and Feige, K. (producers) and Favreau, J. (director). (2008). *Iron Man* [Motion picture]. Marvel Studios.

Feige, K. (producer) and Black, S. (director). (2013). *Iron Man 3* [Motion picture]. Marvel Studios.

Feige, K. and Pascal, A. (producers) and Watts, J. (director). (2021). *Spider-Man: No Way Home* [Motion picture]. Sony Pictures.

Ziskin, I. and Bryce, I. (producers) and Raimi, S. (director). (2002). *Spider-Man* [Motion picture]. Sony Pictures.

Questions for Reflection and Discussion

1. What are some of the most successful "First Day" activities you've used or experienced? Least successful?

2. For what reasons is it helpful and healthy to not share every detail about your "origin story"?

3. What questions would you want students to ask of you? What example questions can you have ready to share?

4. What sort of nicknames did you have for teachers? What nicknames (that you know of) do your students have for you? How do these nicknames impact teacher-student relationships?

5. Do you have an unlisted phone number? What are your thoughts about sharing your contact information with students or parents?

6. Keeping cultural norms in mind, what do you think is the best way to address fellow teachers?

7. How do you respond if a student calls you by your first name (or a nickname)? Is it a big deal, little deal, or no deal?

8. In what ways do teachers "wear a mask" during school hours with students? How might this be helpful or hurtful for classroom instruction and interactions?

9. How can teachers safely navigate social media, both in what they share as well as who they follow or befriend?

References

Anderson, L.W., Krathwohl, D.R., Airasian, P.W., Cruikshank, K.A., Mayer, R.E., Pintrich, P.R., Raths, J., and Wittrock, M.C. (eds.) (2001). *Taxonomy for Learning, Teaching, and Assessing: A Revision of Bloom's Taxonomy of Educational Objectives*. New York: Allyn & Bacon.

Antonelli, W. (2022). How to make your Facebook profile as private as possible. *Business Insider* (28 January). https://www.businessinsider.com/how-to-make-facebook-private.

Arad, A. and Feige, K. (producers) and Favreau, J. (director). (2008). *Iron Man* [Motion picture]. Marvel Studios.

Bendis, B.M. and Coipel, O. (2005/2006). *House of M*. New York: Marvel.

Bloom, B.S. (ed.) (1956). *Taxonomy of Educational Objectives: The Classification of Educational Goals. Handbook I: Cognitive Domain*. New York: McKay.

Byrne, J. (1987). The Secret Revealed! *Superman (Vol. 2) #2*. New York: DC Comics.

Germain, T. (2022). How to use Instagram privacy settings. *Consumer Reports* (26 January). https://www.consumerreports.org/privacy/instagram-privacy-settings-a3036233134/.

Godsey, M. (2016). Why introverted teachers are burning out. *The Atlantic* (25 January). https://www.theatlantic.com/education/archive/2016/01/why-introverted-teachers-are-burning-out/425151/.

Grisham, L. (2014). Teachers, students and social media: Where is the line? *USA Today* (9 April). http://www.usatoday.com/story/news/nation-now/2014/04/09/facebook-teachers-twitter-students-schools/7472051/.

Jenkins, P., Quesada, J., Jemas, B., and Kubert, A. (2001/2009). *Wolverine: Origin*. New York: Marvel.

Johnson, D. (2022). How to change your privacy settings on Twitter. *Business Insider* (18 February). https://www.businessinsider.com/how-to-change-privacy-settings-on-twitter.

Jung, M. (2020). Superman protects his secret identity with more than just glasses. Screen Rant (30 October). https://screenrant.com/superman-secret-identity-glasses-explained-clark-kent/.

Kelly, H. (2022). TikTok privacy settings to change now. *The Washington Post* (24 January). https://www.washingtonpost.com/technology/2022/01/24/tiktok-privacy-settings/.

Lee, S. and Lieber, L. (1968). The parents of Peter Parker! *Amazing Spider-Man Annual (Vol. 1) #5*. New York: Marvel.

Nicieza, F. and Turner, F. (1993). Act one: Sunset breaks. *Cable (Vol. 1) #6*. New York: Marvel.

Shuffelton, A. (2011). On the ethics of teacher-student friendships. In: *Philosophy of Education, 2011 Yearbook* (ed. R. Kunzman), 81–89. Urbana, IL: Philosophy of Education Society. https://www.academia.edu/2065373/On_the_Ethics_of_Teacher-Student_Friendships.

Simonson, L. and Liefeld, R. (1990). A show of power! *New Mutants (Vol. 1) #87*. New York: Marvel.

Simpson, M.D. (2008). The whole world (wide web) is watching: cautionary tales from the "what-were-you-thinking" department. NEA Today. https://www.thefreelibrary.com/The+whole+world+(wide+web)+is+watching%3A+cautionary+tales+from+the...-a0177816289.

Stern, R. and Romita, J. (1997). "There's a man who leads a life of danger!" *Untold Tales of Spider-Man (Vol. 1). #-1*. New York: Marvel.

Walker, T. (2016). Schools need introverted teachers, but avoiding burnout a challenge. NEA Today. https://www.nea.org/advocating-for-change/new-from-nea/schools-need-introverted-teachers-avoiding-burnout-challenge.

Witnessing101. (2012). Why Superman's disguise actually makes sense. HubPages (22 January). https://discover.hubpages.com/literature/Why-Supermans-Costume-Actually-Makes-Sense.

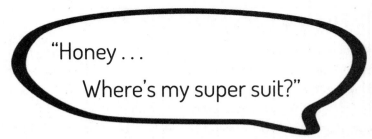

"Honey . . .

Where's my super suit?"

– Frozone,
The Incredibles (2004)

Costumes and Colors

Which superhero has the best costume?

Beauty is in the eye of the beholder, but a few heroes commonly pop up in best-dressed lists from in-the-know places, like *Vanity Fair* (Tashjian 2018), *GQ* (Renwick 2022), and *Insider* (Mitrokostas 2020). In particular, let's focus on characters portrayed in live-action film and television, since teachers deal with the live-action world.

Here are some frequent hero fashionistas:

- Batman.
- Catwoman.
- Wonder Woman.
- Iron Man.
- Black Widow.
- Black Panther.
- Spider-Man (Peter Parker *and* Miles Morales).

Inspired by stylish superheroes, teachers can apply two fundamental fashion tips to their educational wardrobe.

Fashion Tip #1: Functionality

First, a good outfit is functional. This is especially true for live-action costumes. Many of the best film costumes work because they look like something you could actually see in real life. Rather than adhering too closely to garish comic book spandex or colors (more on that later), the designers keep things grounded and user-friendly.

Teachers should consider their daily tasks and possible actions, then dress appropriately. Fabric that breathes, stretches, and covers is a must, along with some comfortable footwear. The website We Are Teachers provides an annual list of recommended shoes, books, sandals, and more (2022). Check out their rankings and compare them with own your favorites. These recommendations focus on comfort concerns for those spending a good portion of their day on their feet. Even so, you'll find a few selections provide a splash of color and pizzazz that may fit some classes and age groups better than others. In most cases, though, look for subtle and simple shoes that support your feet without distracting your students.

Fashion Tip #2: Simplicity

Minimalism is not just a mid-twentieth century art movement, and it's not just for those fed up with too much stuff. We'll talk about messy classrooms in Chapter 4 with respect to Batcaves and secret hideouts. For now, let's stick with clothes. The best superhero costumes keep things simple, while the worst outfits are often just *too much*.

In its review of best and worst cinematic superhero suits, lifestyle website Insider asked designers and stylists to articulate what specifically makes or breaks a costume (Mitrokostas 2020). In discussing bad outfits, these fashion experts use words such as "clunky," "sloppy," "overwhelming," and "in your face." I can't think of any teacher who wants those adjectives describing their appearance (or overall performance).

In terms of attire, resist the urge to add another accessory here or there. Ostentatious superheroes have too many buckles, pockets, and kneepads. Garish teachers can have these, too, along with excessive jewelry or doodads, and a button-laden lanyard that is more fitting for an employee at TGI Fridays.

I remember my elementary music teacher for her multiple turquoise rings. She wore them every day, on at least half of her fingers. When she played piano, her thick rings provided their own percussion accompaniment, clackety-clacking in time with every pressed key. The noise didn't drown out the melody or our voices, but it was a distraction sometimes. Don't let your attire or accessories get in the way of your teaching and students' learning.

Wardrobe Malfunctions

Both of these fashion tips adhere to the ultimate rule for superhero costumes. In the words of superhero stylist Edna E. Mode in *The Incredibles:* "NO CAPES!" (2004). Though impressive when billowing in the breeze, these cumbersome cowls can snag on missiles, catch in jet turbines, get sucked into vortexes, or worse.

Speaking of snags, one day during an internship semester, I arrived at my placement school for an afternoon session. My mentor teacher was wearing his science lab coat. This knee-length jacket wasn't out of the ordinary for a science instructor, but there were no labs or demos that day. Later when we were alone during a plan period, my mentor showed me why he wore the lab coat.

Earlier that morning, the front of his pants got snagged by the waist-high paper towel dispenser at the front table. The sharp metal corner ripped a gaping hole from one pocket to the zipper. This happened in front of his first period class. Quickly, he turned around and slipped inside the supply closet to don his lab coat, which was long enough to hide the tear. After this heroic quick change, he reemerged to the classroom full of wide-eyed students.

"I told them they couldn't say a word to the rest of the school," my mentor said. "And if they kept this secret, I'd buy them each a can of soda pop."

The rest of the day passed and when I returned to school the next afternoon, my mentor teacher proudly lamented that he had to fork over money to buy a case of Dr. Pepper. No one else ever learned about this embarrassing wardrobe malfunction (except for you, dear readers).

I've had my own wardrobe malfunctions from time to time, the most memorable wearing one of my favorite outfits. It was late fall, warm enough to feel like midsummer. As with every school I know, my classroom's air conditioning could never overcome the sweltering heat and humidity. I was wearing a monochrome silver tie and shirt combination—Regis Philbin had made that look famous during his time hosting the *Who Wants to be a Millionaire?* prime time game show. I was no Regis, but I felt like I could hold my students' attention as well as a charismatic TV legend.

During this particular afternoon in class, I was telling one of my anecdotes to illustrate a scientific concept. I don't recall which topic, but it involved me using a meter stick and demonstrating different motions and positions. And it was funny— or at least fun, I thought. But the type of laughter I got from my students didn't sound right. It was less "mildly amused" giggling, and more "disgustedly dismissive" snickering.

"What's wrong?" I asked the class. I distinctly remember one of my students in the front row shaking his head with a smirk and saying nothing. His name was Matt, and he was one of the funniest students I ever knew. Matt eventually moved to Los Angeles and has appeared on network sitcoms and late-night skit TV.

Stuck in the front row of my classroom, Matt just shook his head and said, "Nothing's wrong." But his stifled laughs told me something was off.

Class was soon over, and then I found out what was so funny. It was so hot that day, I had perspired profusely through my armpits, drenching both my undershirt and dress shirt. Regis Philbin never sweat like that on television. The worst part was it probably wouldn't have been noticeable, except for the fact that I repeatedly raised my arms to hold the meter stick aloft, even draping it over both shoulders like I was a yoked ox. But the joke was on me, with yolk on my face and wet stains in my pits.

Ever since this experience, I have always kept a spare stick of deodorant in my desk drawer. It comes in handy during those hot days, during which I'm also careful to keep my arms at my side.

Teachers, *always* check your zippers. And double knot your shoelaces. No one wants to be known as the slobby teacher.

Keep an extra sweater or shirt in your closet for emergencies. Heck, maybe even stow away a spare pair of pants or shoes. You never know when you'll need them. Talk about a lifesaver.

Complementary Colors–Primary Heroes, Secondary Villains

Pause for a moment and picture three different superheroes. What common colors come to mind? Now do the same for three supervillains. What hues and shades do they share?

For classic heroes like Superman, Spider-Man, Wonder Woman, Iron Man, Captain America, and more, we see a lot of reds and blues and yellows. These are primary colors in the traditional sense, as far back as Sir Isaac Newton's very first color wheel (Koontz 2018). In the tradition of comic books, primary colors arose out of necessity. Paper and ink for comics were rather cheap and low quality compared to other printed materials (Fortress of Solitude 2021). To pop off the page, heroes needed to wear costumes with bright primary colors.

Since heroes often wore red, blue, and/or yellow outfits, this left secondary colors like green, purple, and orange for the antagonists. Villains such as the Joker, the Green Goblin, and Lex Luthor all wear some combination of these colors. Heck, just take a look at the Rogues' Gallery for Batman or Spider-Man and notice all of the secondary shades.

There are exceptions of course, including heroes like Green Lantern, Green Arrow, Incredible Hulk, She-Hulk, Gamora, and Hawkeye. And what about primary-hued villains such as Marvel's red heavy Magneto or DC super-baddie Darkseid with his blue boots and onesie?

> "I'm six foot seven and bright green! People are gonna stare no matter how I dress!"

– She-Hulk,
Marvel Graphic Novel:
The Sensational She-Hulk #1 (1985)

Stories with heroes and villains are much more nuanced and complicated than color coding, of course. And there is actually deeper meaning across the spectrum as well. In fact, there are entire fields of study in color theory and fashion psychology that provide insight and application for both heroes and teachers (Mair 2018; McLachlan and Hanson 2016; Miller 2018; Young 2022).

Thought Bubble...
*What are your **favorite colors** to wear when teaching? What **messages** might these colors send to students and colleagues?*

First, let's look more closely at comic book characters.

Red traditionally proclaims passion, boldness, and intensity. Blues convey feelings of loyalty, stability, and trust. Combine these two colors and you see why they show up in so many heroes' costumes: Superman, Wonder Woman, Spider-Man, Captain America, Captain Marvel, Doctor Strange, Thor, and many more.

Throw in a dash of yellow and you add elements of energy, youth, and optimism. Think of the blue-and-gold uniforms of the classic teenage X-Men, or the bright yellow cape worn by Robin, aka Boy Wonder.

Some characters eschew these traditions, such as the mostly yellow Wolverine, who does have energy but not much youth and optimism. (For a while, though, the clawed X-Man did wear a costume that was mostly brown, a color that suggests earthiness, grit, and stability—two out of three ain't bad for a mutant who occasionally succumbs to berserker rage.)

Again, antagonists often get stuck with whatever colors are left, but there is some meaning behind these secondary shades. As a costly dye in ancient times, purple became a symbol for the rich and royalty (Andrews 2018). It's no wonder that Lex Luthor, Brainiac, Galactus, Kingpin, Kang the Conqueror, and other megalomaniacs all use this color in their clothing. Some villains even have purple skin, like the death-obsessed Thanos.

Green is just as common among enemies, a color often associated with illness and greed. You can connect this meaning back to ancient Greek notions about envy causing one's body to overproduce bile (Smith 2007). More recently (but still old), Shakespeare's *Othello* has the famous line about jealousy being "the green-eyed monster." And so we have all kinds of verdant villains. Spider-Man alone faces off against the Green Goblin, Doctor Octopus, the Lizard, the Vulture, Mysterio, Electro, Sandman, Scorpion, and more—all clad in green.

So, what's the lesson here for teachers? Should we wear red, blue, and yellow; and avoid green, purple, and orange?

The answer hinges on a lot of things. Since most teachers aren't fighting supervillains or flying across the sky, we can be a little more selective and discrete with our wardrobe choices. Let's take a look at some of these colors in terms of psychology and professionalism.

Colors in the Classroom

As alluded to earlier, red conveys passion and energy. According to fashion experts, wearing red helps others perceive you as "focused" and "committed" (Giang 2012). Studies have shown that wearing red—even something small like a necktie or scarf—can increase one's persuasive abilities (Centeno 2015). Too much red can have the opposite effect. An entire outfit wrapped in scarlet can communicate "stop." Furthermore, no teacher I know wants to be known as Santa or Mrs. Claus. Subtlety is key.

While red is a go-to color for strength, blue can be equally powerful for opposite reasons. Linked to the sea and sky, blue creates vibes of depth and tranquility, wisdom and truth. Blue's coolness makes it a frequent color of choice for offices and other indoor spaces needing calm and quiet environments. (More on decorating your classroom in Chapter 4.) Teachers may not be able to paint their entire classroom blue, but wearing shades of navy and cyan can help create a calming effect geared toward learning. Again, too much of any color can be a bad thing. A blue outfit in a blue room may put an entire class to sleep.

Let's round out our discussion of traditional primary colors by looking at yellow. This sunny color beams out happiness and youthful enthusiasm, so much so that yellow may work better for teachers of younger students. With yellow (and other bright shades), a little goes a long way. Consider Batman's iconic yellow bat symbol on the chest of his otherwise dim costume. While the emblem's original purpose was for trademark protections (Uslan 2018), later writers have rationalized that the Dark Knight tricks criminals into shooting at the glaring oval (and bulletproof vest underneath) to protect his face. In all seriousness, I hope teachers can add a splash of yellow here and there for much more positive purposes. It's a terrific color for sharing warmth and grabbing attention.

In the same way, there's nothing wrong with purple, orange, green, or any other hue when used well. Everyone has their favorite color and combinations, and different shades come and go with fads and trends. We'll get more into fashion shortly, but first let's talk about one more color—or technically the lack of it.

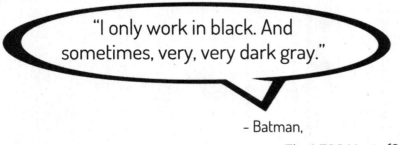

"I only work in black. And sometimes, very, very dark gray."

- Batman,
The LEGO Movie (2014)

Like Batman, black exudes both mystery and confidence. This may prove helpful for establishing authority and respect. Black is also a simple way to communicate elegance and sophistication. But if used too much, black gets bleak—as in death and mourning. To avoid making your classroom feel like a funeral parlor, mix in colors such as those above. And of course, which particular shade or hue differs with each day's circumstances and other classroom dynamics.

I'm not Batman (or am I?), but I often start the school year wearing blacks, blues, and grays. It's not that I'm mourning the start of another term or trying to hide in the shadows. Rather, it's to portray credibility and establish a respectful classroom.

In back-to-school season, most of the students are new to me, and I'm a stranger to them. We'll get to know each other as the year progresses, but the first week or so is not the time to break out my novelty ties or silly socks.

Decades of research supports the notion that teachers should start the school year with proactive and preventative classroom management measures, including procedures and structure to support student learning (Emmer, Evertson, and Worsham 2003; Wong and Wong 2018). Effective teachers begin with more structure, and can then relax as the year progresses. In the same way, I like to dress more formally at the start of the year, and break out my colorful clothing and more casual attire as the semester progresses. My wardrobe changes from August to April, and not just because of the seasons. Likewise, my choice of attire adjusts from Mondays to Fridays, with conscious clothing choices each week based on school events, lesson topics, and the overall community mood.

What (Not) to Wear?

So far, we've mostly shared insight from superhero costumes and colors, but what specifically should teachers wear (or *not* wear)? The short answer is, "It depends." Nevertheless, we can look at research that has examined the impact of teacher dress on student perceptions, as well as related studies.

Students' Perceptions of Teachers Based on Teacher Dress and Appearance

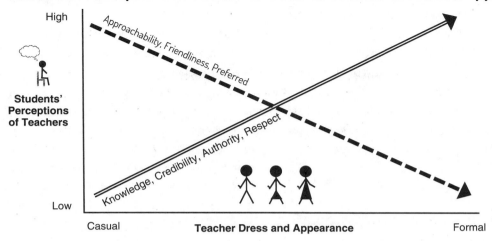

References: Butler & Roesel, 1989; Davis, 1992; Dunbar & Segrin, 2012; Kashem, 2019; Saiki, 2006; Sternberg, 2019

Summary of student perceptions of teacher dress.
What messages do you send with your dress and appearance?

In general, students prefer casually dressed teachers (jeans, untucked shirts, sneakers), whom they perceive as more approachable and friendly, based on appearance alone (Butler and Roesel 1989; Davis 1992; Dunbar and Segrin 2012; Kashem 2019; Saiki 2006). However, many of these same studies find that students regard teachers in casual attire as having less knowledge, authority, and credibility. In other words, teachers who dress more formally (business suits or skirts, ties, collared shirts or blouses) are viewed as smarter and more competent, but less personable. The crisscross graph in the figure encapsulates the relationships found in these studies.

Notice that the research summarized in this graph comes from four different decades, with each era brandishing its own fashion fads and faux pas—and in some cases, reprisals. Look up or think back to the 1980s, 1990s, early 2000s, and more recent times, comparing the hot looks on the runway and in store windows. In spite of all the evolving and revolving styles, these trends between teacher dress and student perceptions persist.

So, what's the solution? Do teachers dress half formally and half sloppily, like Batman villain Two-Face? Probably not. And just as ridiculous is a formal top and casual bottom (or vice versa). The only time the half-and-half approach might work is wearing a dressy shirt or sweater when teaching via videoconference. Just be sure to keep that camera aimed above the waist. Students don't need to see your Aquaman pajama pants. (I have a pair, and they are quite comfy.)

If you follow the provided chart, is there a happy medium or sweet spot right in the middle of intersecting lines? If so, what does that look like? Are jeans allowed? Is it okay to order all your shirts from UnTuckIt.com? Again, it depends.

Mostly, it depends on how you want to portray yourself as a teacher. While presentation relies on many factors such as verbal and nonverbal behaviors, preparedness, and flexibility, first impressions often arise from appearance and attire. And, like these other factors, the clothing you wear can influence your classroom climate on a daily basis. To that end, teachers may need to adjust their outfits from day to day, week to week, or even class to class.

Quick Changes or Gradual Transformations

As Butler and Roesel conclude in their study, "Because of the diversity of roles, it may be that teachers should use different clothing styles depending on the situation and the image to be conveyed" (1989, p. 59). Many superheroes are famous for their variety of costumes worn in comics, movies, TV, videogames, and more: Spider-Man, assorted X-Men, and Iron Man (although his entire suit is more of a gadget). Even Batman doesn't wear black all of the time, as he dons different outfits depending on the task at hand—or however many action figures need to sell in the toy aisle.

As a science teacher, I'm careful to wear my slightly worn pants and older shoes for lessons with messy experiments. And in the days leading up to such labs, I caution my students to do the same, especially if they have favorite clothes they want to keep clean and pristine. We don't plan on spills, but some individuals may want to come prepared. When my physics students test horsepower by sprinting up a stairwell, I'm the first to demonstrate with my pair of running sneakers—the only day I wear them for class. Otherwise, I've got comfy dress shoes that are a better match for my business casual ensemble. Just like heroes, teachers can also change outfits and colors according to the task. Most importantly, wear what's comfortable and appropriate for your classroom lessons. It can change with what you teach, how you teach, when and with whom.

Think back to our examination of different messages and meanings associated with various colors. I mentioned that I typically start the school year wearing black, gray, and blue colors to convey stability and respect. But I don't wear those colors exclusively. As the year goes on, changes obviously occur with the seasons—muted hues in the fall and winter, lighter and brighter colors with the onset of spring.

Even during the week, I purposely select certain outfits or colors. Some days may need a splash of yellow or orange to liven up the classroom—often on a Monday or a Friday after a long week. Other times I know I'm going to have a challenging conversation, and will choose black and red to convey elegance and boldness—more for myself than for those I'm meeting. Or if this conference is with a struggling student and parent, I may wear blue or green to emit feelings of trust and healing. It may not seem like a huge deal, but every little bit helps—even subconsciously. And, of course, it's always fun to get in the spirit and wear school colors during days of special events or competitions.

With colors and clothing styles, consider how you want to represent yourself. It may also depend on the students you have. How old are they? How energetic? What needs are they bringing to your classroom? What objectives do you have for that particular day? Whether you need to foster energy, serenity, authority or something else, your choice of attire can help your efforts. Batman may wear black on most days, but he still keeps his all-white "Camouflage Costume" handy for fighting "North Pole Crimes" (Finger and Kane 1942).

Timeless or Trendy

That said, not all varieties of looks are winners. We've reflected on appealing superhero outfits, as these are the ones that endure. But even classic heroes have worn some cringe-worthy costumes and styles, including "electric blue" Superman, "feral" Wolverine, "harpoon hand" Aquaman, plenty of scantily clad women or beefed-up men, and way too many pockets and shoulder pads.

Let's pick on Superman a little longer, since for nearly three years in the comic books, our esteemed Man of Steel had a tacky Mullet of Steel. The infamous hairstyle, also dubbed the "Super-Mullet," came in the timespan between Superman's death, rebirth, and marriage to Lois Lane (1993/2016, 1996/2021). So in the big picture, a cheesy haircut was probably the least of Clark Kent's concerns. We, however, still bring up this embarrassing phase as one example of the many hilarious times superheroes have followed momentary fads. Such changes may get attention or seem cool for a moment, but they quickly fall out of favor and fade into obscurity, forgotten except for an occasional good laugh.

No one is saying teachers can't sport the latest styles or hairdos. However, do so at your own peril. And consider research that finds students are more interested in a teacher's compassion and competency than in what the teacher wears (Dunbar and Segrin 2012). In another study, 72% of surveyed college students prefer their instructors do *not* follow fashion trends (Mosca and Buzza 2013). Two real teacher heroes come to mind in this topic of uniformity:

- **Teacher Hero #1:** Dale Irby, a retired P.E. teacher in Texas, wore the same outfit on school picture day for 40 years in a row (Kindelan 2013). It started out as a mistake during his first two years of teaching. After noticing the identical polyester shirt and brown sweater-vest in the photographs, Mr. Irby's wife dared him to continue the pattern. This soon became a fun tradition in the years and decades to come. Even though Mr. Irby changed schools and districts, he continued wearing the same picture-day outfit. It was a constant trademark in spite of passing time and changing fashions.

- **Teacher Hero #2:** Another teacher created her own "same clothes" challenge, wearing the same dress to school for 100 straight days (FitzPatrick 2018). Middle school art teacher Julia Mooney, of New Jersey, began her apparel marathon on purpose. Her plan was to teach students and others about sustainability and individuality. She chronicled her project on Instagram, with daily photos displaying the creative ways she accessorized and modified a simple gray dress. Scarfs, aprons, sweaters, and more all contributed to adding variety and adjusting to the seasons and circumstances—including a "healthy living" professional day doing yoga. In an interview with *Good Morning America*, Ms. Mooney explained, "There is no rule that says I cannot wear the same thing every day if I choose to, so I thought why not. I'm just gonna do that and then we can talk about how our clothes really don't define us." This is a helpful reminder that we teach our students so much more than a particular subject or grade level content. Teachers can enlighten kids on many life lessons, and model positive habits through our own behavior.

Dress Codes for Students and Teachers

On the subject of "rules," it is wise to find out if your school has a dress code for staff members. Neat and clean are always "in," with the oft-stated goal for faculty to "dress professionally and appropriately" for their curriculum. Most teacher dress codes address the same hot-button items: tattoos, piercings, exposed skin, frayed jeans, flip-flops—each of these with limitations or outright prohibitions.

Caption Capture: What **dress code** would you create for teachers? List "do's"/"don'ts" here:

Of course, some previously taboo items eventually do become okay in the workplace. Whereas piercings used to be allowed for women's ears only, now we see a lot more jewelry in a lot more people and a lot more body parts. Tattoos are another touchy subject, one more readily accepted in recent years. Nevertheless, there are still questions about how many, subject matter, and visibility. I worked with an elementary pre-service teacher who had tattoos covering both arms all the way down to his wrists. He was a cool dude, and I believe he had a regular gig playing guitar in a local rock band. But for the classroom, this guy was proactive and professional. He told me that during days spent in elementary schools, he planned to wear long-sleeve shirts to avoid unnecessary distractions (or presumptions).

When in doubt, start by dressing conservatively. Social etiquette expert Nancy Mitchell notes that at any job, there's the possibility you could work with as many as four different generations of people (2011). For teachers working at schools, you can add another generation for your students. Each age group has different expectations on appropriate professional dress. Chances are your supervisors will be older than you, and most likely skew on the conservative side of fashion. There's a reason career counselors recommend you "dress like your boss." It's one way to initially align yourself to their example, as you continue to learn and work "on the same side" together.

"When I put that suit on, I thought, 'This is it. This is the moment I become who I'm supposed to be.'"

– Kate Bishop,
Hawkeye,
"Echoes" (2021)

No matter the case, you will want to check with your local district policies and expectations for teacher appearance. And if you see a need for change, bring it up in a professional and appropriate manner.

Whether warranted or not, teachers are often held to a higher standard than most other occupations. This includes how they dress and present themselves in front of students and the community. Harry Wong (of *The First Days of School* fame) echoes this sentiment about standards for teachers: "People look at you and they make perceptions. Right or wrong. Usually it's wrong. That's a reality of life. . . . How you dress so shall you be perceived. And as you are perceived, so shall you be treated. Always dress better than your students. If you don't care how you look, how can they care about you?" (2018).

I've taken this "dress better than your students" message to heart, with a memorable experience in the opposite dynamic. At the first high school where I taught, our student athletes dressed up on days they had a game later in the afternoon or evening. In place of T-shirts or sweatshirts with jeans or shorts, they came to school wearing dresses or skirts, slacks, and shirts with neckties. Many of these kids wore outfits nicer than most teachers. I was one of these teachers, and one day this juxtaposition hit me as odd and off-putting. Adding to the awkwardness was the fact that this particular day was a casual Friday, meaning most teachers were wearing jeans and other casual clothing. Walking around the school, it was hard to discern between student and teacher based on appearance alone. And to be honest, some of the dressed-up students carried themselves in a more mature manner than some of the casually dressed adults. As I stood in the hallway, I decided then that to help present myself as a professional educator, I would always dress as formally as my students—no matter if it was game day, casual Friday, or any other day of the week.

$uper $aver!
Check CLEARANCE and SALES RACKS for cheap new clothing. These may be "out of season," so save them for the next year! Timeless!

When addressing wardrobe choices, it's important to consider underlying bias issues. Many of these items typically apply to women, who often receive more scrutiny when it comes to appearance (Awashti 2017; Bell 2016; Ellemers 2018; Rees 2018). Plus, there are all kinds of considerations for cultural context, community expectations, equity, and inclusion (Pearlman 2019). Some schools are leading the way with anti-shaming and gender-neutral student dress codes (Haller 2019; McClellan 2018; Tucker 2018). Let's hope that more districts follow and apply the same principles to their staff expectations. Even so, when it comes to teacher dress, we at least have some guidance and cautionary tales from superheroes—wear clothes that are functional, simple, timeless, with colors coordinated to context and classroom circumstances.

Work only in black?

Not always.

What about capes?

Still no.

To Be Continued!

Further Reading

McLachlan, B. and Hanson, A. (2016). Superhero color theory. *Comics Alliance*. https://comicsalliance.com/tags/superhero-color-theory/.

Shooter, J., Stern, R., DeFalco, T. et al. (2007). *Spider-Man: Birth of Venom*. New York: Marvel.

Whedon, J. and Cassaday, J. (2004/2012). *Astonishing X-Men Ultimate Collection: Book 1*. New York: Marvel.

Further Viewing

Feige, K. and Pascal, A. (producers) and Watts, J. (director). (2017). *Spider-Man: Homecoming* [Motion picture]. Sony Pictures.

Niswander, S. (2015/2016). The design of comic book superheroes. NerdSync Productions. https://www.youtube.com/playlist?list=PLPEShH2LWsQA1y bbbyfywk1Mn53DSQZql.

Walker, J. (producer) and Bird, B. (director). (2004). *The Incredibles* [Motion picture]. Walt Disney/Pixar Studios.

Questions for Reflection and Discussion

1. What is your school's dress code policy for teachers and staff? How does this compare with the student dress code?

2. What do you like about your favorite outfit for teaching? When do you wear it?

3. Monitor how your students respond or behave depending on your teaching attire. What patterns do you notice?

4. If you have any wardrobe malfunction stories (as a teacher or student), what happened? What lessons did you learn?

5. What do you think about the career recommendation to "dress like your boss"?

6. What are some cultural or regional considerations to make in regard to choosing what to wear (or not to wear)?

7. If you have slightly used (or unused) teacher clothing, donate it to a thrift store. If younger colleagues don't need them, other customers and professionals will!

References

Andrews, E. (2018). Why is purple considered the color of royalty? *History*. https://www.history.com/news/why-is-purple-considered-the-color-of-royalty.

Awashti, B. (2017). From attire to assault: clothing, objectification, and de-humanization–a possible prelude to sexual violence? *Frontiers in Psychology* 8 (338). doi: 10.3389/fpsyg.2017.00338. https://www.ncbi.nlm.nih.gov/pmc/articles/PMC5344900/pdf/fpsyg-08-00338.pdf.

Bell, B. (2016). Why workplace dress codes have troubled women for decades. *Newsweek* (16 May). https://www.newsweek.com/high-heels-and-workplace-460312.

Butler, S. and Roesel, K. (1989). The influence of dress on students' perceptions of teacher characteristics. *Clothing and Textiles Research Journal* 7(3): 57–59.

Centeno, A. (2015). Why you should wear red if you want to be persuasive. *Business Insider* (6 March). https://www.businessinsider.com/wear-red-to-be-persuasive-2015-3.

Davis, M.A. (1992). Age and dress of professors: influence on students' first impressions of teaching effectiveness. Doctoral dissertation. Virginia Polytechnic Institute and State University.

Dunbar, N.E. and Segrin, C. (2012). Clothing and teacher credibility: an application of expectancy violations theory. *International Scholarly Research Network* 2012.

Ellemers, N. (2018). Looks do matter, especially for work, and also at work. *Psychology Today* (7 September). https://www.psychologytoday.com/us/blog/social-climates/201809/looks-do-matter-especially-women-and-also-work.

Emmer, E.T., Evertson, C.M., and Worsham, M.E. (2003). *Classroom Management for Secondary Teachers, Sixth Edition*. Boston: Allyn & Bacon.

Evertson, C.M., Emmer, E.T., and Worsham, M.E. (2003). *Classroom Management for Elementary Teachers, Sixth Edition*. Boston: Allyn & Bacon.

Finger, B. and Kane, B. (1942). Batman: The North Pole Crimes. *World's Finest (Vol. 1) #7*. New York: DC Comics.

FitzPatrick, H. (2018). Here's why a New Jersey middle school teacher is wearing the same dress for 100 days. *Good Morning America* (28 November). https://www.goodmorningamerica.com/style/story/jersey-middle-school-teacher-wearing-dress-100-days-59452012

Fortress of Solitude. (2021). The surprising reason Spider-Man wears red & blue (27 November). https://www.fortressofsolitude.co.za/the-surprising-reason-spider-man-wears-red-blue/.

Giang, V. (2012). An expert reveals the one color you should wear to your next interview. *Business Insider* (8 March). https://www.businessinsider.com/an-expert-reveals-the-one-color-you-should-wear-to-when-trying-to-impress-an-interviewer-or-important-client-2012-3.

Haller, S. (2019). Virginia school district adopts dress code that isn't sexist! Students helped draft rules. *USA Today* (15 July). https://www.usatoday.com/story/life/parenting/2019/07/15/gender-neutral-dress-code-gets-approval-roanoke-virginia-school-district/1734009001/.

Jones, G., Jurgens, D., Kesel, K. et al. (1993/2016). *Superman: The Return of Superman*. New York: DC Comics.

Jurgens, D. (1996/2021). *Superman & Lois Lane: The 25th Wedding Anniversary Deluxe Edition*. New York: DC Comics.

Kashem, M.A. (2019). The effect of teachers' dress on students' attitudes and students' learning: Higher education view. *Education Research Journal* 2019 (3): 1–7.

Kindelan, K. (2013). Texas teacher dons same yearbook outfit for 40 years. *ABC News* (2 July). https://abcnews.go.com/blogs/lifestyle/2013/07/texas-teacher-dons-same-yearbook-outfit-for-40-years.

Koontz, A. (2018). A history of color. Caltech Letters (29 May). https://caltechletters.org/science/history-of-color-1.

Lin, D. and Lee, R. (producers) and Lord, P. and Miller, C. (directors). (2014). *The LEGO Movie* [Motion picture]. Warner Bros. Pictures.

Mair, C. (2018). *The Psychology of Fashion*. New York: Routledge.

McClellan, J. (2018). California school's no-shame dress code empowers students to wear what they want. *USA Today* (21 August). https://www.usatoday.com/story/life/allthemoms/2018/08/21/san-francisco-bay-area-schools-no-shame-dress-code-allows-tube-tops-and-torn-jeans/1052718002/.

McLachlan, B. and Hanson, A. (2016). Superhero color theory, part I: the primary heroes. Comics Alliance (2 June). https://comicsalliance.com/superhero-color-theory-primary-heroes/.

Miller, J. (2018). The dress doctor is in. *The New York Times* (12 April). https://www.nytimes.com/2018/04/12/fashion/fashion-psychologist.html.

Mitchell, N. (2011). MC lectures: social etiquette with Nancy Mitchell. Montgomery College. https://www.youtube.com/watch?v=livmmoZHokQ.

Mitrokostas, S. (2020). We had fashion experts critique 14 famous superhero suits, from Catwoman to Spider-Man. Insider (22 January). https://www.insider.com/best-and-worst-superhero-suits-according-to-fashion-experts-2020-1.

Mosca, J.B. and Buzza, J. (2013). Clothing and the effects on a teacher's image: how students view them. *Contemporary Issues in Education Research* 6 (1): 59–66.

Pearlman, S. (2019). "Professional appearance" in the workplace under scrutiny. *Forbes* (24 September). https://www.forbes.com/sites/stevenpearlman/2019/09/24/professional-appearance-in-the-workplace-under-scrutiny/?sh=69889f0c3412.

Rees, E. (2018). Clothes do not make the woman: what female academics wear is subject to constant scrutiny. Times Higher Education (5 April). https://www.timeshighereducation.com/features/clothes-do-not-make-woman-what-female-academics-wear-subject-constant-scrutiny.

Renwick, F. (2022). We've ranked the most stylish Marvel characters of all time. *GQ Magazine* (1 April). https://www.gq-magazine.co.uk/fashion/article/marvel-most-stylish-characters.

Saiki, R. (2006). Communicating effectively: teaching lessons about dress for the workplace. *Journal of Family and Consumer Sciences Education* 24 (1): 1–13.

Smith, K. (2007). The meaning of green with envy. Sensational Color. https://www.sensationalcolor.com/green-with-envy/.

Sternberg, R. (2019). The link between teacher dress and student decorum. American Association of School Administrators. https://www.aasa.org/SchoolAdministratorArticle.aspx?id=9720.

Tashjian, R. (2018). The top 10 best-dressed superheroes. *Vanity Fair* (6 June). https://www.vanityfair.com/style/photos/2014/06/best-dressed-superheroes.

Tucker, J. (2018). Alameda schools' new dress code: tube tops are in, shaming girls is out. *San Francisco Chronicle* (19 August). https://www.sfchronicle.com/bayarea/article/Alameda-schools-new-dress-code-Tube-tops-are-13167331.php.

Uslan, M. (2018). How & why Batman got his yellow oval. Batman-on-Film.com 13 (September). https://batman-on-film.com/4263/history_batman-yellow-oval-why-how_m-uslan_9-13-18/.

Walker, J. (producer) and Bird, B. (director). (2004). *The Incredibles* [Motion picture]. Walt Disney/Pixar Studios.

We Are Teachers. (2022). Take care of your feet with these 50+ comfy teacher shoes. https://www.weareteachers.com/teacher-shoes/.

Wong, H.K. and Wong, R. (2001). *The Effective Teacher, Part 4: Procedures and Routines*. Mountain View, CA: Harry K. Wong Publications.

Wong, H.K. and Wong, R. (2018). *The First Days of School: How to Be an Effective Teacher, 5th Edition*. Mountain View, CA: Harry K. Wong Publications.

Young, C. (2022). *The Color of Fashion: The Story of Clothes in Ten Colors*. London: Welbeck Publishing.

> "Look, this isn't New York.
> We don't do cosmic battles every five
> minutes, okay? We have standards."

– Ms. Marvel,
Ms. Marvel #33 (2018)

Living and Learning in Your Universe

It's an age-old debate that rivals Coca-Cola vs. Pepsi.

Which is better, Marvel or DC? My choice is easy: *both*.

But for the sake of teaching and learning, there is a clear winner: Marvel is best.

That's because the Marvel Universe exists in the "real" world. DC has its heroes crusading in imaginary cities such as Metropolis, Gotham City, Keystone City, and so on. Marvel launched its heroic age by firmly establishing characters that live "right outside your window" (Lee 2017). Spider-Man is a kid from Queens; Captain America proudly hails from Brooklyn. Even Doctor Strange's mystical mansion has the precise address of 177A Bleecker Street, New York City, New York, 10012, in the heart of Greenwich Village. (Search for "Sanctum Sanctorum" in New York and you'll find it on MapQuest and Google Maps.)

Admittedly, the Marvel Universe does have its share of fantasy settings–fictional countries like Black Panther's Wakanda and Dr. Doom's Latveria, and the prehistoric tropical Savage Land hidden somewhere in Antarctica. Moreover, both Marvel and DC dabble in the limitless "multiverse" with alternate realities or timelines, which basically creates an "anything goes" approach. Even so, since its inception, the Marvel Universe has always leaned heavily into more realistic characters living more down-to-earth (Earth-616, to be exact). DC, on the other hand, feels a little more distant in places such as Metropolis (utopian New York City) and Gotham City (dystopian New York City).

"We're a long way from Budapest."

— Hawkeye,
Avengers: Endgame (2019)

Keeping It Real

Teachers can take inspiration from the Marvel Universe by cultivating classrooms that reflect the real world. Note that I do *not* use the terms "real-world learning" or "real-life application." Both phrases are common and celebrated among schools, but problematic. Be careful with their hidden messages that all other kinds of learning are not "real," or an implication that everything else done in the classroom is "fake." In truth, all learning should exist in the real world and have meaning and application to students' lives.

Philosopher and progressive John Dewey is noteworthy for his efforts in promoting "real" education (Durst 2010; Fallace and Fantozzi 2017; Knoll 2016). He put these ideas to the test in 1896 by founding the Laboratory School at the University of Chicago. It was a "micro-society" for children, oriented toward applied learning, democratic ideals, and problem-solving (Mayhew and Edwards 1936). Students mastered academic concepts and practical skills by actually using them. A school garden grew out of science investigations, mathematical computations, analysis of anthropology and historical developments, and more. When they needed someplace to store supplies and tools, the kids built a barn. Throughout these various projects, students got plenty of practice using collaboration, communication, creativity, and critical thinking. Interestingly, these "Four Cs" arose to prominence a hundred years later with the "21st Century Learning Skills" movement (NEA 2012; P21 2008). We'll talk more about "super" skills and tools in Chapters 5 and 6, but for now let's consider this progressive teaching approach in light of your own personal universe.

First off, what does your classroom look like? Does it reflect the real marvelous world, or does it feel distant and disconnected? You may not have the facilities to help students build a barn or cultivate a garden—and if such experiences don't connect with students' lives, you may not want to anyway. Nevertheless, how can you design a classroom space that engages students and promotes authentic learning?

Caption Capture: Draw your **ideal classroom**. Include table/desk arrangements, stations, teacher desk, technology, doors/windows, décor, etc.

The ultimate educational setting for superheroes is Xavier's School for Gifted Youngsters (still love that name). The original campus for Marvel's X-Men—which also has a real address at 1407 Graymalkin Lane, Westchester County, North Salem, New York, 10560—has everything a teacher needs to prepare superpowered mutants to protect a world that hates and fears them. Sure, you've got your classrooms, a cafeteria, playgrounds and ball fields, residential wings, and other boarding school staples. But at Xavier's, you also have a hidden jet hangar, the mutant-tracking computer Cerebro, and the training simulator Danger Room—complete with its hard-light holographic technology able to construct anything from obstacle courses to robotic villain replicas. Talk about progressive! I bet even John Dewey would be impressed.

Dream all they want, most teachers can't afford their own private mansion and campus with cutting-edge technology. Heck, some of us don't even have our own classroom or personal desk. Regardless, there are still things any teacher can do to elevate their space into an educational haven. Let's begin by looking at research on classroom design and consider implications for our own real-life learning spaces.

Classrooms of SIN!

A fascinating body of research has combined neuroscience and architecture, bringing together three critical design themes: naturalness, individuality, and stimulation (Barrett and Barrett 2010). Shuffle those three ideas and you get SIN—their idea, not mine. SIN is not the most pleasant acronym, but it's certainly memorable! (I would even argue that quality teachers demonstrate this trio of traits, too, during their daily interactions and instruction. Alas, labeling a teacher as "SINful" gets nothing but bad press.) When applied to learning spaces, the SIN model provides powerful insight and application for teachers in organizing their classrooms.

Each SIN theme is further broken down into component variables. Stimulation deals primarily with complexity and color, both of which impact how exciting or relaxing a classroom makes you feel. (For discussion of color psychology, see Chapter 3.) Individualization pertains to the personal connections, flexibility, and ownership traits that support each learner and learning task. Finally, naturalization addresses parameters affecting physical comfort: light, sound, air quality, temperature, and even links to nature.

In their research of over 150 classrooms in 27 different primary (elementary) schools, Barret et al. (2015) found that naturalness elements make up half the impact of all design elements on student learning. This emphasis on physical comfort shouldn't be a surprise to anyone who has heard of Abraham Maslow's "Hierarchy of Needs" (1943). People require their basic needs to be addressed before they are able to attend to other matters. The other two areas—stimulation and individualization—are still important, however, each accounting for about a quarter of the overall impact on learning.

After examining schools, classrooms, and student achievement data, Barret and his colleagues—experts in the intersecting fields of architecture, engineering, and human impact—proposed seven key traits of "good classroom features" that can improve student learning. I'll resist calling them the "Sinful Seven" and instead summarize these design elements in a diagram I've created and dubbed . . . the "Heptagon for Higher Learning!"

Although naturalness elements (light, temperature, and air quality) form almost half of the entire shape, the two other SIN factors—stimulation (complexity, color) and individualization (ownership, flexibility)—take up a big chunk of design parameters. The researchers behind this model note that some of these seven features fall under the control of the "user." In other words, the teacher can directly manipulate these elements to help students learn. While Barrett and his colleagues focus on color, complexity, and ownership, I believe teachers can shape many other classroom components, too. It may not be a monumental change or immediate transformation, but there are creative ways to modify spaces to their maximum potential.

"Heptagon For Higher Learning" – 7 Features of Good Classroom Design

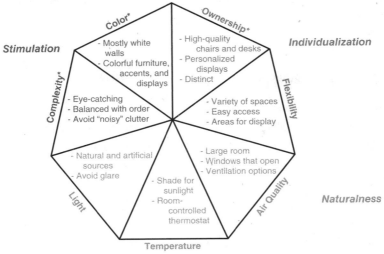

Color*
- Mostly white walls
- Colorful furniture, accents, and displays

Ownership*
- High-quality chairs and desks
- Personalized displays
- Distinct

Stimulation

Individualization

Complexity*
- Eye-catching
- Balanced with order
- Avoid "noisy" clutter

Flexibility
- Variety of spaces
- Easy access
- Areas for display

Light
- Natural and artificial sources
- Avoid glare

Temperature
- Shade for sunlight
- Room-controlled thermostat

Air Quality
- Large room
- Windows that open
- Ventilation options

Naturalness

Reference: Barrett, Davies, Zhang, and Barrett, 2015   *Identified as "strongly usage-related classroom features"*

The Heptagon for Higher Learning demonstrates seven features of good classroom design. What features can you control?

Natural Light and Life

Only the most powerful superheroes can move the planet Earth, but any teacher can block a glaring sun by adding indoor curtains or window shades (or even taping up a poster to cover the transparent spot). Lamps with soft white lightbulbs help offset blinding fluorescent lights. They also add a warmer ambiance to windowless rooms. Oscillating fans provide a cool breeze and more circulation to stuffy spaces. And if air quality is really bad, invest in a good purifier.

Houseplants may not actually do much for cleaning the air, but they have been found to help reduce stress levels and increase productivity and concentration (Lee et al. 2015; Nieuwenhuis et al. 2014). Adding a succulent or other durable species can also

$uper $aver!
Want cheap (or free) PLANTS to decorate your classroom space? Contact the nearest horticulture club—school, 4-H, scouts, etc. Also look for Arbor Day giveaways (last Friday in April)!

enhance your classroom's color, complexity, and distinctiveness. But don't become Poison Ivy and turn your tidy classroom into a tangled Savage Land jungle. (That last sentence included both a DC and Marvel reference, for anyone keeping score.) Don't have a green thumb? Try a few plastic or fake plants. Or find other living or nonliving items attuned to nature—rocks, seashells, fish tanks, hermit crabs, artwork, and so on.

No matter how you decorate and design your classroom, use the space to support students and their learning. Some features may be immovable—walls, doors, windows—but many other objects are flexible to varying degrees—bookshelves, filing cabinets, computers, rugs, and the most important two: chairs and desks.

Musical Chairs (and Desks)

One big decision for classroom layout is how to arrange student desks. This question also applies to two-person tables and similar furniture for students to sit and work. The traditional, or vertical, layout lines desks into columns and rows, all facing the teacher at the front of the room. However, there many other possible arrangements, including nonlinear pods or clusters of desks where students face each other in small groups, as well as desks arranged in a semicircle or horseshoe shape ("U"), or other letters like "T" or "L."

Just like the clothes a teacher wears, the classroom space can look very different depending on students, subject, strategies, and more. Consider your context and vision in light of research on classroom seating types, including the studies summarized in the following chart.

Research on Classroom Layout*

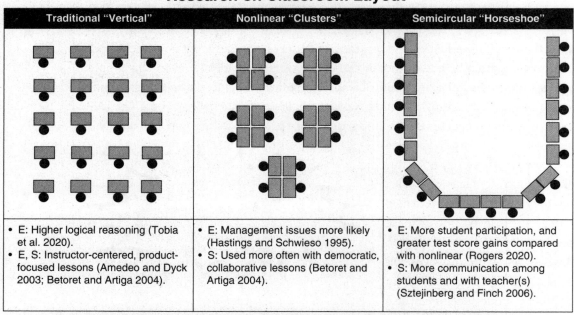

Traditional "Vertical"	Nonlinear "Clusters"	Semicircular "Horseshoe"
• E: Higher logical reasoning (Tobia et al. 2020). • E, S: Instructor-centered, product-focused lessons (Amedeo and Dyck 2003; Betoret and Artiga 2004).	• E: Management issues more likely (Hastings and Schwieso 1995). • S: Used more often with democratic, collaborative lessons (Betoret and Artiga 2004).	• E: More student participation, and greater test score gains compared with nonlinear (Rogers 2020). • S: More communication among students and with teacher(s) (Sztejinberg and Finch 2006).

*School/Age Level Studied: E = Elementary/Early Childhood; S = Secondary (Middle, High School)

Summary of classroom layout research.
What arrangements work best for you and your students?

What do your students need to be successful? What is the best way for them to learn content and participate in your lessons? What other goals do you have for your students? Are there specific students with specific needs? They may benefit in a particular location or orientation in your room. There is evidence that individuals near the front actually do better, all things being equal. In a study of first-year college students, students were randomly assigned seats in a lecture hall at the beginning of the semester. Those who started near the front had higher marks for both participation and course grades (Perkins and Wieman 2005).

Also think about your own strengths and weaknesses. If maintaining on-task students is a struggle for you, you might want to start with students seated individually in columns facing the front. You don't have to keep a single seating plan the entire time. As you and the students get to know each other—and as classroom procedures become more routine—you can transition to layouts that foster more peer interactions.

My sixth grade homeroom teacher began the school year having the students sit in a traditional vertical desk arrangement. But as time went on—marked by the start of a new nine-week quarter—our classroom shuffled into more complex and collaborative arrangements. I distinctly remember a season when all of our desks formed a large square-ish U-shape around the room. Every student had a clear view of the front chalkboard and teacher table, and we could see each other, too. Plus, there was a nice wide-open space in the middle of the room for presentations and projects. Later in the year, we sat in pods of four desks each, two students on each side facing the other pair. In our last seating chart, our teacher knew us well enough to allow students to pick neighbors. Still, he kept some semblance of control by assigning each group's location in the room. As the teacher, you have final say on where students can sit. Again, how much freedom of choice you allot depends on your students, skills, and goals.

Thought Bubble . . .
*What is a **"must-have"** feature for your classroom? Decorations? Furniture? Etc.*

Declarative Decorations

A classroom's layout communicates expectations about the learning environment and students' contributions. Similar messages appear through decoration and other symbolic objects (Cheryan et al. 2014). Think back to the classical classroom standards in America. Presidential portraits and U.S. flags emphasize patriotism and leadership. How you adorn your classroom space can either inspire or intimidate students, so be thoughtful in your decorative decisions.

Inspirational posters, infographics with key content, and student products can all present a supportive arena for learning. It's also important to include artwork and displays that celebrate all students and their cultures, recognizing underrepresented populations without reverting to tokenism (Kelly 2007). However, be careful to not overdo it with extraneous clutter that can distract students or dilute key elements. Ultimately, your classroom is part of the real world in their lives, and it should enrich ongoing learning and growth.

$uper $aver!
Live near a college? At the end of each semester, check curbsides around dormitories and apartments for discarded furniture—tables, chairs, rugs, lamps—FREE!

You Are the Real Clock King

During my undergraduate years in college, our general physics classes always met in the same large lecture hall—big enough to fit the entire University of Nebraska Cornhusker Marching Band. I learned a lot of Newtonian mechanics and quantum theory in that room, having sat in it for at least three semesters in a row. But what I remember most about those sessions was the clock. You couldn't miss it. It had a traditional analog dial, bold black numbers on a massive white circle face—at least three feet in diameter. And, worst of all, the huge thing hung on the front wall directly above the instructor's lectern.

Thankfully, the clock did not emit an annoying tick-tock sound. But it did have a pencil-thin second hand that steadily, slowly, mercilessly circled the clockface . . . every . . . single . . . minute . . . of class. After a while, you didn't notice the incessant second hand. But you couldn't stop your eyes from glancing over the instructor's shoulder, and cringe as the clock's other hands glacially trudged along. I vaguely recall learning about time dilation in our Modern Physics course. I experienced it firsthand during each epochal class.

When I got my first teaching job, the first thing I noticed upon walking into my new classroom was the clock. Although much smaller than the college physics monster, it also hung on the front wall above the teacher's table. But not for long. I snatched the battery-powered timepiece and switched it to the back of the room.

Now, instead of my students counting down every minute, I could more easily glance at the classroom clock to check the time. And surprisingly, I never caught myself wishing the day to go faster. In fact, it was the complete opposite. I monitored the clock so we wouldn't run out of time. When you're the teacher, each lesson goes by in a flash. And there's no greater compliment than hearing your students say, "Over already? That was fast."

> "This is the one place where I can relax and work undisturbed! No one suspects its existence, and no one can penetrate the solid rock out of which it is hewn!"
>
> – Superman,
> *Action Comics* #241 (1958)

Where Is Your Hideout?

Each teacher also needs a place for themselves. Where do you plan lessons, follow up with email, score papers, record grades, and get other things done? For many teachers, such a space is in the very classroom where you work with students all day. But even in this larger area, you should have a "zone" for yourself—your desk, computer, cabinets, personal supplies, and mementos.

During class with kids, you probably don't spend much time at your desk. I recommend you keep students away from that area, too. You respect their space and belongings, and they should give you the same courtesy. I never let my students sit in my cushy swivel office chair, no matter how hard they beg. This rule is not just to limit access to sensitive materials and maintain confidentiality. It also reduces chances for anyone to put a tack or anything else in my seat!

Whether your workspace is in the classroom, a nearby office or closet, or somewhere else, consider it your personal Batcave. Batman doesn't just fight crime on the streets of Gotham. He also spends a lot of time in his underground lair. In fact, I'd argue "The World's Greatest Detective" does most of his preparation, research, and reflecting in the safe confines of the Batcave. Like Batman, teachers require a private (or semiprivate) space for these same important tasks. Our days with students make up the heart of what we do. But we also need noninstructional time in our secret hideouts.

At the high school where I first taught science, my hideout was a teacher desk in the corner of the classroom. Personally, my most productive moments came at the end of the day after everybody else left. During the day, plan periods typically filled up with trips to the copier machine or bathroom, catching up on emails or phone messages, resetting science lab stations, and more. There was never enough time during my plan period for actual planning, especially during those first few years. You may be able to focus and make fast decisions about upcoming lessons or materials during such downtime without students, but I usually had to wait until everyone was long gone—students *and* staff.

This meant staying late after school or coming back after dinner for some work sessions, but I always finished feeling ready and prepared for the next lesson or unit or beyond. Additionally, I could update students' grades on a daily basis. This quick turnaround time was important to me. Teachers expect students to meet deadlines; we should model the same habit. Not every day required grading, but there was always a make-up paper or missing assignment to check off.

Even though I spent a lot of late afternoons and/or nights at my teacher desk, it never felt like extra work. In a quiet school, I could listen to music and enjoy myself. Plus, I never brought work home with me. There was a clear demarcation between professional and domestic life. Think of how Batman has to take a secret passageway to move from Wayne Manor to his underground lair. All I did was walk two blocks from my apartment, but the transition helped maintain a balance between school and home.

Putting a Personal Touch on Personal Space

That said, I still brought a little of my personal life to my work. Like other symbolic objects in the classroom, I could share my own décor and curios. Unlike Batman and his Batcave, I didn't have huge memorabilia like a mechanical *T. rex* or giant penny. Such superhero souvenirs would be distracting and potentially dangerous in the classroom. But I did keep a few family photos and plenty of geeky science toys, along with trinkets that revealed a diverse interest in music, sports, nerd culture, and much more.

Such familiar objects were beneficial for my mental and emotional health. They helped keep me grounded. A quick glance during the day could instill a warm memory or spark a smile. They also provided students a window into my life beyond the classroom, showing them that teachers are people, too, with their own families, hobbies, and goals. How much you want to share is up to you, knowing how comfortable you are revealing a little bit of your backstory (see Chapter 2 for more about sharing personal info).

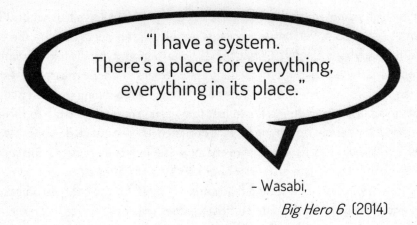

"I have a system.
There's a place for everything,
everything in its place."

– Wasabi,
Big Hero 6 (2014)

Be True to Your School(s)

Two decoration recommendations can shed light on your history and also promote academic aspirations for your students. In their book *The First Days of School*, Harry and Rosemary Wong encourage teachers to frame and hang diplomas in their classrooms, comparing the practice to other professions: "When you walk into a doctor's office, you see degrees, certificates, and licenses nicely framed and neatly hung on the wall in columns and rows. The same is true in the offices of accountants, pharmacists, and even mechanics, with their Mr. Goodwrench certificates." Noting that "teachers are in the diploma business," the Wongs conclude, "Effective teachers display their diplomas with pride" (1998, p. 317).

Many teachers have multiple degrees and certificates, and all of these are fair game for highlighting your accomplishments and expertise. In addition to college and beyond, I recommend teachers post their high school diplomas. This is what most of our students will accomplish first, and your example can give them a preview of their own academic milestones. If you're worried about dated diplomas revealing your age, don't be. Most kids don't care, and they all think we're ancient anyway.

A second suggested decoration is at least one artifact from each alma mater. Where did you attend college? Sure, institutional names appear in formal script on your diplomas. But teachers can elevate awareness by displaying pennants with recognizable logos and mascots. Hang one for every college or university you've attended and graduated. Not only does this further enhance your educational pedigree, it exposes students to a life of intellectual and geographic exploration. Some schools do this for their teachers, lining the hallways with college banners or posting mascot decals on classroom windows.

I'm always amazed to learn where colleagues in education have studied and lived. Moreover, it's another opportunity to bond over common favorites or friendly rivals. Students can join this fun, too. More importantly, they can join conversations about college and further learning as an obvious "next step." This isn't just for high schools, either. Buildings with all ages of kids can elevate awareness. It's never too early to plan or dream about the future. And that certainly has real-world impact!

> **Caption Capture:** In addition to diplomas or degrees, **what other credentials and highlights** can you display in your teaching space?

Meanwhile, at the Hall of Justice . . .

The Batcave isn't Batman's only hangout, and teachers shouldn't stay stuck at their desks. Obviously, during class time they move about the room and interact with students. But even during noninstructional moments, teachers should get away from their private workspaces from time to time.

Superhero teams have all kinds of headquarters, but one of the most famous locations is the Hall of Justice. First featured in the *Super Friends* cartoon of the 1970s and 80s, the Hall of Justice is the gathering place for Superman, Wonder Woman, Batman, and other Justice League members. It's a useful analogy for teachers, as each of these superheroes has their own home base, city, or even planet to patrol and protect. Despite these individual responsibilities, the Justice League heroes meet to tackle big problems and help each other. Are alien "Watermen" extracting silicon from the ocean and disrupting ecosystems? Aquaman can bring his Super Friends together at the Hall of Justice to figure out a solution (Freiberger et al. 1973).

"If you want to get to know any place, you have to start with the people first."

– Peggy Carter,
Agent Carter,
"The Iron Ceiling" (2015)

Schools don't have a Hall of Justice, but they do have workrooms, conference rooms, and teacher lounges. Where do you go to meet up with colleagues and help each other out? Maybe your district has weekly team meetings or regular professional days (see Chapter 9 for more teamwork ideas). Unfortunately, these sessions' agendas are often already full, or an urgent issue needs faster resolution. For me, the best opportunity for meeting teacher colleagues was the lunch hour—or to be more accurate, the 15-minute meal. This midday break was basically a brief respite for scarfing down a quick bite and friendly conversation before returning to afternoon classes.

When I was new, I ate lunch in the teachers' lounge and hardly spoke a word. Each minute was precious, since I first had to hurry to the cafeteria for food. (When you're a bachelor, school lunch is tasty, easy, and cheap.) After cutting in line—one perk of being a teacher—and filling my tray, I'd zip to the teachers' lounge and dive in. I was so busy eating that I didn't have time to talk. Occasionally I might pose a question or seek advice. But mostly I would listen to my colleagues, who represented every department, age group, and experience level. These listening sessions gave me tremendous insight about students, staff, school history, and more. (As an added bonus, my quiet demeanor developed into an assumption by my peers that I was rather smart and introspective.)

Every once in a while, however, a dismal mood would hover over the staff lounge at lunch. It could be for any number of reasons. Someone might have had a rough morning. Students may have been fidgety or fussy. The weather was gloomy (or too nice). Whatever the case, at times the dreary state would linger for a few days. Conversation often turned into complaints. Our teachers' lounge was no longer a comfortable haven, but rather a cranky hive. Or to continue our superhero analogy, the Hall of Justice became the Hall of Doom (and gloom).

During these contentious seasons, I would bypass the teachers' lounge and hoof it back to my classroom for silent dining. Sure, this trip across school grounds took more time, and my hot lunch was closer to room temperature by the time I wolfed it down. But at least I could eat in my own room and eat in peace.

A Secret Sanctum Sanctorum

Doctor Strange's Sanctum Sanctorum isn't as well-known as other superhero hideouts. And in truth, its location isn't that much of a secret (Google it, remember?). Still, the enchanted townhouse is described as Doctor Strange's place to escape reality. Sounds nice, doesn't it? Or maybe you prefer the Fortress of Solitude, Superman's secluded getaway in the Arctic. Either place offers a welcome break from life's usual hustle and bustle.

Maybe you can't escape reality, but every teacher needs daily moments for themselves. These slivers of quiet time don't have to be lengthy. When I taught high school with a busy plan period, I still found a few precious minutes between making copies or writing emails. During the doom-and-gloom teachers' lounge days, I ate in my classroom with the door locked and the lights off. Maybe I even listened to some gentle music at low volume. For those 15 minutes of munching, I entered my very own Sanctum Sanctorum. Refreshed and refueled, I could then return my attention to the students and afternoon tasks.

Not all teachers have a classroom to call home, however. In such cases, it's vital to understand that a secret hideout doesn't have to be a permanent area. Maybe you can find a closet or hallway nook for a temporary respite. Schools are full of interesting little spaces.

Do you have the title of "Floating Teacher"? (Almost sounds like a superhero.) Although a rolling cart has far less surface area, you can still personalize it with similar decorations as you would for a room or desk. Take a look at the cart figure for a summary of floating teacher tips, including references with additional ideas (Bulion 2015; Dubois and Luft 2014; Frommert 2022; Will 2019). Turn your cart into the ultimate "Teach-Mobile"—a portable hub of inspiration and information.

Tips for Floating Teachers Using a Cart

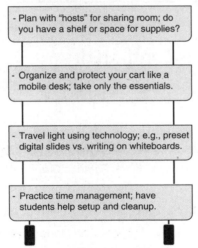

- Plan with "hosts" for sharing room; do you have a shelf or space for supplies?

- Organize and protect your cart like a mobile desk; take only the essentials.

- Travel light using technology; e.g., preset digital slides vs. writing on whiteboards.

- Practice time management; have students help setup and cleanup.

References: Bulion 2015; Dubois and Luft 2014; Frommert 2022; Will 2019.

Tips for floating teachers. To what extent do these tips apply to all teachers?

Superhero hideouts come in all shapes and sizes, spaces and places—everything from skyscrapers to satellites, mansions to sewers. Perhaps it's more accurate to think of a secret hideout as a state of mind. As I mentioned previously, at my first teaching job I walked to and from school nearly every day. This habit astonished my teenage students, who repeatedly questioned why I didn't take my car. I answered that driving isn't all that new and cool after you turn 20. Honestly though, the brief, brisk morning walk energized me. And the journey back and forth was always time well spent, giving me precious moments to preview and review each day. So, I guess my first secret hideout was a two-block stretch of sidewalk.

I know another teacher who drives to school, but always parks in the spot farthest from the building entrance. His colleagues joke that he picks this location to avoid any car dings and scratches—whether unintentional or intentional. The real reason, he says, is so he can spend the lengthy walk thinking of an individual, and how he can make a positive difference in their life that day. He told me if there's ever a morning he can't come up with someone's name, he'll quit teaching. That was a few years ago, but the last I heard, he's still teaching.

So, whatever you have for a secret hideout (and wherever it is), consider how you maintain that special place. And use that space to reflect, retool, and recharge in your efforts to be a better teacher.

No Danger Room required.

 ## To Be Continued!

Further Reading

Brown, R.A., Araújo, D., Bustos, N., and Aguirre, C. (2022). *Shuri and T'Challa: Into the Heartlands (An Original Black Panther Graphic Novel)*. New York: Marvel Comics/Scholastic.

Busiek, K. and Ross, A. (1994/2010). *Marvels*. New York: Marvel Comics.

Lobdell, S. (1993). *X-Men: Survival Guide to the Mansion*. New York: Marvel Comics.

Stern, R., Buscema, J., and Palmer, T. (1986/2010). *Avengers: Under Siege*. New York: Marvel Comics.

Further Viewing

Feige, K. (producer) and Coogler, R. (director). (2018). *Black Panther* [Motion picture]. Marvel Studios.

Feige, K. (producer) and Derrickson, S. (director). (2016). *Doctor Strange* [Motion picture]. Marvel Studios.

Peters, J. and Guber, P. (producers) and Burton, T. (director). (1989). *Batman* [Motion picture]. Warner Bros. Pictures.

Shuler Donner, L. and Winter, R. (producers) and Singer, B. (director). (2000). *X-Men* [Motion picture]. 20th Century Fox.

Shuler Donner, L., Winter, R., and Arad, A. (producers) and Ratner, B. (director). (2006). *X-Men: The Last Stand* [Motion picture]. 20th Century Fox.

WatchMojo. (2015). Top 10 Superhero lairs. https://www.youtube.com/watch?v=E6iMTh-_Mnw.

Questions for Reflection and Discussion

1. What are pros and cons of a teacher living in the same community where they teach?

2. Review the seven traits of good classroom features reported by architectural researchers Barret et al. (2015)–light, temperature, air quality, complexity, color, ownership, and flexibility.

   - Which of these can you control in your classroom? What could you change right now?
   - If something is "impossible" to change, what are some creative solutions for improving it?

3. How much clutter is too much?

4. What other accommodations are needed for your unique classroom and specific students?

5. What personal items do you use to decorate your classroom or workspace? How do students respond to these decorations?

6. How does your school celebrate college and career possibilities through decoration? What could you do to elevate students' awareness even more?

7. Where do you go to get things done? Where do you go to get away and have time for yourself?

8. How much time or space do you need to transition between school life and home life?

9. How much time do you spend in the teachers' lounge or workroom? What kind of atmosphere or attitude do these spaces emit? Where else do you hang out with fellow teachers?

10. What sort of conversations do you have with fellow teachers online and through social media? How do these compare with your in-school interactions?

References

Amedeo, D. and Dyck, J.A. (2003). Activity-enhancing arenas of designs: a case study of the classroom layout. *Journal of Architectural and Planning Research* 20 (4): 323–343.

Barrett, P. and Barrett, L. (2010). The potential of positive places: senses, brain and spaces. *Intelligent Buildings International* 2: 218–228.

Barrett, P., Davies, F., Zhang, Y., and Barrett, L. (2015). The impact of classroom design on pupils' learning: final results of a holistic, multi-level analysis. *Building and Environment* 89: 118–133.

Betoret, F.D. and Artiga, A.G. (2004). Trainee teachers' conceptions of teaching and learning, classroom layout and exam design. *Educational Studies* 30 (4): 355–372.

Bulion, L. (2015). The pains and pleasures of the "floating" teacher. Education World. https://www.educationworld.com/a_curr/curr278.shtml.

Cheryan, S., Ziegler, S.A., Plaut, V.C., and Meltzoff, A.N. (2014). Designing classrooms to maximize student achievement. *Policy Insights from the Behavioral and Brain Sciences* 1 (1): 4–12.

Dubois, S.L. and Luft, J.A. (2014) Science teachers without classrooms of their own: a study of the phenomenon of floating. *Journal of Science Teacher Education* 25 (1): 5–23. doi:10.1007/s10972-013-9364-x.

Durst, A. (2010). John Dewey and the beginnings of the laboratory school. In: *Women Educators in the Progressive Era*, 9–24. New York: Palgrave Macmillan.

Fallace, T. and Fantozzi, V. (2017). The Dewey school as triumph, tragedy, and misunderstood: exploring the myths and historiography of the University of Chicago Laboratory School. *Teachers College Record* 119 (2): 1–32.

Freiberger, F., Gilbert, W., Kahn, B., Robbins, D., Rotcop, K., Sharp, H., Weiss, A., and Williams, M.S. (writers) and Nichols, C.A. (director). (1973). The Watermen. In: *Super Friends* (producers J. Barbera, W. Hanna, L. Marshall, and I. Takamoto). Hanna-Barbera Productions.

Frommert, C. (2022). 3 tips to make life easier as a floating teacher with no set classroom. Edutopia (3 June). https://www.edutopia.org/article/3-tips-make-life-easier-floating-teacher-no-set-classroom.

Hastings, N. and Schwieso, J. (1995). Tasks and tables: the effects of seating arrangements on task engagement in primary classrooms. *Educational Research* 37: 279–291.

Kelly, H. (2007). Racial tokenism in the school workplace: an exploratory study of black teachers in overwhelmingly white schools. *Educational Studies* 41 (3): 230–254. doi:10.1080/00131940701325712.

Knoll, M. (2016). John Dewey's Laboratory School: theory versus practice. Presentation at the International Standing Committee for the History of Education Conference, Chicago (17–20 August).

Lee, M., Lee, J., Park, B., and Miyazaki, Y. (2015). Interaction with indoor plants may reduce psychological and physiological stress by suppressing autonomic nervous system activity in young adults: a randomized crossover study. *Journal of Physiological Anthropology* 34 (21): 1–6.

Lee, S. (2017). A message from Stan Lee. Marvel Entertainment. https://www.youtube.com/watch?v=sjobevGAYHQ.

Maslow, A.H. (1943). A theory of human motivation. *Psychological Review* 50 (4): 370-96.

Mayhew, K.C. and Edwards, A.C. (1936). *The Dewey School: The Laboratory School of the University of Chicago, 1896-1903*. New York: D. Appleton-Century Company, Inc.

National Education Association. (2012). An Educator's Guide to the Four Cs: Preparing 21st Century Students for a Global Society.

Nieuwenhuis, M., Knight, C., Postmes, T., and Haslam, S.A. (2014). The relative benefits of green versus lean office space: three field experiments. *Journal of Experimental Psychology: Applied* 20 (3): 199–214.

Partnership for 21st Century Learning. (2008). 21st Century Skills, Education & Competitiveness: A Resource and Policy Guide. Battelle for Kids. http://www.p21.org/storage/documents/21st_century_skills_education_and_competitiveness_guide.pdf.

Perkins, K.K. and Wieman, C.E. (2005). The surprising impact of seat location on student performance. *The Physics Teacher* 43: 30–33.

Rogers, K.W. (2020). The effects of classroom seating layouts on participation and assessment performance in a fourth grade classroom. *Journal of Learning Spaces* 9 (1): 31–41.

Sztejnberg, A. and Finch, E.F. (2006). Adaptive use patterns of secondary school classroom environments. *Facilities* 24 (13/14): 490–509.

Tobia, V., Sacchi, S., Cerina, V. et al. (2020). The influence of classroom seating arrangement on children's cognitive processes in primary school: the role of individual variables. *Current Psychology* 41: 6522–6533. Advance online publication. https://doi.org/10.1007/s12144-020-01154-9.

Will, M. (2019). Tips for 'floating' teachers: how to survive without a classroom of your own. *Education Week* (8 August). https://www.edweek.org/teaching-learning/tips-for-floating-teachers-how-to-survive-without-a-classroom-of-your-own/2019/08.

Wong, H.K. and Wong, R.T. (1998). *The Days of School: How to Be an Effective Teacher, Second Edition*. Mountain View, CA: Harry K. Wong Productions, Inc.

> "Taste, touch, smell, hearing . . .
> all my senses were heightened! Except
> perhaps for that secret ingredient
> called . . . common sense!"

– Daredevil,
Daredevil #58 (1969)

 Strengths and Superpowers

If you could have any superpower, what would it be?

Flight? Super strength? Invulnerability?

What superpowers could a teacher use?

Super speed would be nice for grading papers. Telepathic mind reading might help to understand what each student is thinking. (Well, not *everything* a student thinks about; more like curriculum-exclusive telepathy.)

Man Without Fear and With-It Teachers

Personally, I'd appreciate having Daredevil's "Superhuman Sensory System" in the classroom. Marvel's "Man Without Fear" has a whole array of enhanced senses that would come in handy. Amplified hearing could detect whispered comments and movements, even to the point of knowing whether someone is telling the truth based on the sound of their heartbeat.

One drawback to super senses would be having super-smelling abilities. While it might prove easier to distinguish between identical twins (based on their body odor alone), an oversensitive nose would quickly reach its fill in a classroom full of kids. Still, the overall "radar sense" would be terrific to observe what's going on in class, taking in data from all sorts of angles. One could pay attention to each individual and monitor progress, struggles, and other behaviors at a superhuman level. Also, a teacher would essentially possess "eyes in the back of their head," a true advantage in any busy classroom.

All things considered, however, I'm not quite ready to douse myself with radioactive slime in hopes of gaining these powers. For now, I'll survey my classes the old-fashioned way, walking around with observant eyes and attentive ears, keeping my head on a swivel. There's a name for this power in the educational world: "with-it-ness" (Kounin 1970). Effective teachers are "with-it" in the classroom. They are alert, always watching even when it doesn't seem like it.

While "with-it-ness" is an ongoing awareness during class time, teachers can take proactive steps to prepare themselves and their lessons. Here's a list of recommendations from Madeline Kovarik (2008), co-author of *The ABC's of Classroom Management*:

- Cultivate positive, caring relationships with students.
- Keep the classroom space open with no hidden spots or line-of-sight obstructions.
- Plan transitions at key moments (beginning, switching activities, dismissing).
- Move and position yourself to face students from different sides of the room.
- Address misbehavior issues immediately and with minimal interruption to the learning of others.

A "with-it" teacher is prompt when dealing with discipline issues, maintaining respect, and preventing off-task behavior before it gets out of control. Like Daredevil, you can be vigilant and ready to intervene when necessary and without fear.

Caption Capture: Daredevil is Marvel's *"Man Without Fear."* What about YOU? **Fill in the blank(s):**

I am the . . .

"Teacher Without _____."

Or the . . .

"Teacher WITH _____."

Fantastic Teaching Powers

For further inspiration and insight on teacher powers, look no further than the Fantastic Four. This heroic quartet not only launched the Marvel Age of Superheroes, they also exemplify many traits of *fantastic* teaching.

Mr. Fantastic (Reed Richards)

Egocentric name aside, Mr. Fantastic is as famous for his amazing intellect as much as his elastic superpowers. Like the Fantastic Four's leader, teachers must be *smart*. Intelligence alone doesn't make a great teacher, but it certainly helps. According to a 2017–2018 survey by the Institute for Education Sciences, over half (58%) of all public school teachers have a postbaccalaureate degree (e.g., master's, educational specialist, or doctorate degree). But learning doesn't stop after a diploma. Isn't that what lifelong learning is all about?

You and I may not be as brilliant as Reed Richards, but we can do our best to study and develop a rich, robust understanding. This growing knowledge base should not be limited to our particular subject(s), but include all the arts and sciences, and—perhaps more importantly—research on how people learn and applicable teaching strategies. Chapter 9 talks more about integrated curriculum and collaborations, so for now, consider how a holistic view of disciplines can enhance your own content knowledge and lesson designs.

> "I've got powers you haven't even dreamed of!"

– Mr. Fantastic,
Fantastic Four #56 (1966)

Teachers must also be *flexible*. You don't have to wear a uniform made of unstable molecules (though it'd be cool to try), but you must be ready to bend, twist, and stretch if you want to stay sane. I have a colleague who worked as a teacher, administrator, professor, and even state school board member, committing her entire career to education. She tells new teachers that all of them should have the same middle name: Flexible. She may not be envisioning the ever-elastic Mr. Fantastic, but I'm confident she speaks the truth from years of experience in classrooms and schools. Notice that she doesn't say all teachers must be charismatic, good at managing students and time, highly organized, and so on—although I'm sure all of these help, too. The number one thing this lifelong educator recommends for new teachers is an ability to adjust, oftentimes in the midst of the moment.

You may not be diving into the Negative Zone like the Fantastic Four (although sometimes maybe your classroom does feel like a pocket universe of contracting anti-matter). Nevertheless, you can follow Mr. Fantastic's example of changing plans and paradigms when exploring unexpected events.

Human Torch (Johnny Storm)

Teachers should be able to instantly "flame on" and fire up their students. I'm speaking figuratively here, of course. (Safety first!) Think back to your most influential teachers. I bet each of them inspired you through their enthusiasm for learning. It didn't matter what subject or grade level they taught. These teachers brought a genuine *warmth* to their classroom. Such energy can vary in terms of volume and theatrics—no one says you have to dance on tables or high-five all your students—but there's a passion that permeates every lesson. It kindles the classroom and makes it glow.

Fantastic teachers also have a healthy *sense of humor*, much like the Fantastic Four's resident jokester. Ever since the quartet's early days, Johnny Storm has used pranks and quips to lighten the mood during life-or-death adventures. You don't have to be a comedian, but it certainly helps to laugh every once in a while.

Early in their careers, every teacher hears the adage, "Don't smile 'til Christmas" (or a similar midwinter milestone). The underlying notion is that a teacher gains respect and control by maintaining a stern façade. Not only does this stoic approach run counter to the need for "warm" classrooms, it also has been

debunked as a myth for decades (Andersen and Andersen 1987; Redman 2006). Additional research finds that humor can reduce stress and classroom tension and increase student rapport and content retention (Buskist et al. 2002; Duffy and Jones 1995; Jeder 2015).

While inviting humor in the classroom, teachers should avoid unnecessary and unethical ridicule or victimization (Cocorada 2008; Gorham and Christophel 2009). Ed Dunkelblau, former president of the Association for Applied and Therapeutic Humor (I bet their conferences are a hoot), is an advocate for "no hurt" humor and adds the following recommendations for teachers (summarized by Elias 2015):

- Insert "Easter eggs" in tests, homework, and other assignments for students to find—recurring jokes or puns, pop culture references, familiar allusions, and so on.
- Post funny quotes and cartoon/comic strips in your room.
- Have a "Joke Friday" to share subject-related humor during timely transitions or "brain breaks."
- Invite students to bring jokes and funny materials they find or create themselves that connect to content learned in class. (Prescreened by the teacher, of course.)

One of my favorite quotes is from comedian Tina Fey: "You can tell how smart people are by what they laugh at." The more someone learns about a topic, the more often they will notice humorous asides, puns, and analogies.

I would argue that the smartest people also laugh at themselves. They understand that nobody has it all put together. We each make mistakes, and most goofs deserve a chuckle followed by a better try the next time. On the first day of school, I ask my students, "Who will make a mistake in the upcoming year?" Before anyone in class can respond, I quickly raise my hand. I explain that as their teacher, I will have my own share of errors. Furthermore, I tell my students that missteps are understandable for each one of them. It is through these experiences that we grow. Throughout the year, my use of self-deprecating humor shows students it's okay to laugh and move on.

Invisible Woman (Susan Storm-Richards)

Here's where we get a little more profound. Teachers are often most effective when they stay out of the spotlight. Instead, they put the primary focus on students, encouraging them to take responsibility and leadership in the learning process. A common motto used among educators is to relinquish the classroom role of "sage on the stage" and become a "guide on the side." Sometimes, that guide is so good the students hardly notice the teacher's presence. Nevertheless, the teacher still plays a vital role in the classroom—they may be *invisible* at times, but they haven't vanished completely. In addition to planning and preparation, the teacher continually engages students as active members in a learning community, helping them make decisions and make sense of information.

This is not a complete shift from teacher-centered to student-centered classrooms, but rather a third option, which Morrison (2014) calls a "*learning*-centered model . . . both teachers *and* students are learners, both constituencies transform information into knowledge and, arguably, motivations and strategies for those transformational processes flow in both directions" (p. 10, emphases in original). A fantastic teacher knows when to appear and disappear at key moments, based on their under-standing of the lesson and awareness of their students. They know when to allow freedom and when to provide parameters, when to give guidance and when to encourage exploration.

> "One invisible girl can sometimes accomplish more than a battalion!"

–Invisible Woman,
Fantastic Four #3 (1961)

In many ways, Susan Storm has the most powerful abilities among her team-mates. Not only can she turn invisible, she can also produce invisible force fields for both offensive and defensive purposes. Teachers must also do their best to *protect* students and colleagues from all kinds of hazards, unseen or otherwise.

In most states, American teachers are mandatory reporters of suspected child abuse and neglect. Be aware of your students, watching and listening, and report concerns to school social workers and law enforcement, if necessary. If you're not sure, ask a colleague or supervisor, maintaining confidentiality and trust. Teachers can find resources from their local and state agencies, as well as organizations such as Child Welfare Information Gateway, the Office of Juvenile Justice and Delinquency Prevention, the National Child Traumatic Stress Network, the U.S. Department of Education's Office of Safe and Supportive Schools, among others. (See the References section of this chapter.) Likewise, agencies such as the Anti-Bullying Alliance in the United Kingdom and StopBullying.gov in the United States provide tools and tips for teachers to fight bullying in their schools and communities.

We talk more about working with colleagues and other stakeholders in later chapters, but keep in mind that a teacher's protective role also applies to their fellow educators. Speak up for your schools and profession. Celebrate accomplishments and be a positive voice. Invisibility is an instructional asset in the classroom, but teachers must also project ourselves into the wider world and conversations about education. Remember, we're the experts in this stuff, with degrees and everything.

The Thing (Ben Grimm)

In addition to protecting students, fantastic teachers also need to protect themselves. Like the ever lovable, blue-eyed Thing, teachers must be *thick-skinned*. We have to withstand a daily barrage of gripes and wisecracks that rival Doctor Doom's sorcery blasts. Teaching can be tough, and it requires tough teachers. Another term for this is "grit," defined by early grit researcher Angela Lee Duckworth as "passion and perseverance for very long-term goals," "having stamina," and "sticking with your future day-in, day-out; not just for the week, not just for the month, but for years" (2013). Grit speaks to one's determination and durability, especially during challenging situations.

Over six decades, the Thing has battled fellow Marvel heavyweight the Incredible Hulk over 60 times (Cimino 2021). More significantly, the Thing has a losing record. But he keeps fighting back and fighting through impossible odds. Teachers who do the same will ultimately make a difference that lasts. Duckworth and her colleagues report that grit is a key predictor for teacher effectiveness and retention, accounting for those who "survive and thrive" in educational careers (Robertson-Kraft and Duckworth 2014). Additional research has found that grit-based performance depends greater on a teacher's perseverance than on their passion (Baraquia 2020). In other words, while it's important to have a purpose and passion for teaching (as discussed in Chapter 1), what matters more is sticking with it and pushing through the hard days. During these difficult times, look to Ben Grimm and his rocky hide for inspiration.

To use another metaphor, teachers should be judicious in deciding when "It's clobberin' time!" Even fantastic teachers have students who occasionally act out worse than a hoard of Mole Man's Moloids. We can't simply exile these misguided minions into Subterranea. But we can't allow class clowns to ruin everyone else's opportunity to learn, either. It takes wisdom (sometimes a Reed Richards-level of intellect) to know how to squash misbehavior without squashing the student (emotionally, that is—we're still speaking metaphorically here).

Effective classroom management also requires a mix of courage and compassion. This gets even harder when emotions run high. Richard Curwin, author of *Discipline with Dignity* (2014), recommends a two-step process. The first goal is stabilization to calm things down, followed by intervention to address the issue with respect and empathy. Nevertheless, there are times when immediate action is required. This could be anything from major safety precautions to minor behavior redirections occurring moment by moment. In such scenarios, the "with-it" teacher must also be a "deal-with-it" teacher.

Even the best teachers aren't perfect in determining when and how to manage, discipline, and/or overlook student actions and attitudes. Nobody is flawless. But we can all strive to be fantastic.

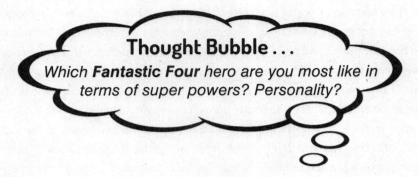

Thought Bubble...

*Which **Fantastic Four** hero are you most like in terms of super powers? Personality?*

Earthbound (and Effective) Teacher Powers

Alas, most of us will not travel outside the protection of Earth's atmosphere and get bombarded by cosmic radiation. And even if we did, we're more likely to get cancer than cool superpowers (NASA 2019). Thanks a lot, science.

So, in addition to fantastic teacher powers—figurative, yet still real—let's take a closer look at some earthbound strengths and skills.

If you examine literature in teacher competency, a few common phrases pop up that refer to professional prowess. These may not arise from cosmic rays, but they are pretty universal among educators and researchers. Some of you may have come across these terms before. And you probably have your own collection of educational acronyms and abbreviations in your particular field of expertise. To keep things simple, I focus on some general teaching items that each have more precise applications to specific subjects and grades.

"The greatest power on Earth is the magnificent power we all possess . . . the power of the human brain!"

– Professor X,
X-Men #2 (1963)

Content Knowledge (CK)

Obviously, teachers must know something about what they are teaching. Numerous studies have found positive correlations between higher student achievement scores and teachers with stronger content knowledge, or CK. Interestingly, a lot of this research focuses on mathematics education (Clotfelter, Ladd, and Vigdor 2007; Guimarães et al. 2013; Harbison and Hanushek 1992; Hill et al. 2008). Another study found that math teachers who have a more conceptual view of mathematics taught with this approach, as opposed to those who focused on rote memorization and rules (Tchoshanov 2011). Additionally, students are prone to struggle in the same areas of content where their teachers are weakest (Tchoshanov, Lesser, and Salazar 2008).

Regardless of subject, content knowledge is more than a mere collection of facts or skills. In comparing novices and experts of various fields, psychologists have found that experts don't just know more, they also *think* differently. "[E]xpertise requires something else: a well-organized knowledge of concepts, principles, and procedures of inquiry" (Bransford, Brown, and Cocking 2000, p. 239). A teacher who possesses true CK has a rich, robust mastery of fundamental principles along with key relationships and applications.

This does not mean you must know everything about your subject. Rather, you possess a firm framework of understanding from which you perceive and relate concepts. In a way, teachers with solid content knowledge have both a big-picture view as well as a pinpoint awareness of noteworthy exemplars, exceptions, and connections. "The teacher need not only understand *that* something is so; the teacher must further understand *why* it is so, on what grounds its warrant can be asserted, and under what circumstances our beliefs in its justification can be weakened or denied" (Ball, Thames, and Phelps 2008, p. 391, emphases in original). This description sounds like an expert to me.

But knowing your stuff is not the only ingredient for successful teaching. If that were the case, our most brilliant minds would be the best teachers. And we all know intelligent people who know a lot about something, but are lousy when it comes to helping others learn it. Effective teachers need more superpowers than just smarts.

Pedagogical Knowledge (PK)

Additional research into student achievement has found many other influential teacher attributes beyond content knowledge. These factors include classroom management, relationship building, feedback, and instructional strategies (Hattie 2003; 2012). In other words, effective teachers don't just know what to teach, but how to teach.

The fancy phrase for this type of understanding is "pedagogical knowledge," or PK. Pedagogy is a favorite term for educators, often defined as "the art and science of teaching" (Marzano 2007). Teachers with sound PK are able to plan lessons with purposeful instruction and interactions. You may know people like this, who seem capable of teaching anything. Through preparation, practice, and personal talents, these teachers can implement key strategies and behaviors to engage students. Here are some example components of a quality teacher's general PK (König et al. 2011; Voss, Kunter, and Baumert 2011):

- General structure of lesson plans and objectives.
- Student motivational methods.
- Classroom management and maintaining on-task behaviors.
- Time management and transitions.
- Cooperative and individual learning tasks.
- Assessment strategies.
- Adaptive and differentiated instruction.

Lee Shulman—more on him in a minute—says that pedagogical knowledge is able to "transcend subject matter" (1987, p. 8). Sounds impressive, no? Unfortunately, general PK can only go so far. It's hard to lead students through a subject field about which you know very little. Even though I am certified to teach science, I've been a substitute teacher in all kinds of classrooms, including foreign language and vocal music. It's fun for a day or so, but beyond that I'm pretty worthless. Know your limits.

Historically, stakeholders have debated between the merits of content knowledge and pedagogical knowledge as the primary element for preparing teachers. Like a lot of trends in education, relative popularity of CK or PK swings back and forth like a pendulum. Both have value, but either one by itself is insufficient. In the midst of the 1980s reform movements—including *A Nation at Risk* (1983) and the rise of National Board Certification (1987)—Stanford educational scholar Lee Shulman proposed a third option—PCK.

Pedagogical Content Knowledge (PCK)

Basically, PCK is an educational Reese's Peanut Butter Cup. Shulman combined the chocolate CK and peanut butter PK to create something better. Or, if you prefer a relatively obscure superhero reference, PCK is like DC's Firestorm—a nuclear-powered hero created from the fusion of high schooler Ronnie Raymond and adult physicist Martin Stein (Conway and Milgrom 1978). (Don't ask me how it works. That's comic book science.)

Back to reality, Shulman has written extensively about the limits of CK and PK as singular elements in teacher preparation and proficiency. In particular, he was concerned with how novice teachers transform into expert educators. In presenting the various knowledges developed by teachers, Shulman highlights the important role of pedagogical content knowledge (PCK): "It represents the blending of content and pedagogy into an understanding of how particular topics, problems, or issues are organized, represented, and adapted to the diverse interests and abilities of learners, and presented for instruction" (1987, p. 8). There is power in this amalgamation, since such knowledge has direct application to a particular curriculum and classroom setting. Shulman lists several items teachers may include in their personal PCK collection, each applicable to individual topics (1986):

- Analogies and metaphors.
- Illustrations, stories, and examples.
- Demonstrations and explanations.
- Alternative representations and rephrasings.
- Common "tricky spots" and student misconceptions.
- Questions and problems.

Instead of just knowing "what" (CK) or having a general grasp of "how" (PK), a teacher can use these PCK elements (and others) to target specific situations.

This all sounds wonderful, but unfortunately PCK also has its limits. First, PCK can be so precise that it loses value outside of a single scenario. Indeed, there is a challenge to unpacking which particular aspects of PCK are useful or not (Baxter and Lederman 1999; Gess-Newsome 1999; Loughran et al. 2001; Meredith 1995; Settlage 2013). Given the hundreds of lessons occurring every school year, a teacher relying on PCK may collapse under the burden of shuffling all the different stories and tricks for each individual lesson. Also, some students may get sidetracked by too many analogies or metaphors. Distracted, they could lose sight of the actual content they're supposed to learn.

Secondly, a lot of PCK comes through experience, including trial and error. It certainly follows a "whatever works" philosophy for teaching and learning. If one particular story works to help students understand a concept, terrific! If not, well, what else can you try? Depending on students' diverse backgrounds, they may or may not connect with your own frame of reference or cultural touchstones. Shulman himself acknowledges the strain of building up PCK into a viable teacher power: "Since there are no single most powerful forms of representation, the teacher must have at hand a veritable armamentarium of alternative forms of representation, some of which derive from research whereas others originate in the wisdom of practice" (1986, p. 9).

If you're a veteran teacher, no doubt you have already assembled a functional collection of PCK. This includes applying your knowledge of content and general pedagogy. It also involves direct experience and reflection of what students find meaningful and memorable in terms of your subject. By all means, use what works and share it with your colleagues. Even so, every teacher has their own personality and experiences they can apply to lessons. What works for you may not work for others. (See the section entitled "Weird Superpowers.")

Whenever you do teach something new, you probably sense a disequilibrium and trepidation toward empty spots in the curriculum. How will you fill these holes with relevant and rigorous instruction? Sure, you have content standards, course materials, and pacing guides, but no lesson can actually teach itself. That's your job. What do you do? You could rely on PCK, but that may require stumbling through some rough days until you get your footing.

Research-Aligned Framework for Teaching (RAFT)

One more acronym, and RAFT can mean many things to many different people and professions. (Just be careful looking it up in the Urban Dictionary; "F" can be a tricky letter.) In the Marvel Universe, the RAFT is a maximum-security prison for superpowered criminals (Bendis and Finch 2005). Jail has obvious negative connotations, but on the bright side, think of RAFT as a protective institution. Teachers can use a research-aligned framework as a safe haven to support their decisions and inform reflection. But rather than locking in villains, this RAFT provides a secure base for launching instruction.

There are all kinds of conceptual models and theoretical frameworks in the field of education. Open any textbook for teachers and you'll find concept maps, flowcharts, and visual schematics illustrating such ideas. One thing they have in common—aside from a lot of boxes and circles and arrows and linking lines—is a reference to educational research and scholarly writings.

> **Caption Capture:** Sketch your own **diagram or flowchart** illustrating what you regard as KEY elements and relationships for effective teaching:

Credible research should be the foundation for any teacher's decisions and actions. The opposite of this is to chase the latest fad making the rounds at school in-service meetings or on social media. Professional development is important, but those who have taught for more than a few years are apt to notice and comment, "We've seen this before. It isn't new." In such cases, consider déjà vu to be a good sign. Something that is rebranded or repackaged probably came from a central tenet in education that spans decades.

Sure, new ideas come up. But the stuff that lasts builds on top of established research. The thing to watch out for is an "original" or "groundbreaking" conceit that claims to revolutionize education as we know it. Such notions appear "innovative" because they have no connection to quality research or sound learning theory. As a result, any sense of "fresh and new" will inevitably spoil and rot.

Getting back to frameworks for teaching, the ones that endure are those that align with research and provide practical application. Different schools and subject fields may focus on one particular framework or another, or even possible combinations. Some have become tools for teacher development, evaluation, and self-reflection (e.g., Clough, Berg, and Olson 2009; Colton and Sparks-Langer 1993; Danielson 2002; 2007; Marzano 2007; 2017; Squires 2004). Others provide a system for planning and teaching, applicable for entire courses, separate units, or even single lessons (Engelman 2001; Meyer, Rose, and Gordon 2014; Wiggins and McTighe 2005). All of these RAFTs emphasize teacher decision-making about the multiple dimensions of classroom instruction. Regardless of the framework, several common themes arise:

- Consideration of student traits (cultural, cognitive, affective, etc.).
- Well-defined vision for student outcomes.
- Planning of procedures, sequence, and materials.
- Classroom instruction, management, and interactions.
- Student actions and evidence of learning (assessment).
- Reflection and evaluation of teaching.
- Professionalism and ethical responsibilities.

Depending on the individual framework, some of these categories contain several more subtopics and detailed components. Many include elements found above with respect to content knowledge (CK), pedagogical knowledge (PK), and pedagogical content knowledge (PCK). A RAFT takes such "teacher powers" into account and equips teachers to do their job.

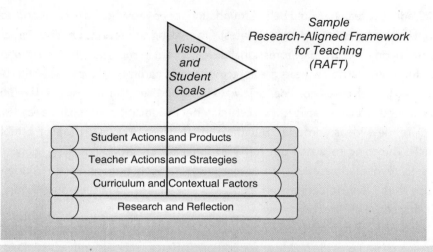

Sample Research-Aligned Framework for Teaching (RAFT)

Vision and Student Goals

Student Actions and Products

Teacher Actions and Strategies

Curriculum and Contextual Factors

Research and Reflection

An example RAFT (research-aligned framework for teaching). What elements guide your teaching and keep it afloat?

Are there drawbacks to emphasizing a research-aligned framework for teaching? I'll admit that some of the models can get quite cumbersome. This may be due to lengthy text or intricate diagrams, but it's understandable given the complex nature of teaching. At the same time, RAFTs are not as specific when it comes to direct classroom application. But rather than dismissing research and theory as fluff, consider how such a framework can keep your teaching afloat. As one RAFT developer explains, a framework "tells teachers what to think about rather than what to do" (Squires 2004, p. 352).

Effective teachers are informed and reflective. They make purposeful choices and take thoughtful actions, as opposed to following the latest craze or dogma. In this way, teachers guided by a research-aligned framework are able to develop and analyze instruction like true educational experts. Their teaching is not trendy, but rather *timely* and *timeless*. That's a pretty nifty superpower.

Weird Superpowers

Super ventriloquism, super eating, and super dancing.

These are all lesser known (and much weirder) superpowers of the Man of Steel himself, Superman. Most of these oddball antics occurred just once or twice in a zany comic book story (e.g., Bates and Swan 1975; Bernstein and Boring 1961;

Burkett and Schaffenberger 1979). Even so, you never know when one of these bizarre abilities might come in handy.

Do you have any weird superpowers? If you're like most teachers (and Superman), you can probably gulp down a quick lunch while on the go. But what else can you do that makes you special? Consider how you can use these unique skills and traits to enhance your teaching. For example, I used to play my trumpet to help students learn about the physics of sound.

What about you? Are you musically talented? Artistic? Athletic? Magical? These talents don't necessarily have to be "weird," but they may be a terrific addition in the classroom. If you're stumped for inspiration, search for "family friendly party tricks" on the Internet. You can also find books with all kinds of ideas (Davis 1991; Holcombe 2016). Turn these "totally useless skills" into pedagogical tools for lessons, bellwork, brain breaks, and more memorable learning experiences.

> **Caption Capture:** List any "weird superpowers," unusual talents, or hobbies you could harness to **enhance your classroom teaching:**

 ## To Be Continued!

Further Reading

Higgins, E. (2022). The saga of Marvel's highly debatable power-level cards. Polygon (21 March). https://www.polygon.com/22981576/marvel-cards-90s-power-levels.

Leong, T. (2013). *Super Graphic: A Visual Guide to the Comic Book Universe*. San Francisco: Chronicle Books.

Mack, D. and Quesada, J. (2010). *Daredevil/Echo: Parts of a Hole*. New York: Marvel Comics.

Schedeen, J. (2015). Superman's weirdest superpowers. IGN (4 February). https://www.ign.com/articles/2015/02/04/supermans-15-weirdest-superpowers.

Waid, M., Rivera, P., and Martin, M. (2011/2012). *Daredevil, Vol. 1*. New York: Marvel Comics.

Waid, M., Wieringo, M., and Buckingham, M. (2002/2011). *Fantastic Four by Waid & Wieringo Ultimate Collection, Book 1*. New York: Marvel Comics.

Further Viewing

Feige, K. (producer) and Boden, A. and Fleck, R. (directors). (2019). *Captain Marvel* [Motion picture]. Marvel Studios.

Milchan, A., Foster, G., and Arad, A. (producers) and Johnson, M.S. (director). (2003). *Daredevil* [Motion picture]. 20th Century Fox.

Safran, P. (producer) and Sandberg, D.F. (director). (2019). *Shazam!* [Motion picture]. Warner Bros.

Walker, J. and Paradis Grindle, N. (producers) and Bird, B. (director). (2018). *Incredibles 2* [Motion picture]. Walt Disney/Pixar Studios.

Questions for Reflection and Discussion

1. What are deliberate ways a teacher can practice "with-it-ness" in the classroom?

2. Which Fantastic Four trait(s) do you exhibit the most as a teacher: smart, flexible, fired up, humorous, invisible, protective, gritty, tough? Which FF trait(s) do you wish to add or improve? How can you do this?

3. Of the following types of teacher knowledge–Content Knowledge (CK), Pedagogical Knowledge (PK), Pedagogical Content Knowledge (PCK)–which is your strongest? Which is your weakest? How have you grown in each of these areas? How can you grow more in each?

4. What do you think of the phrase "good teaching is good teaching"? How accurate is it?

5. What sorts of conceptual models or theoretical frameworks have you witnessed in different organizations or programs? What did you find useful? Confusing?

6. In what ways can a Research-Aligned Framework for Teaching (RAFT) keep you buoyant and afloat?
   - To continue this analogy, describe storms or squalls with potential to sink your teaching.
   - What are the tides and currents that come and go?
   - How do you avoid or remove dead weight that pulls you down?
   - How can you help others stay afloat and seek calmer waters?
   - What other nautical or buoyancy aspects work well with this RAFT analogy?

7. How would you respond to the comment, "A real teacher doesn't have time to deal with theoretical fluff."?

8. What educational trends have you found revolutionary or revelatory? Helpful? Redundant?

9. What are some "weird superpowers" or unique talents you've witnessed in other teachers? How did they enhance classroom instruction? Any drawbacks or distractions?

References

Andersen, J.F. and Andersen, P.A. (1987). Never smile until Christmas? Casting doubt on an old myth. *Journal of Thought* 22 (4): 57–61.

Ball, D.L., Thames, M.H., and Phelps, G. (2008). Content knowledge for teaching: What makes it special? *Journal of Teacher Education* 59 (5): 389–407.

Baraquia, L.G. (2020). Development of a teacher grit scale (TGS): predicting the performance of educators in the Philippines. *The New Educational Review* 60 (2): 165–177.

Bates, C. and Swan, C. (1975). Superman's Energy-Crisis! *Action Comics (Vol. 1) #454*. New York: DC Comics.

Baxter, J.A. and Lederman, N.G. (1999). Assessment and measurement of pedagogical content knowledge. In: *Examining Pedagogical Content Knowledge: The Construct and Its Implications for Science education* (eds. J. Gess-Newsome and N.G. Lederman, 147–161. Dordrecht, the Netherlands: Kluwer Academic Publishers.

Bendis, B.M. and Finch, D. (2005). Breakout! Part 1. *New Avengers (Vol. 1) #1*. New York: Marvel Comics.

Bernstein, R. and Boring, W. (1961). Superman: The War between Supergirl and the Superman Emergency Squad! *Action Comics (Vol. 1) #276*. New York: DC Comics.

Bransford, J., Brown, A., and Cocking, R. (eds.). (2000). *How People Learn: Brain, Mind, Experience, and School*. Washington, DC: National Research Council.

Burkett, C. and Schaffenberger, K. (1979). Private Life of Clark Kent: Super-Disco Fever. *Superman Family (Vol. 1) #196*. New York: DC Comics.

Buskist, W., Sikorski, J., Buckley, T., and Saville, B.K. (2002). Elements of master teaching. In: *The Teaching of Psychology: Essays in Honor of Wilbert J. McKeachie and Charles L. Brewer* (eds. S.F. Davis and W. Buskist), 27–39. New York: Routledge.

Child Welfare Information Gateway. (2019). Mandatory reporters of child abuse and neglect. https://www.childwelfare.gov/topics/systemwide/laws-policies/statutes/manda/.

Cimino, J. (2021). Hulk vs Thing. Hero Envy (12 April). http://hero-envy.blogspot.com/2012/04/hulk-vs-thing.html.

Clotfelter, C., Ladd, H., and Vigdor, J. (2007). How and why do credentials matter for student achievement (NBER, Working Paper #12828). Cambridge, MA: National Bureau of Economic Research.

Clough, M.P., Berg, C., and Olson, J.K. (2009). Promoting effective science teacher education and science teaching: A framework for teacher decision-making. *International Journal of Science and Mathematics Education* 7 (4): 821–847.

Cocorada, E. (2008). *Evaluation and Microviolence in the School Environment*. Brașov, Romania: Transilvania University of Brașov Publishing House.

Conway, G. and Milgrom, A. (1978). Make Way for Firestorm! *Firestorm (Vol. 1) #1*. New York: DC Comics.

Curwin, R. (2014). Classroom management: the intervention two-step. Edutopia (4 February). https://www.edutopia.org/blog/classroom-management-intervention-two-step-richard-curwin.

Danielson, C. (2007). Enhancing professional practice: a framework for teaching, second edition. Association for Supervision and Curriculum Development.

Danielson, C. (2002). Enhancing student achievement: a framework for school improvement. Association for Supervision and Curriculum Development.

Davis, R. (1991). *Totally Useless Skills*. New York: Perigree Books/Putnam.

Department of Health and Human Services. (n.d.) Stop Bullying. www.stopbullying.gov.

Duckworth, A.L. (2013). Grit: the power of passion and perseverance. TED Talks Education. https://www.ted.com/talks/angela_lee_duckworth_grit_the_power_of_passion_and_perseverance.

Duffy, D.K., and Jones, J.W. (1995). Creating magic in the classroom. In: *Teaching Within the Rhythms of the Semester* (eds. D.K. Duffy and J.W. Jones), p. 27–54. San Francisco: Jossey-Bass.

Elias, M.J. (2014). Using humor in the classroom. Edutopia (30 March). https://www.edutopia.org/blog/using-humor-in-the-classroom-maurice-elias.

Engleman, L. (ed.). (2001). *The BSCS Story: A History of the Biological Sciences Curriculum Study*. Colorado Springs, CO: Biological Sciences Curriculum Study.

Fiske, E.B. (1986). Carnegie panel plans to establish nationwide teacher certification. *The New York Times* (16 May). https://www.nytimes.com/1986/05/16/us/carnegie-panel-plans-to-establish-nationwide-teacher-certification.html.

Gess-Newsome, J. (1999). Pedagogical content knowledge: an introduction and orientation. In: *Examining Pedagogical Content Knowledge: The Construct and Its Implications for Science Education* (eds. J. Gess-Newsome and N.G. Lederman), 3–17. Dordrecht, the Netherlands: Kluwer Academic Publishers.

Gorham, J. and Christophel, D.M. (1990). The relationship of teachers' use of humor in the classroom to immediacy and student learning. *Communication Education* 39: 46–62.

Guimarães, R., Sitaram, A., Jardon, L. et al. (2013). The effect of teacher content knowledge on student achievement: A quantitative case analysis of six Brazilian states. Population Association of America 2013 Annual Meeting Program, New Orleans (11–13 April).

Harbison, R. and Hanushek, E. (1992). Educational performance of the poor: lessons from rural northeast Brazil. World Bank (p. 81–177).

Hattie, J. (2003). Teachers make a difference: What is the research evidence? Paper presented at the ACER Research Conference, Melbourne, Australia (October). http://research.acer.edu.au/research_conference_2003/4/.

Hattie, J. (2012). *Visible Learning for Teachers: Maximizing Impact on Learning*. New York: Routledge.

Hill, H., Ball, D., and Schilling, S. (2008). Unpacking pedagogical content knowledge: conceptualizing and measuring teachers' topic-specific knowledge of students. *Journal for Research in Mathematics Education* 39 (4): 372–400.

Holcombe, C. (2016). *Party Tricks, Magic and Puzzles: Easy to Learn Tricks and Puzzles to Entertain Family and Friends*. Scotts Valley, CA: CreateSpace.

Institute of Education Sciences. (2021). Characteristics of public school teachers. https://nces.ed.gov/programs/coe/indicator/clr.

Jeder, D. (2015). Implications of using humor in the classroom. *Procedia–Social and Behavioral Sciences* 180: 828–833.

König, J., Blömeke, S., Paine, L. et al. (2011). General pedagogical knowledge of future middle school teachers: on the complex ecology of teacher education in the United States, Germany, and Taiwan. *Journal of Teacher Education* 62 (2): 188–201.

Korobkin, D. (1988). Humor in the classroom: Considerations and strategies. *College Teaching* 36 (4): 154–158.

Kounin, J. (1970). *Discipline and Group Management in Classrooms*. New York: Holt, Rinehart & Winston.

Kovarik, M. (2008). Being a with-it teacher. *New Teacher Advocate* 10 (Winter).

Kramer Ertel, P.A. and Kovarik, M. (2014). *The ABC's of Classroom Management: An A-Z Sampler for Designing Your Learning Community, Second Edition*. New York: Routledge/Kappa Delta Pi.

Loughran, J., Milroy, P., Berry, A. et al. (2001). Documenting science teachers' pedagogical content knowledge through papers. *Research in Science Education* 31: 289–307.

Marzano, R.J. (2007). The art and science of teaching: A comprehensive framework for effective instruction. Association for Supervision and Curriculum Development.

Marzano, R.J. (2017). *The New Art and Science of Teaching: More Than Fifty New Instructional Strategies for Academic Success*. Bloomington, IN: Solution Tree Press.

Meredith, A. (1995). Terry's learning: some limitations of Shulman's pedagogical content knowledge. *Cambridge Journal of Education* 25 (2): 175–187.

Meyer, A., Rose, D., and Gordon, D. (2014). *Universal Design for Learning: Theory and Practice*. Wakefield, MA: CAST Professional Publishing.

Morrison, C.D. (2014). From 'sage on the stage' to 'guide on the side': a good start. *International Journal for the Scholarship of Teaching and Learning* 8 (1): Article 4.

National Aeronautics and Space Administration. (2019). Why space radiation matters. https://www.nasa.gov/analogs/nsrl/why-space-radiation-matters/.

National Board for Professional Teaching Standards. (2022). Mission and history. https://www.nbpts.org/about/mission-history/.

National Child Traumatic Stress Network. (2008). Child trauma toolkit for educators. https://www.nctsn.org/resources/child-trauma-toolkit-educators.

National Children's Bureau. (2022). Anti-bullying alliance. anti-bullyingalliance.org.uk.

National Commission on Excellence in Education. (1983). A nation at risk: The imperative for educational reform. https://www2.ed.gov/pubs/NatAtRisk/index.html.

Office of Elementary and Secondary Education. (2022). Safe & supportive schools. U.S. Department of Education. https://oese.ed.gov/offices/office-of-formula-grants/safe-supportive-schools/.

Office of Juvenile Justice and Delinquency Prevention. (2011). Trauma-informed care for children exposed to violence: "tips for teachers." https://www.justice.gov/sites/default/files/defendingchildhood/legacy/2011/09/19/tips-teachers.pdf.

Redman, P.D. (2006). *Don't Smile Until December, and Other Myths About Classroom Teaching*. Thousand Oaks, CA: Corwin Press/Sage Publications Company.

Robertson-Kraft, C. and Duckworth, A.L. (2014). True grit: trait-level perseverance and passion for long-term goals predicts effectiveness and retention among novice teachers. *Teachers College Record* 116 (3). https://journals.sagepub.com/doi/10.1177/016146811411600306.

Settlage, J. (2013). On acknowledging PCK's shortcomings. *Journal of Science Teacher Education* 24: 1–12.

Shulman, L.S. (1987). Knowledge and teaching: Foundations of the new reform. *Harvard Educational Review* 57: 1–22.

Shulman, L.S. (1986). Those who understand: Knowledge growth in teaching. *Educational Researcher* 15 (2): 4–31.

Squires, G. (2004). A framework for teaching. *British Journal of Educational Studies* 52 (4): 342–358.

Tchoshanov, M.A. (2011). Relationship between teacher knowledge of concepts and connections, teaching practice, and student achievement in middle grade mathematics. *Educational Studies in Mathematics* 76: 141–164.

Tchoshanov, M.A., Lesser, L.M., and Salazar, J. (2008). Teacher knowledge and student achievement: revealing patterns. *NCSM Journal of Mathematics Education Leadership* 10 (2): 38–48.

Voss, T., Kunter, M., and Baumert, J. (2011). Assessing teacher candidates' general pedagogical/psychological knowledge: test construction and validation. *Journal of Educational Psychology* 103 (4): 952–969.

Wiggins, G.P. and McTighe, J. (2005). *Understanding by Design*. Alexandria, VA: Association for Supervision and Curriculum Development.

> "I have everything for an emergency in my utility belt . . . except money to pay for our food and drink!"

– Batman,
World's Finest #186 (1969)

 Gadgets and Gizmos

Superpowers are great and all, but it also helps to have one or more helpful tools at the ready. Consider some popular superheroes and their gadgets and weapons. Wonder Woman has her lasso and bracelets. Thor holds the enchanted hammer Mjolnir. Captain America carries his trusty Vibranium shield. Heck, even Spider-Man has his mechanical web-shooters (unless you're Tobey Maguire). These heroes already possess special abilities, but they take crime fighting up a notch by adding accessories to the mix.

Teachers, do you see the parallel for your classroom? In addition to a framework of knowledge and fantastic strengths, heroic teachers utilize an assortment of useful tools.

What's in Your Utility Belt?

Batman is the best known hero for his gadgets and gizmos, which he carries about in his trusty utility belt. Hidden around his waist are all kinds of clever items, each within arm's reach when the need arises: Batarangs, grappling hook and cable, smoke bombs, lock picks, laser torch, a SCUBA-like "rebreathing apparatus," first-aid kit, even a chunk of green kryptonite, plus many more. Batman doesn't stop at his belt, either, with additional secret accessories in his costume, along with much bigger toys: Batmobiles, Batplane, Batcopter, Batglider, and pretty much any other kind of Bat-vehicle you can imagine.

Teachers may not have the Bat-budget or storage space for so much stuff, but we can still learn from Batman's example. He doesn't use all of these tools and gadgets equally. We see the Caped Crusader use Batarangs and grappling rope quite often. Shark repellent or glue globules? Not so much.

The same goes for teachers. In your classroom, you probably have a go-to collection of tools and materials. What do you use most often in your day-to-day instruction? What are your favorite resources and strategies? Like Batgear, the most frequently used gadgets are portable, functional, and applicable toward a variety of situations. Still, some items are more effective than others depending on the need. Let's take a closer look at materials first, before we dive into strategies and the *ultimate* education tool.

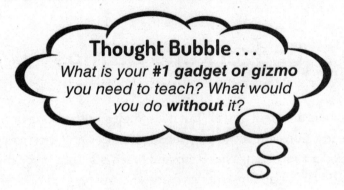

Thought Bubble . . .
What is your #1 gadget or gizmo you need to teach? What would you do without it?

Meaningful Materials

The typical classroom contains all kinds of school supplies—books, pencils, pens, markers, paper, scissors, tape, glue, and more. Depending on your subject and grades, you'll have other materials at your disposal. In addition to using things that are appropriate for student age and class topic, also consider what objects you feature to foster meaningful learning. Ask yourself, what will truly resonate with my students?

I mostly teach science, a subject that often stirs up images of chemicals, equipment, and specimens. We use such items for experiments and demonstrations, but not all materials come from this supply. Where possible, I try to incorporate objects and tools students find familiar from everyday experience.

For example, if an activity requires containers for storing or mixing liquids, I bypass glass beakers and flasks in favor of salvaged Styrofoam or plastic cups from nearby restaurants. (This also is an opportunity to teach the three Rs—reduce, reuse, recycle.) For a demonstration of chemical properties, I skip the stockroom and go straight to the kitchen or grocery store. Why waste concentrated hydrochloric acid when I can use vinegar instead?

In addition to being cheaper and safer, common materials are more recognizable. My students learn how science is not exclusive to the laboratory. By using familiar and accessible materials in my lessons, I help them see science all around them.

Seek a similar relevance when choosing illustrations or examples of whatever content you are teaching. And strive to add substance. Classrooms are wonderful arenas to discuss and imagine ideas. But if we're not careful, our thinking space gets clogged up with abstractions. Students may struggle with misconceptions and confusion if there is no tangible experience to which they can attach these concepts. Unlike Professor X or other telepaths, teachers cannot psionically project images into the minds of our students. This is where our instructional tools come in handy. And what we choose for materials or medium can make a big difference.

Do not simply rely on a textbook. Provide students the most concrete representations of whatever content they are learning. The following figure shows the wide range of concrete to abstract representations. I call it the "Teaching Tools Tangibility Scale," and I'll use two more X-Men characters to help this illustration. On one end are objects considered "most real," or concrete. Think of this side in terms of Colossus, the mutant who transforms into "organic steel." On the opposite end is Shadowcat, who can turn her body intangible like a ghost. Both extremes are useful in their own way, and there are many other types between them.

Teaching Tools Tangibility Scale

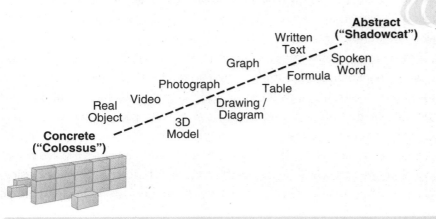

The Teaching Tools Tangibility Scale.
Which types of tools do you use most often? Which can you use more?

When starting any unit, it's best to approach the content using the real thing. Of course, this is not always feasible for a variety of reasons—cost, accessibility, safety, and other logistical concerns. In a lesson about volcanoes, for example, most of us cannot easily take our students to witness an active eruption. If the real object is not possible, find the next best representation. Instead of a volcano field trip, teachers could show video footage of various types. Additionally, there's the classic three-dimensional model. Students can use clay, papier-mâché, and other supplies to create physical replicas.

When using models and similar exemplars, however, watch out for students developing additional misconceptions. In the case of volcano models, the traditional bubbly baking soda/vinegar mixture has very little in common with the actual movement of molten rock during eruptions. A tactful teacher might go further and challenge students to develop a better model, one that more accurately represents volcanic structure and geological mechanisms.

As you move from concrete to abstract teaching tools, the likelihood increases for more confusion and misconceptions. A particular diagram component or drawing style may obscure features that a photograph can clearly present. Going further, a data table or formula with symbols creates additional levels of complexity. That's not to say we never use such text-based tools. But in most cases, these representations shouldn't be students' only exposure to content.

Getting back to Batman and his utility belt, often the best approach is a combination of tools. The Caped Crusader may start with his night vision Bat-goggles to scope out a shady scene, then switch to a lock pick or grapple gun for a closer look. When taking out a mob of villains, Batman might employ Batarangs, bolas, smoke bombs, and more—all during the same fight. Common knowledge tells us that you truly understand something when you can explain, show, and apply that knowledge in multiple ways. The reverse application, then, is to use multiple representations of a concept to help students truly learn it.

Still, some content is best taught in a particular manner. When learning poetry, students typically read or listen to samples, then hopefully create and perform some of their own poems. The same goes for music. I argue that what they're learning and using is the "real thing." Even so, teachers can support this content by using visual tools or examples, where appropriate. In most math lessons, students deal with numbers in some shape or manner. Except for younger ages, such activities involve actual digits and symbols written down. But all math levels benefit from strategic inclusion of visual aids, whether they appear as real objects, models, diagrams, graphs, or other forms.

Technology: Vision or Ultron?

So far, I haven't brought up the use of technology. Depending on people's experiences and goals, they may view technology as benevolent and miraculous (like Vision, the android Avenger) or treacherous and maddening (like the Avengers' villain Ultron). Either way, technology can be a powerful force.

It's also important to remember that technology is not just a device you plug in or power up. The wheel is a form of technology. So is a wooden pencil with a graphite core and eraser. (Travel back in time a few centuries and show our ancestors a crayon box with 64 colors and a built-in sharpener. You would blow their minds!) Since the dawn of civilization, technology has been all around us. This includes schools and classrooms, whether we're talking about slates and chalkboards or smartboards and Wi-Fi. But for the sake of this conversation, let's focus on electronic varieties.

Digital devices are absent from the Teaching Tools Tangibility Scale because they can skew toward either concrete or abstract representations. An interactive software simulation, for example, can help students manipulate and visualize phenomena. Such content might otherwise be impossible to examine in a classroom. But it's still not real. And in some cases, a simulation may distort scales of time or size. This shift may be to increase usability or simplify variables, but teachers will still want to call students' attention to these changes.

Electronic gadgets and resources can be terrific tools—when used appropriately. Be vigilant that your students don't treat technology as a "magic box" (Olson and Clough 2001). For example, calculators are great for quick computations, but students still need to understand what they're doing. Do the displayed numbers make sense? Students should estimate and predict solutions to check their work, avoiding the assumption that whatever value appears on screen is the correct answer.

Teachers of older grades, should you let students use phones in the classroom? It depends on how they'll use them. Instead of a constant distraction, phones and other portable devices can become helpful tools in an instructional arsenal. The key is inclusion—and exclusion—at pivotal times for the greatest learning potential.

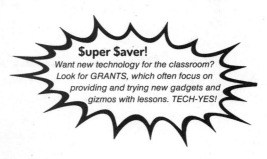

$uper $aver!
Want new technology for the classroom? Look for GRANTS, which often focus on providing and trying new gadgets and gizmos with lessons. TECH-YES!

Magic Bullets, Quick Fixes, Power Rings, and Ultimate Nullifiers

The most dangerous pitfall with any tool or technology is expecting it to fix every lesson. Most teachers know this, alluding to the favorite adage that there is no "magic bullet" or "quick fix" in education (Cepeda 2017; Peterson 2011; Sharma 2017). In the Marvel Universe, such a tool is called the Ultimate Nullifier. The Fantastic Four first brandished this weapon to ward off Galactus from eating Earth, since they had no other option (Lee and Kirby 1966). Unfortunately, the Ultimate Nullifier has enough power to also destroy the entire galaxy, so it's a good thing no one had to actually use it. Hooray for *deus ex machina*!

Magic bullets, quick fixes, and Nullifiers are objects of fiction. They don't exist in reality, and certainly not in classrooms. Still, it would make things a lot easier, wouldn't it? And it's tempting to latch onto a trendy tool or technology with hopes of erasing all difficulties. But to be honest, a lot of genuine learning comes through the struggle and effort. Whatever resource you use, be sure it doesn't become another obstacle in the way of understanding. No classroom tool produces instant comprehension; the best ones engage and support students in the process.

Another danger is to assume teaching tools will replace the actual teacher. Different instructors with the same resources can produce wide-ranging results. The actual quality of a build relies on the skill of the builder as much as it does the tools they use. Or consider the Power Ring wielded by assorted Green Lanterns in the DC Universe. Over the years, various Green Lantern heroes have helped (or harmed) galaxies depending on their competency, creativity, and character. I would argue that the same traits in teachers impact any lesson's ultimate success.

> "The ring's just a tool . . . .
> Being a hero depends on what's in
> your heart, and in your mind."

— John Stewart,
Green Lantern #70 (1996)

The Ultimate Educational Tool

In the end, the most important instructional resource in every classroom . . . is *you*!

I'm speaking to teachers here, whom research has found to be the most influential classroom factor for student learning and school success (Hattie 2008, 2015;

Penick, Yager, and Bonnstetter 1986; Rockoff et al. 2011). Beyond better test scores, a high-quality teacher can impact students in the long-term, elevating their likelihood of high school graduation and college enrollment (Jackson 2018), college graduation (Lee 2018), and even increasing their lifetime income (Chetty, Friedman, and Rockoff 2014).

If you are the ultimate tool (I mean that in a good way), how do you function? In other words, what does a teacher actually do?

Effective teachers exhibit a variety of traits, and precise behaviors may depend on the classroom context. Nevertheless, the following sections discuss some common actions that are essential for quality instruction.

Questioning

A key teaching behavior for engaging and assessing students is asking questions. Not all questions are equal, however. Unfortunately, research has found that a vast majority (70 to 80%) of questions asked by teachers require nothing more from students than reciting facts or guessing simple answers (Bergman and Morphew 2014; Gall 1984; Watson and Young 1986).

In his thought-provoking book *Why Don't Students Like School?* (2009) cognitive scientist Daniel Willingham notes, "Sometimes I think that we, as teachers, are so eager to get to the answers that we do not devote sufficient time to developing the question" (p. 20). Don't settle for mere recall or rote memorization. Instead, challenge yourself (and your students) to use more open-ended questions. Such prompts encourage conversation, reflection, creativity, and critical thinking from students' extended answers. Examples include the following:

- "What do you think might happen if . . . ?"
- "How does that compare with . . . ?"
- "Tell me about what you are thinking."
- "What if . . . ?"
- "For what reasons might . . . ?"
- "How would you . . . ?"

Another way to elevate your prompts is to use "higher order thinking" verbs from Bloom's educational taxonomy (Anderson and Krathwohl 2001; Bloom 1956). Throughout classroom instruction, incorporate words like "compare," "interpret," "justify," "predict," "prioritize," "decide," and similar stimulative actions.

With quality questions and purposeful prompts, you not only raise the intellectual atmosphere of the classroom. You also will gain a better understanding of what your students are truly thinking. You can assess their progress throughout every lesson. Such insight will guide your teaching, starting with your next question.

> **Caption Capture:** Write down **questions or phrases** you habitually use in the classroom. Cross out any that are rote or restrictive, then **replace them with better** prompts and responses.

Responding

After a student speaks, how do you respond? Your reaction can be just as important—maybe more so—than your initial question. Typically, though, teachers' responses are limited to simple affirmation, rejection, or repetition (Weiss et al. 2003).

Obviously, criticizing or rejecting students' ideas (intentionally or unintentionally) will deter their future participation and eagerness to learn. Likewise, always telling students the answer without challenging them to think stifles their development of critical analysis, curiosity, and creativity.

Counter to common thought, praising students also hinders students' learning. A review of the research reveals that excessive praise actually lowers students' confidence, autonomy, motivation, and reflection (Brophy 1981; Dweck 2007; Larrivee 2002; Sæverot 2011). At best, praise should be specific, private, unexpected, and used sparingly. In general, though, praise is overrated.

Praise and rejection are both *teacher*-centered responses, in that students rely on the teacher to judge the worth of their ideas. A better instructional approach is using *student*-centered responses.

One type of student-centered response is using students' contributions and calling classmates' attention to these ideas. For example, a teacher may ask the class, "What do the rest of you think?" or "How could we use that?" Such a response increases positive and productive interactions among students, not just with the teacher.

Another student-centered response is asking individuals to elaborate on their ideas. This reply is often applicable when a student gives a short answer. When you ask for elaboration, you can draw out further details of the students' thinking. This gives the teacher another opportunity for assessment (checking for understanding) and gives classmates more information to consider. Here are some examples:

- "What do you mean by . . . ?"
- "Tell me more about . . ."
- "How does that compare to . . . ?"
- "For what reasons . . . ?"
- "How did you . . . ?"

Notice that you do not elaborate or clarify *for* the student, but rather prompt *them* to explain, paraphrase, or justify their reasoning. Asking for elaboration works whether the student's idea is seemingly correct or incorrect. This habit of "symmetrical responding" decreases attention toward right/wrong and emphasizes students' thinking, learning, and continued participation.

Conveying Nonverbal Behaviors

Actions speak louder than words, and this applies to classroom interactions, too. In addition to what teachers say, *how* they say it can have a profound impact on students' engagement and learning.

Maybe you have heard estimates that up to 93% of communication is unspoken, or nonverbal. This number first appeared from research done in the 1960s (Mehrabian and Ferris 1967; Mehrabian and Wiener 1967) and deals with very specific parameters (voice recordings of single words, facial photographs) and tasks (discerning emotions). Nevertheless, teachers can still consider the power of all their various nonverbal behaviors. This includes the combined use of facial expressions, eye contact, posture and gestures, proximity, intonation, and more (Babad 2009).

Intonation—or tone of voice—is critical for clear, engaging communication. Consider how you come across to your students. Is your voice comforting? Encouraging? Enthusiastic? Confident? Condescending? Do you clearly enunciate your words? Adjust the speed and volume of your voice to accentuate comments. Avoid flat or monotone speech that invokes slumber. Reflect on your passion for teaching and reaching students. Show this energy through animated intonation and word inflection.

Voice tone is easier to understand when you add meaningful mannerisms and expressions (Van den Stock, Righart, and de Gelder 2007). To cultivate an inviting classroom, use welcoming gestures with open palms, as opposed to closed fists or crossed arms. Counting on your fingers shows that you expect answers from multiple students. Nodding acknowledges student contributions without using excessive praise. And as mentioned in the last chapter, don't forget to smile! Together with eye contact, a gentle grin (not a maniacal Joker face) conveys authenticity and attracts others to pay attention (Krumhuber, Manstead, and Kappas 2007; Little, Jones, and DeBruine 2011).

Listening and Noticing

In his heroic book for teachers *We Got This* (2019), Brooklyn teacher Cornelius Minor argues that teachers can transform their classrooms, schools, and communities by taking one important step: listening. While this receptive action occurs in many contexts, it is particularly vital for our interactions with students. As Minor notes, "teaching is not a monologue. It's a dialogue" (p. 12).

An effective teacher prioritizes listening to the point where it becomes a habit or an "orientation" (Davis 1994). In another book called *When to Speak up and When to Shut up* (isn't that a great title?), behavior consultant Michael Sedler (2003) notes the distractions and dangers of the opposite approach: "Too often we are so focused on our own thoughts and what we are going to say that we miss the essence of what the other person is saying" (p. 101). An effective teacher is an effective listener, often silencing themselves in favor of their students.

Related to listening, we must work at "noticing" our students, an action defined as "making sense of how individuals process complex situations" (Jacobs, Lamb, and Philipp 2010, p. 171). Instead of jumping to judgment, our initial steps should be listening and noticing what thoughts students share. Insight gained from these moments equip us to help students resolve challenging concepts or circumstances.

Waiting and Thinking

To listen and notice students, effective teachers provide the time necessary for students to speak and think. Many educators are familiar with the research-supported practice of wait-time, the moment of silence after a teacher asks a question. Designated "wait-time I," these seconds are critical for students to reflect and think before providing answers. Equally important is "wait-time II," which is the time teachers wait after the students talk. More recently, the terms "think-time I" and "think-time II" have been introduced to emphasize the purpose of these moments (Walsh and Sattes 2015).

Whatever you call it, waiting longer after someone speaks encourages additional thinking and robust discussion. Not only do kids extend their answers and respond to one another, but teachers also talk less and ask better questions (Rowe 1986, 1996; Tobin 1986, 1987). The classroom climate becomes that of a multidimensional conversation, as opposed to a one-sided lecture.

Utility and Synergy

Like all the gadgets and materials in your teaching utility belt, relative use of these instructional behaviors depends on classroom conditions. And often multiple tools must work together for the best results—good questions and wait-time, interesting visual aids, functional technology, a captivating smile, and more.

That said, teachers may need to set aside one resource or action from time to time. There are moments when you can't pose an open-ended question or provide extended wait-time. For example, during a science laboratory lesson, I won't hesitate to act or speak up when students are seconds away from causing a dangerous accident. Or if a student is having a particularly rough morning, it's not in their best interest for me to press them with additional prompts.

No matter the case, effective teachers always maintain a well-equipped utility belt—full of the best tools and synergetic skills. They are ready to craft a culture of learning, reflecting, supporting, and challenging one another in daily lessons. And they always watch for useful items or strategies to add to their collection.

"Just because something works *doesn't* mean it *can't* be improved."

– Princess Shuri,
Black Panther (2018)

Sharpen the Saw (and Your Skills)

How do you get better? In the words of legendary coach Vince Lombardi: "Practice does not make perfect. Only *perfect* practice makes perfect." The following suggestions may not be perfect, but they're a good start for getting better!

- **Get connected!** Join educational organizations and conferences, especially those in your specific fields of study. State groups are helpful, since they are often a closer-knit bunch and cheaper than national associations. Through social media, connect and follow respected teachers and other educational leaders.
- **Read up!** An added perk of professional memberships is receiving journals and newsletters. Peruse professional publications (not just blogs or Pinterest) to get fresh ideas and the latest news.
- **Cheat sheet!** Since it's often hard to spontaneously conjure an open-ended question or student-centered response, write these down ahead of time. These could be lesson-specific in your plans, or general sentence starters you post on the classroom wall or keep on a "cheat sheet" card at your desk or in a pocket.
- **Spy on your peers!** Watch your colleagues teach, whether it's a quick glance while you walk by their room or an official observation during a plan period or brief downtime. In particular, look for the best teachers in your building—although you can still learn what *not* to do from poor examples. (I talk more about mentors in future chapters.)
- **Spy on yourself!** Use your favorite camera-equipped device to record and review your teaching. You don't have to show the footage to anyone but yourself, which can alleviate privacy concerns (more on this in Chapter 8). Even if you watch or listen to only a few minutes, you'll gain powerful insight about your current teaching and get ideas on where to improve. Plus, your students may notice you modeling that lovely habit of lifelong learning!

 **To Be Continued!**

Further Reading

Ashford, S. (2021). DC: top 10 weirdest things on Batman's utility belt. Comic Book Resources (15 July). https://www.cbr.com/dc-comics-batman-utility-belt-strange-items/.

Bendis, B.M. and Caselli, S. (2019). *Ironheart: Riri Williams*. New York: Marvel Comics.

Biskup, A.J. (2014). *Batarangs and Grapnels: The Science Behind Batman's Utility Belt (Batman Science)*. North Mankato, MN: Capstone Press.

Lee, S., Kirby, J., Buscema, J., and Byrne, J. (2019). *Fantastic Four: Behold . . . Galactus!* New York: Marvel Comics.

Waid, M., Busiek, K., Stern, R. et al. (2021). *Captain America: Heroes Return–The Complete Collection, Volume 1*. New York: Marvel Comics.

Further Viewing

Conli, R. (producer) and Hall, D. and Williams, C. (directors). (2014). *Big Hero 6* [Motion picture]. Walt Disney Studios.

DC Kids. (2021). Batman's utility belt. Batcomputer Archives. https://www.youtube.com/watch?v=2sLjn1BWPBk.

Feige, K. (producer) and Black, S. (director). (2013). *Iron Man 3* [Motion picture]. Marvel Studios.

Feige, K. (producer) and Coogler, R. (director). (2018). *Black Panther* [Motion picture]. Marvel Studios.

Feige, K. (producer) and Whedon, J. (director). (2015). *Avengers: Age of Ultron* [Motion picture]. Marvel Studios.

Igla, J. and Feige, K. (producers) and Thomas, R., Templemore-Finlayson, A., and Ellwood, K. (directors). (2021). *Hawkeye* [Television series]. Marvel Studios.

Yamaguchi, T. (Producer) and Mizusaki, J. (director). (2018). *Batman Ninja* [Motion picture]. Warner Bros. Pictures.

Questions for Reflection and Discussion

1. What are your favorite go-to gadgets and gizmos for the classroom? What tools or materials do you find irreplaceable?

2. After reviewing the Teaching Tool Tangibility Scale, decide and describe the best tools for teaching the following topics:
   - Poetry forms (e.g., narrative, free verse, sonnet, haiku, limerick).
   - Types of polygons (e.g., triangle, quadrilateral, pentagon, etc.).
   - Three branches of U.S. government (legislative, executive, judicial).
   - Properties of solids, liquids, and gases.
   - Other: _____ .

3. What are your recommendations for cheaper alternatives or bargains to keep personal costs to a minimum?

4. Where have you experienced technology as a barrier to learning, instead of the intended asset? How do you ensure the focus remains on learning?

5. How do you prepare for the inevitable tech failure? (No Wi-Fi, electrical power, etc.) What is your backup plan?

6. In which of the following behaviors do you excel—questioning, responding, nonverbal, listening, noticing, wait-time—and in what ways?
   - Which of these behaviors do you need to improve?
   - How will you get better?

7. Think of a past or present hobby or skill where you're particularly successful or the best you know. What's your recipe for success? List all the elements that helped you get there. How can you use similar elements to improve and be the best possible teacher?

References

Anderson, L.W. and Krathwohl, D.R. (eds.) (2001). *Taxonomy for Learning, Teaching, and Assessing: A Revision of Bloom's Taxonomy of Educational Objectives*. New York: Longman.

Babad, E. (2009). Teaching and nonverbal behavior in the classroom. In: *International Handbook of Research on Teachers and Learning* (eds. L. Saha and A. Dworkin), 817–827. New York: Springer.

Belfield, C., Bowden, A., Klapp, A. et al. (2015). The economic value of social and emotional learning. *Journal of Benefit-Cost Analysis* 6 (3): 508–544.

Bergman, D.J. and Morphew, J.W. (2014). Comparing classroom interactive behaviors of science and non-science pre-service teachers. *Journal of Classroom Interaction* 49 (2): 4–10.

Bloom, B.S. (ed.) (1956). *Taxonomy of Educational Objectives: The Classification of Educational Goals. Handbook I: Cognitive Domain*. New York: D. McKay Co., Inc.

Brophy, J. (1981). On praising effectively. *Elementary School Journal* 81 (5): 269–78.

Cantrell, S. and Kane, T.J. (2013). Ensuring fair and reliable measures of effective teaching: culminating findings from the MET Project's three-year study. Bill & Melinda Gates Foundation

Cepeda, E. (2017). Commentary: Technology is no magic bullet for U.S. schools." *Las Vegas Review-Journal* (12 March). https://www.reviewjournal.com/opinion/comentary-technology-is-no-magic-bullet-for-u-s-schools/.

Chetty, R., Friedman, J.N., and Rockoff, J.E. (2014). Measuring the impacts of teachers II: teacher value-added and student outcomes in adulthood. *American Economic Review* 104 (9): 2633–2679.

Colburn, A. (2000). An inquiry primer. *Science Scope* 23 (6): 42–44.

Davis, B. (1994). Mathematics telling: Moving from telling to listening. *Journal of Curriculum and Supervision* 9: 267–83.

Gall, M. (1984). Synthesis of research on teachers' questioning. *Educational Leadership* 42 (3): 40–47.

Hattie, J. (2015). The applicability of visible learning to higher education. *Scholarship of Teaching and Learning in Psychology* 1 (1): 79–91.

Hattie, J. (2008). *Visible Learning: A Synthesis of over 800 Meta-Analyses Relating to Achievement*. New York: Routledge Press.

Jackson, C.K. (2018). What do test scores miss? The importance of teacher effects on non-test score outcomes. *Journal of Political Economy* 126 (5): 2072–2107.

Jacobs, V., Lamb, L., and Philipp, R. (2010). Professional noticing of children's mathematical thinking. *Journal for Research in Mathematics Education* 41 (2): 169–202.

Krumhuber, E., Manstead, A.S.R., Cosker, D. et al. (2007). Facial dynamics as indicators of trustworthiness and cooperative behavior. *Emotion* 7 (4): 730–735.

Lee, S.W. (2018). Pulling back the curtain: Revealing the cumulative importance of high-performing, highly qualified teachers on students' educational outcome. *Educational Evaluation and Policy Analysis* 40 (3): 359–381.

Lee, S. and Kirby, J. (1966). The Startling Saga of the Silver Surfer! *Fantastic Four (Vol. 1) #50*. New York: Marvel.

Little, A.C., Jones, B.C., and DeBruine, L.M. (2011). Facial attractiveness: evolutionary based research. *Philosophical Transactions of the Royal Society B: Biological Sciences* 366 (1571): 1638–1659.

Mehrabian, A. and Ferris, S. (1967). Inference of attitudes from nonverbal communication in two channels. *Journal of Consulting Psychology* 31: 248–252.

Mehrabian, A. and Weiner, M. (1967). Decoding of inconsistent communications. *Journal of Personality and Social Psychology* 6: 109–114.

Minor, C. (2019). *We Got This: Equity, Access, and the Quest to Be Who Our Students Need Us to Be*. Portsmouth, NH: Heinemann.

Olson, J.K. and Clough, M.P. (2001). Technology's tendency to undermine serious study: a cautionary note. *The Clearing House* 75 (1): 8–13.

Penick, J.E., Crow, L.W., and Bonnstetter, R.J. (1996). Questions are the answer: a logical questioning strategy for any topic. *The Science Teacher* 63 (1): 27–29.

Penick, J.E., Yager, R.E., and Bonnstetter, R.J. (1986). Teachers make exemplary programs. *Educational Leadership* 44: 14–20.

Peterson, S. (2011). There's no magic bullet to improve education." *Penn Live* (31 May). https://www.pennlive.com/editorials/2011/05/theres_no_magic_bullet_to_impr.html.

Rockoff, J.E., Jacob, B.A., Kane, T.J., and Staiger, D.O. (2011). Can you recognize an effective teacher when you recruit one? *Education Finance and Policy* 6 (1): 43–74.

Rowe, M.S. (1986). Wait-time: slowing down may be a way of speeding up. *Journal of Teacher Education* 37 (1): 43–50.

Rowe, M.S. (1996). Science, silence, and sanctions. *Science and Children* 34 (1), 35–37.

Sedler, M. (2003). *When to Speak up and When to Shut up*. Grand Rapids, MI: Revell.

Sharma, C.B. (2017). There is no quick fix in education. *The Pioneer* (30 November). https://www.dailypioneer.com/2017/columnists/there-is-no-quick-fix-in-education.html.

Tobin, K. (1986). Effects of teacher wait time on discourse characteristics in mathematics and language arts classes. *American Educational Research Journal* 23 (2): 191–200.

Tobin, K. (1987). The role of wait time in higher cognitive level learning. *Review of Educational Research* 5: 69–95.

Van den Stock, J., Righart, R., and de Gelder, B. (2007). Body expressions influence recognition of emotions in the face and voice. *Emotion* 7 (3): 487–494.

Walsh, J.A. and Sattes, B.D. (2015). A new rhythm for responding. *Educational Leadership* 73 (1): 46–52.

Watson, K. and Young, B. (1986). Discourse for learning in the classroom. *Language Arts* 63 (2): 126–133.

Weiss, I.R., Pasley, J.D., Smith, P.S. et al. (2003). Looking inside the classroom: a study of K-12 mathematics and science education in the United States. Horizon Research. https://www.horizon-research.com/horizonresearchwp/wp-content/uploads/2013/04/complete-1.pdf.

Willingham, D.T. (2009). *Why Don't Students Like School?* San Francisco, CA: Jossey-Bass/Wiley.

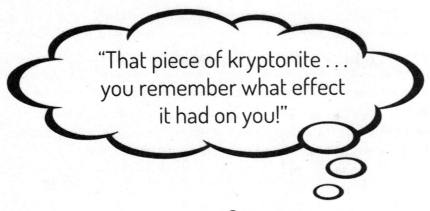

"That piece of kryptonite . . . you remember what effect it had on you!"

– Superman,
The Adventures of Superman,
"The Meteor of Kryptonite" (1945)

Vulnerabilities

In addition to strengths and gadgets, most superheroes have vulnerabilities. The most famous of these is Superman and kryptonite—radioactive rocks created when his home planet Krypton exploded.

What Color Is Your Kryptonite?

Kryptonite comes in many shapes and sizes, as do the challenges faced by teachers. Nevertheless, there are common pitfalls in day-to-day school life that require attention and intervention. The following sections discuss different kinds of kryptonite and their effects, and include an exploration of similar vulnerabilities we must overcome as teachers.

Green Kryptonite: Weakness

The best-known form of kryptonite is also the most common. Called "Green K" for short, it has appeared in comics, cartoons, movies, even a music video by rock band 3 Doors Down (that last one may have been lime Jell-O). Exposure to green kryptonite means debilitating pain and momentary weakness for Superman and fellow Kryptonians. The Man of Steel becomes frail and feeble whenever he is near the stuff, and prolonged contact can be fatal.

Teachers can suffer similar symptoms. In fact, I would argue the biggest threat to our teaching is an overall sense of weakness. It's doubly dangerous as both a cause and effect.

Start with the basics. Most educators are familiar with the work of psychologist Abraham Maslow. I name-dropped him in Chapter 4's discussion of classrooms and workspace but consider how Maslow's "Hierarchy of Needs" (1943) applies not only to students, but teachers as well. What happens if our welfare is neglected? Teachers will have a hard time helping students reach their full potential if they also are running on empty.

Lights Out!

Are you getting enough rest? Sleep deprivation is a danger to all kinds of people, but it can produce dire consequences in the classroom. School days are stressful enough, and only get worse for a tired teacher suffering through mood swings, memory issues, compromised immunity, and more. In one study, nearly two-thirds of all responding teachers (64%) reported feeling drowsy during the day (Amschler and McKenzie 2010). Moreover, 25% of them admitted sleepiness seriously hindered their work on a daily basis. What's wearing out these teachers? In this same study, 43% said they slept an average of six hours *or fewer* each night. That's far short of the nightly seven to nine hours of sleep recommended for adults by health organizations (CDC 2017; Olson 2021).

It's not just the quantity of sleep that matters either. We benefit from *quality* sleep, too, which relates to the extent we can unwind or switch off from work. A second study found that teachers with higher "job strain" spent more time thinking about work during nonwork hours (Cropley, Dijk, and Stanley 2006). These same teachers also reported worse quality of sleep, even though there was no difference in sleeping hours compared with other teachers.

Shut Off!

So, it's not just a matter of getting more sleep, although that's a start. Teachers must also find ways to disconnect from work when away from school. One step I recommend is literally leaving work at work. Don't take papers home to grade. The place you live should be a safe haven where you can tend to yourself. (See the discussions of "Fortress of Solitude" and "Sanctum Sanctorum" in Chapter 4.) Once you bring stacks of exams or essays (or worse, lesson plans) through your front door, you've violated the boundaries of personal time and space.

"Keeping work at work" may mean you have to stay at school late or come in early to get things done. You can focus on the job while you're there, just like you can focus on your own relaxation and rejuvenation at home. At one juncture in my life, I found an *occasional* weekend afternoon to be the best time to plow through paperwork piles. The school building was usually empty, I could crank up some motivational music, and I got brownie points whenever my principal noticed. Yes, this was technically overtime during noncontract hours. And truthfully, I could probably have managed to cram these tasks into my weekday schedule. But it was time well spent, so my days during school hours were not so rushed.

Please don't take this as a recommendation to work unpaid overtime. This is just what worked for me during one particular season of life. I was single, lived two blocks from school, and didn't have a computer of my own. Nowadays, I'm married with kids, have a 35-minute commute (when traffic is good), and use a portable laptop. Needless to say, my daily approach to work has changed. Not better or worse, just different. Each teacher needs to figure out what works for them.

Another solution is to seriously reconsider how much paperwork is necessary. A review of research finds that excessive grading occupies teachers' time and attention, so much so that they are unable to reflect and refine their lessons (Schinske and Tanner 2014). What assignments do students really need to complete to develop and demonstrate understanding? How can you monitor and measure their learning efficiently and effectively? One recommendation is using more in-class activities and discussions to emphasize key information and assess student thinking. Other time-saving tools are detailed rubrics to highlight and pinpoint feedback—as opposed to composing similar comments over and over again—and color-coordinated markings to indicate performance level of key items in the unit or project (Diaz 2020).

Reach Out!

How else can you unwind and detach from the job? Don't do it by yourself. Cultivate a supportive network of family and friends and spend time with them outside of work. Additional research has found that teachers are more likely to get bogged down with work-related thoughts when they are alone (Cropley and Purvis 2003). As an introvert myself, participating in a community can sometimes feel like more work, but it's worth the effort. You don't have to be a social butterfly, but it's okay to come out of your cocoon every once in a while.

Interactions don't have to be face-to-face or in a crowd. As a young single teacher in a strange new town, my earliest support system was 130+ miles away. It was my mom. (What can I say? I was a mama's boy, which does sound like a superhero.) Over the phone, my mother patiently listened and allowed me to vent about frustrations. She also encouraged me as I realized poignant triumphs, no matter how small. And we could talk about other things besides school and students. Nowadays, my wife lends an ear and sympathetic shoulder for the tougher days. It helps that neither my wife or mom work in schools; both have helped me stay grounded and connected to the rest of the outside world.

Who are your personal allies and trustworthy confidants? Think of individuals you don't see in schools every day. Think also of which people you can serve and support in return.

Caption Capture: Write down names of your **personal allies** and "trusted confidants" here. If you need to protect their identities, use initials or nicknames! ☺

Rest Up!

Avoiding weakness requires more than a healthy daily routine. It's also vital to take breaks to elude the daily grind. Obviously, the weekend is sacred time. If you prefer to use Saturdays or Sundays for grading or planning, make this a rare occasion. Once a month is enough. Get away from school physically and mentally, which I know is easier said than done.

To be transparent, it wasn't until my third year teaching when I could regularly walk out my classroom on Friday afternoons and not think about school until Monday morning. That's how long it took for me to be familiar with lessons so that preparation was smoother and quicker. Veteran teachers, maybe you needed more or less time depending on the circumstances or your own skills. New teachers, it does get better. (And starting out, remind yourself that "good enough" is indeed good enough.)

The same respite pattern is true for that lovely time of year called summer break. Note that I don't call it summer *vacation*, because that's not the case for most teachers. Some of you work for year-round schools and get shorter, more frequent breaks from classes. Regardless of the term or time span, teachers hardly ever go on lengthy vacations. Sure, you may take trips or enjoy seasonal events. But most teachers spend their breaks doing more work.

According to data analyzed by the Pew Research Center, about 1 in 6, or 16% of all public school teachers work a second job in the summer (2019). This number gets higher for newer teachers, peaking at 32% of those in their first year. In addition, many teachers are busy in the summer with additional coursework and graduate programs, professional conferences or workshops, curriculum planning sessions for the upcoming year, or sometimes all of the above (Cohen 2019; Riggs 2015).

For some teachers, these experiences do count as a break of sorts. Away from the daily demands of meeting students' immediate needs, they can pause and address their own learning and development. But it still helps to enjoy a momentary reprieve from school and educational endeavors.

Consider the true origins of Superman's kryptonite. I'm not talking about radioactive rocks leftover from planet Krypton's explosion. Instead, let's learn from the genesis of the actual story idea. Superman cocreator Jerry Siegel initially thought up the concept of a deadly mineral, but it first appeared in *The Adventures of Superman* radio drama series (Downey 2018). More than a narrative decision, kryptonite was a logistical necessity. Superman radio actor Bud Collyer needed to rest his voice, or otherwise risk losing it from overuse. So, to maintain the production output, scripts introduced kryptonite as a way to put the main hero (and voice) on the sidelines for a few episodes while other characters took up the slack.

If even Superman (or least his voice actor) needs to take time off, so do teachers. Learn the power of saying "No" or "Not now." I have a colleague who keeps a whiteboard next to her desk that lists of all her current job duties. The list is color-coordinated and full of various tasks–classes, committees, programs, and so on. This whiteboard is useful whenever someone (i.e., a supervisor) stops by to ask if she can add another project to her responsibilities. In response, my colleague can refer to the whiteboard's list and ask, "Which current task should we remove and replace with this new one?" She doesn't do this all the time, but it comes in handy as a reminder of her ongoing job demands. And even if you don't share such a list with your colleagues or boss, you can keep one for yourself as a reference and safeguard against overdoing it.

Caption Capture: Make a list of all your **work-related tasks** – committees, teams, coaching, sponsoring, etc. If you run out of room in this space, decide what you can remove!

Be selective in your professional choices in favor of a better "Yes" to yourself. Find time for personal enjoyment, too. Travel every once in a while. Exercise on a regular basis. Start a new hobby. For me, my two early self-care activities were playing trumpet and playing basketball. I still do both, along with bicycling, jogging, creative writing, and assorted family adventures. All of these pastimes are healthy for both body and mind. Whatever you choose, prioritizing self-care will help you overcome the weakening burden of a busy schedule.

Caption Capture: List your favorite **self-care activities** that promote physical, mental, and emotional health.

How to Answer the Interview Question "What Is Your Greatest Weakness?"

Are you interviewing for a new teaching position? A common question asks about your greatest weakness as a teacher. How do you answer? Avoid trite replies like "I care too much," or the ultimate brownnoser "I work too hard." Not only are these answers super hokey, they're also borderline disingenuous. At best, such a response may get you an annoyed eye roll; at worst, the interviewer quickly ends the session and bids you farewell.

Instead, be honest and appropriate about your personal pitfalls. This can reveal astute self-awareness and reflection. Also, add an action plan for how you are working to improve. Share specific goals and steps you've taken to address these struggles. (Again, be honest.) Are you a perfectionist? What have you done to set reasonable standards and measure progress? Do you prefer working alone to the point of seclusion? How are you reaching out to foster collaboration with fellow educators or community partners? According to job search engine and employment website Indeed.com (2022), "By presenting both the problem and the solution, you can transform your weakness into a strength."

Red Kryptonite: Unpredictability

Green kryptonite is not the only kind to watch out for. Another variety is "Red K," known for its unpredictability. Over the decades, exposure to red kryptonite has resulted in all kinds of changes in Superman: rapid aging, rapid hair growth, extra limbs, shrinking, mental instability, amnesia, and my personal favorite—turning into a dragon. Thankfully, these transformations are temporary. But the erratic effects are what make red kryptonite so risky. No two chunks have the same results.

It's hard to prepare for Red K when you don't know what it will do. A similar vulnerability rears its head for many teachers—lack of planning. When teachers are unprepared and lessons go unplanned, disaster is sure to follow. The unpredictability arises in different forms of impending doom—bored students, chaotic classrooms, unsafe situations, unclear instructions, incorrect content, general confusion, and more.

Yes, teachers need to be flexible, which I've already noted is a fantastic superpower to have in the classroom (see Chapter 5). And spontaneity is one of my favorite parts of the teaching experience. Despite the best-laid plans, things still go awry. You can't prepare for every scenario. Unexpected events, fickle students, and faulty technology are bound to happen during the year. But as teachers, we should do our part to have our materials and ourselves ready for each lesson. You can't alter instruction unless you first have something to adjust. Teachers must plan ahead.

Planning requires time to reflect on key concepts and critical components of each activity. Not only do we prepare for academic content, but also the procedures and transitions that enable students to learn and work together. This does not mean lesson plans should be multipage and minutiae-filled tomes. Too much detail can bog teachers down and distract us from actually teaching. After studying hundreds of lesson plans and evaluating effectiveness, Womack et al. (2015) conclude, "The key issue for lesson planning is *certainty*—not exhaustiveness" (p. 12, emphasis in original).

There are all sorts of lesson plan models and templates to use, and your district or department probably has a particular favorite or recommendations. Many schools even provide content-specific lesson plans for their teachers in repositories called "district pacing guides," "unit instructional guides," or similar titles. These resources are especially helpful for beginning teachers working through new curriculum. Since novice teachers encounter many challenges in their first year or so, high-quality lessons can serve as a "lifeline" for staying afloat (Goodwin 2016; Sultana 2001).

Prescribed lessons may also help weaker teachers who need additional guidance in supporting students, as one study of math teachers found (Jackson and Makarin 2016). Even so, I balk at a blanket recommendation that all teachers simply wait for lessons to fall from the sky (or district curriculum office). Such a passive approach echoes the old proverb "Give someone a fish, feed them for a day. Teach them to fish, feed them for a lifetime." Effective teachers don't settle for prefabricated lessons; they improve upon them or craft totally new ones to serve their unique classrooms.

Keep in mind, too, that as the classroom teacher you still have final say and decisions in what and how to teach your students. Through experience and insight, you'll gain a better understanding of your content and students. Soon, you won't have to refer to such mass-produced commodities. Instead, you will activate your vast repertoire of methods using meaningful materials and purposeful tools (see Chapters 5 and 6).

Gold Kryptonite: Permanent Powerlessness

Teachers must be keenly involved in decisions impacting not only the classroom, but their entire school, community, and beyond. This purposeful approach is essential to avoid the effects of gold kryptonite. In Superman's world, "Gold K" takes away Kryptonians' powers forever. In the educational world, powerless teachers suffer an equally dismal fate—as do their students.

In my experience, I've encountered two forms of powerless teachers. The first are often newer to the profession, and they fall into a common trap of passive acquiescence. Sure, we should all respect our supervisors and follow chain of command. And when you start your career, you have plenty to learn from established colleagues and policies. This includes accepting support in the form of prewritten lessons and curricula guides, as alluded to previously. If we're not careful, however, such lifelines can become tripwires to professional growth, or tethers that hold back our potential. Whether it's intentional or not, teachers relinquish their professional expertise. As a result, they become pushovers and curriculum consumers, as opposed to active producers and advocates.

Veteran teachers can also assume this passive habit, but there is another form of powerlessness that is just as problematic. Rather than being easily swayed, these teachers are stolid stick-in-the-muds. Whenever you hear comments like "It's been tried already" or "That'll never work," chances are the speaker has developed a powerless persona. Maybe such resistance is due to living through cycles (and recycles) of various standards, assessments, and other high-stakes initiatives. Or perhaps teachers grow apathetic because no one has ever listened to their ideas. After feeling ignored for too long, they disengage from colleagues and the wider school community.

Teachers: beware of either form of powerlessness. You still may be able to function in the day-to-day classroom. But apathy and passivity can both limit your overall influence and long-term impact. Look for opportunities to share your expertise, which is not the same as experience. Speak up when it matters, and I don't mean grumble or complain. You don't have to expound sage wisdom, either. On the contrary, the most useful comments can come in the form of questions. (Use the same teacher tools outlined

Chapter 6.) Just like in the classroom, you can catalyze productive conversations, dig deeper into the issues, and invite others to participate. That's powerful stuff.

White Kryptonite: Kills All Plant Life

This one is a bit of a stretch, but stick with me for a bit. White kryptonite is a little-known variety, found in only a few obscure Superman stories. Basically, "White K" kills all plant life. While this comes in handy for fighting off viral vegetation or pathogenic microbes, let's consider the potential danger for teachers. What happens if you stop growing?

Over the course of a career, you can expect different seasons. Depending on circumstances, you'll face assorted challenges and find various victories. Teachers are vulnerable, however, when they stay too long in a stagnant phase. Humorist Will Rogers noted this danger with his famous quote: "Even if you're on the right track, you'll get run over if you just sit there."

White kryptonite is especially hazardous because it has no limits. All plants are susceptible, whether from Earth, Krypton, or any other planet. In the same way, a teacher's lack of growth can poison the progress of others nearby. This includes our colleagues—young and old—as well as our students in the classroom. How can teachers advocate for lifelong learning when we don't strive for the same habit ourselves?

What are you doing to grow and get better? (Review the suggestions in the section "Sharpen the Saw (and Your Skills)" in Chapter 6.) Growth could be taking a formal class—anything from graduate coursework to a community outreach event. It may be professional development (PD) or personal enrichment. Start a new hobby. You might think it has nothing to do with your educational career, but I bet you'll discover it enhances your teaching in some way or another.

$uper $aver!
Get PAID for PD! Select workshops, classes, and other professional development opportunities that come with a stipend, college credit, or FREE supplies.

Remember the adage that you don't truly learn something unless you teach it to someone else. Sure, this pertains to content knowledge, but also consider ways you can teach others about teaching. Invite potential teachers to shadow and observe your classroom. Welcome college students and interns to assist for a semester or longer. (I talk more about mentoring others and leaving a legacy in Chapters 10 and 11.) Such collaborations can vary in commitment and official capacity. Nevertheless, you will grow from these experiences, as will your educational colleagues. Most importantly, together you can cultivate a thriving community of lifelong learners and truly mean it.

Summary of Teachers' Kryptonite Types: Symptoms, Sources, and Remedies

Color	Symptoms	Possible Sources	Remedies
Green	- Fatigue - Feebleness	- Lack of sleep - Overstressed	- Get rest - Unplug - Connect with others
Red	- Unprepared - Unpredictable - Constant stumbles	- Lack of planning - "Murphy's Law" (*If anything can go wrong, it will.*)	- Plan ahead - Start with provided resources
Gold	- Powerlessness - Helplessness	- Passive acquiescence - Apathy - Overreliance on others	- Speak up/ask questions - Take charge of your choices
White	- Lack of growth - Infecting others	- Stuck in a rut - Repeating same mistakes	- Try something new - "Sharpen the saw" - Partner with other "lifelong learners"

Summary of kryptonite types for teachers.
What are your "weak spots"? How can you overcome them?

Feet of Clay

Beyond the examples here, there are other colors of kryptonite in Superman stories—blue, black, orange, purple, even periwinkle (Baltazar and Franco 2013). Each type produces varying effects. Teachers can have just as many areas of vulnerability.

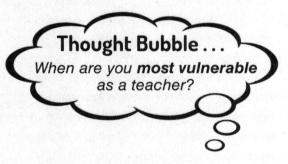

Thought Bubble . . .
*When are you **most vulnerable** as a teacher?*

Take heart in accepting that we all have personal pitfalls. In the 1960s, Stan Lee helped revitalize Marvel Comics—and revolutionize comic books in general—by creating imperfect characters. "Most of the new super heroes sent out into the world . . . were being noticed and embraced both for their special powers—and for their very human weaknesses" (Thomas 2006, p. 44). The Fantastic Four bickered like a real family. Spider-Man was a wise-cracking hero, but Peter Parker struggled with teenage insecurities. Iron Man, Thor, and Doctor Strange all had inflated egos. The X-Men whined to Professor X about mutant schoolwork and practice drills.

Story-wise, flawed superheroes are a lot more interesting. School-wise, our missteps are opportunities to remain authentic and present teachable moments. Admitting vulnerability—while maintaining professional boundaries—may actually help build rapport and positive student relationships. With a healthy sense of humor (see Chapter 5), teachers can admit their mistakes, model humility, and practice perseverance. No one is perfect, but we should all strive to get better.

Kindness Is Not a Weakness

Do you struggle with being "too nice" in the classroom? This is a common trap, to the point that some teachers let students bully them. Effective teachers maintain a climate of on-task learning and positive relationships. While it's important to set boundaries for appropriate school behavior, watch out that you don't mistake being mean and tough with being a strong teacher. Likewise, don't confuse gentleness and kindness as signs of a weak teacher. Discipline is necessary, as is holding students accountable and dealing with management issues for the benefit of the class. But you don't have to raise your voice or blow your top over every little infraction. ("Hulking out" works in comic books, but not in the classroom.)

Early in the year, I would inform my students that I was *not* going to yell at them. (It was a useful reminder to myself, too.) Certainly, I would address management issues as they arose. But with the exception of urgent safety matters, I avoided shouting or screaming. Some students found this gentler approach to be abnormal based on their past experiences. It was a teachable moment that someone can be direct and deal with conflict in a respectful, caring manner.

"Caring about the vulnerable isn't a weakness! It is my biggest strength!"

- Supergirl,
Supergirl #27 (2019)

More and more, teachers must tend to students' social and emotional well-being as well as their intellectual needs (Durlak et al. 2011). A little kindness goes a long way. Or consider the words of children's rights advocate and parenting author L.R. Knost (2013): "Gentleness is not weakness. Just the opposite. Preserving a gentle spirit in a heartless world takes extraordinary courage, determination, and resilience."

To Be Continued!

Further Reading

Cooke, D. and Sale, T. (2019). *Superman: Kryptonite*. New York: DC Comics.

Freeman, B.P. (1945). The meteor of kryptonite (Chapters 1 and 2). *The Adventures of Superman* (radio program transcripts). The Generic Radio Workshop, Vintage Radio Script Library. https://www.genericradio.com/series/superman.

Micheline, D., Layton, B., Romita Jr., R., and Infantino, C. (1979/2006). *Iron Man: Demon in a Bottle*. New York: Marvel Comics.

O'Neill, D. and Swan, C. (1971/2021). *Superman: Kryptonite Nevermore*. New York: DC Comics.

Shammans, N. and Ali, N.H. (2021). *Ms. Marvel: Stretched Thin (Original Graphic Novel)*. New York: Marvel Comics/Scholastic.

Waid, M. and Porter, H. (2000/2021). *JLA: Tower of Babel*. New York: DC Comics.

Further Viewing

Bader, H.J. (writer) and Tomonaga, K. (director). (1996). A little piece of home [Television series episode]. In: *Superman: The Animated Series* (producers P. Dini and B. Timm. Warner Bros.

Feige, K. (producer) and Favreau, J. (director). (2010). *Iron Man 2* [Motion picture]. Marvel Studios/Paramount Pictures.

Montgomery, L. (producer and director). (2012). *Justice League: Doom* [Motion picture]. Warner Home Video.

Spengler, P. (producer) and Donner, R. (director). (1978). *Superman: The Movie* [Motion picture]. Warner Bros.

Questions for Reflection and Discussion

1. Personally, what color of kryptonite do you find most dangerous to your teaching and learning? How so?

   - Green/weakness
   - Red/unpredictability
   - Gold/powerlessness

- White/lack of growth
- Other?

2. As a teacher, when are you at your weakest? How can you prepare for these circumstances and prevent negative effects?

3. How good are you at keeping work at work? What strategies or routines do you follow to protect your time and health?

4. Review your list of current work-related tasks—committees, teams, coaching, sponsoring, and so on. What other responsibilities do you have for your family, community, and so on? If you feel overwhelmed, whom can you contact about reducing your workload?

5. Stan Lee's revolutionary take on superheroes was to give them human faults and foibles. In what ways can teachers use their own flaws to strengthen their classroom instruction and interactions?

6. How comfortable are you being open about your vulnerabilities in the classroom? How could this openness enhance your teaching? How could it backfire?

References

Amschler, D.H. and McKenzie, J.F. (2010). Perceived sleepiness, sleep habits and sleep concerns of public school teachers, administrators and other personnel. *American Journal of Health Education* 41 (2): 102–109.

Baltazar, A. and Franco. (2013 March). *Superman Family Adventures #9*. New York: DC Comics.

Centers for Disease Control and Prevention. (2017). How much sleep do I need? Sleep and sleep disorders. https://www.cdc.gov/sleep/about_sleep/how_much_sleep.html.

Cohen, M. (2019). 'I do not have 2-3 months off': Teachers on summer break or working, a lot. *USA Today* (11 July). https://www.usatoday.com/story/news/education/2019/07/11/teachers-summer-break-jobs-work-living-wage/1524677001/.

Cropley, M., Dijk, D., and Stanley, N. (2006). Job strain, work rumination, and sleep in school teachers. *European Journal of Work and Organizational Psychology* 15 (2): 181–196.

Cropley, M. and Millward Purvis, L. (2003). Job strain and rumination about work issues during leisure time: a diary study. *European Journal of Work and Organizational Psychology* 12 (3): 195–207.

Diaz, E. (2020). How to spend less time grading. Edutopia (22 December). https://www.edutopia.org/article/how-spend-less-time-grading.

Downey, M. (2018). The weird and wonderful history of kryptonite. DC Comics (5 April). https://www.dccomics.com/blog/2018/04/05/the-weird-and-wonderful-history-of-kryptonite.

Durlak, J.A., Weissberg, R.P., Dymnicki, A.B. et al. (2011). Enhancing students' social and emotional development promotes success in school: results of a meta-analysis. *Child Development* 82: 474–501.

Goodwin, B. (2016). Research matters: novice teachers benefit from lesson plans. Association for Supervision and Curriculum Development. https://www.ascd.org/el/articles/novice-teachers-benefit-from-lesson-plans.

Indeed Editorial Team. (2022). List of weaknesses: Examples of what to say in an interview. Indeed.com. https://www.indeed.com/career-advice/interviewing/list-of-example-weaknesses-for-interviewing (accessed 3 December 2022).

Jackson, C.K. and Makarin, A. (2016). Can online off-the-shelf lessons improve student outcomes? Evidence from a field experiment. *National Bureau of Economic Research* Working Paper 22398. https://www.nber.org/system/files/working_papers/w22398/w22398.pdf.

Knost, L.R. (2013). *The Gentle Parent: Positive, Practical, Effective Discipline*. Saint Cloud, FL: Little Hearts Books, LLC.

Olson, E.J. (2021). How many hours of sleep are enough for good health? Mayo Clinic (15 May). https://www.mayoclinic.org/healthy-lifestyle/adult-health/expert-answers/how-many-hours-of-sleep-are-enough/faq-20057898.

Riggs, L. (2015). The myth of a teacher's 'summer vacation.' *The Atlantic* (2 July). https://www.theatlantic.com/education/archive/2015/07/myth-of-teacher-summer-vacation/397535/.

Schaeffer, K. (2019). About one-in-six U.S. teachers work second jobs–and not just in the summer. Pew Research Center (1 July). https://www.pewresearch.org/fact-tank/2019/07/01/about-one-in-six-u-s-teachers-work-second-jobs-and-not-just-in-the-summer/.

Schinske, J. and Tanner, K. (2014). Teaching more by grading less (or differently). *CBE Life Sciences Education* 13 (2): 159–166.

Sultana, Q. (2001). Scholarly teaching: applications of Bloom's taxonomy in Kentucky's classrooms. Third Annual Conference on Scholarship and Teaching, Bowling Green, KY.

Thomas, R. (2006). *Stan Lee's Amazing Marvel Universe*. New York: Sterling Publishing Co., Inc.

Womack, S.T., Pepper, S., Hanna, S.L., and Bell, C.D. (2015). Most effective practices in lesson planning. ERIC Research Report No. ED553616. https://files.eric.ed.gov/fulltext/ED553616.pdf.

> "You're an amazing creature, Spider-Man.
> You and I are not so different."
>
> – Green Goblin,
> *Spider-Man* (2002)

8 Archenemies

Every good hero deserves a terrible villain. And the greatest heroes have a whole lot of enemies. Batman not only has the Joker, but also Penguin, Poison Ivy, Two-Face, the Riddler, Bane, Scarecrow, and more. Spider-Man often spars with the Green Goblin, but he spends just as much time battling Doctor Octopus, the Vulture, Mysterio, the Lizard, Venom, Carnage, Kraven the Hunter, Chameleon, and many others.

A variety of villains provides avenues for different types of stories. One adversary attacks with brute force, while another devises a mental trial or emotional threat. Altogether, a robust Rogues' Gallery creates ongoing obstacles for our heroes, keeping them on their toes. Even so, most protagonists have a singular antagonist—an archenemy—who appears time and again, ready for another clash.

Superman has Lex Luthor. Captain America has Red Skull. Wonder Woman and Cheetah. Thor and Loki. Professor X and Magneto.

Many of these classic pairings have existed so long that they may even work together for a season. Still, they never quite see eye to eye, and soon end up fighting again fist to fist (or mind to mind).

Teachers also encounter a colorful cast of characters, some who present assorted challenges throughout the school year. Still, whom would you consider your archenemy? Who is the single foe lurking in the shadows, waiting to thwart your efforts? The answer may surprise you.

Let's start with a list of usual suspects, and examine how each of them are *not* the actual enemy. Then we'll get to the *true* adversary of effective teachers.

Not the Enemy #1: Students

One day after school, a teacher friend stopped by my classroom. He was clearly agitated, flustered, and frustrated in a way that was at odds with his normal easy-going and fun-loving self.

My colleague slumped into a nearby chair and said, "I got angry with my class today." After a long sigh and wipe of his brow, he continued, "A teacher can't stay angry at their students. It's like a swimmer getting angry at water."

Some days it may feel as though you face wave upon wave of students. Like a fickle sea, the waters are calm for a spell, but can churn turbulent with the smallest change in weather. (Snow days, anyone?) Figuratively or literally, all kinds of events and stimuli can disrupt a student's mood and behavior. Lack of sleep. Food insecurity. Family tensions. Something said by a peer or teacher. Celebrity gossip. Combine all of these and apply them to an entire classroom of kids. Is it any wonder students are goofy or carefree one day, and glum or crabby the next?

And isn't the same true for you and me? We're all human. We all have different things going on in life—some good, some bad. Sometimes a lot more one way or the other. And sometimes we're just in a mood, without any reason why. If that's the case for us adults, imagine the inexplicable changes in our students.

> "Kids. You can't control 'em. No matter how hard you try."
>
> - Agatha Harkness,
>   *WandaVision*,
>   "On a Very Special Episode..." (2021)

While cause and effect can often be unclear, there are resources to help us teachers help our students. A big body of research and theory has tackled the issue of classroom management and discipline. Your school or department probably follows a certain program or model. Whatever it is, there is power in consistency. Nevertheless, some systems may work better for certain situations than others. In one of my classes for future (pre-service) teachers, we research a handful of discipline models and examine key elements of each. Ultimately, as a group, we compile items that frequently appear in these different approaches. One of the most common ingredients is students' motivation for their behavior (Charles 2014; Dreikurs 1968; Jones 2007).

A lot of these ideas are not new, but deserve a teacher's review with every batch of fresh-faced students you encounter. Why do students act a certain way in the classroom? Go beyond outward appearances and look to the reasons. Misbehavior often arises from the results of "mistaken goals" (Dreikurs 1968). Is a student seeking attention?

Avoiding it? Are they testing power dynamics of the classroom? Or does a student want revenge? Some of these goals may sound like villainous behavior, but they are simply a child's way of figuring out their place among peers. And let's be honest, haven't we all had similar feelings at various points in our lives? Effective teachers provide a safe learning environment, and they help students find positive ways to meet their needs.

Caption Capture: What **common elements** do you notice in misbehaving students? What are your **solutions or strategies** to help them?

Sometimes, students "misbehave" because they are unaware of expectations. A key element of productive classrooms is clear communication of expected behaviors, along with purposeful practice of routines and procedures (Canter 2010; Rogers 2015; Wong and Wong 2018). Teachers strengthen these efforts by inviting student contributions (Albert 1996), encouraging responsible choices (Glasser 1998), and building relationships (Curwin, Mendler, and Mendler 2018). We also can lead by example, modeling the appropriate behaviors ourselves (Ginnott 1972). This means maintaining self-control, staying on task, and going easy on the sarcasm. Such efforts combine to foster collaborative classrooms as opposed to combative battlefields. With focused objectives and boundaries, teachers lead their students as fellow allies in learning.

Not the Enemy #2: Parents

In a nationwide survey, teachers identified parental involvement as the number one factor for improving students' success (Metropolitan Life 2002). In another survey a decade later (2013), engaging parents was the third highest challenge reported by both teachers and school principals (outranked only by meeting the individual needs of diverse learners and managing budgets).

Obviously, parents play a key role in students' education. Data from decades of studies back up the link between parental involvement and student achievement (Constantino 2008; Hill and Tyson 2009). Unfortunately, many teachers struggle with how to work alongside parents and families. As a pre-service teacher once told me, "I'm scared of my students' parents."

I would argue that many parents have mutual feelings about teachers and schools. Whether justified or not, a lot of people hold negative memories and ongoing trepidation toward educational institutions. Nevertheless, teachers and parents are not enemies. We are on the same side, with the common goal of raising healthy, intelligent, compassionate citizens who contribute to their communities and society.

A common goal does not mean completely identical, however. Likewise, how you raise your children (real or hypothetical) may or may not match how someone else raises theirs. In her book *Every Teacher's Guide to Working with Parents* (2005), Gwen Rudney elaborates: "We know that there is not *one* kind of family. We also need to remember that there is not one kind of *successful* family" (p. 75, emphases in original). Keeping such differences in mind, teachers can work to lower barriers and partner with parents to support students.

"Family isn't just who you're related to.
It's who cares for you and takes care of you."

– Invisible Woman,
Fantastic Four #14 (2013)

In addition to parental involvement, another term used in this context is "family engagement," defined by the National Association for Family, School, and Community Engagement as "a shared responsibility in which schools and other community agencies and organizations are committed to reaching out to engage families in meaningful ways and in which families are committed to actively supporting their children's learning and development" (NAFSCE 2010, p. 1). Effective teachers do their part to actively contribute to this network, inviting and interacting with assorted caretakers and stakeholders involved in students' lives.

Family engagement includes going beyond reactionary strategies such as the traditional parent-teacher conference, phone calls about concerning behavior, or general newsletters (Gray 2001). Instead, consider proactive and cooperative efforts promoting two-way communication and contributions. How can you involve your students' families? Community outreach? Cultural traditions? Interactive homework? Project-based learning? Guest speakers (on-site or online)? Field trips (real or virtual)?

$uper $aver!
Many parents enjoy providing FREE services for their child's school—guest speakers, field trips, FOOD, and other freebies! They'll be honored you asked (after checking with your administration).

Some initiatives may run yearlong, while others are seasonal events. They can range from district-wide programs to classroom-specific plans. You might learn your students need more than what the school provides, and develop something that engages families even further. Better yet, maybe you can share this idea with others and expand it for broader impact.

Find out what your school already does, and what gaps may exist in reaching the community. And find new methods based on research and practice. The National Parent Teacher Association has created Standards for Family-School Partnerships (PTA 2010), and provides multiple tools for teachers and schools. Organizations such as the Global Family Research Project (formerly from the Harvard Graduate School of Education) and the Center on School, Family, and Community Partnerships (Johns Hopkins University) possess a wealth of research and resources. Additionally, local and state education organizations can be another outlet for serving families, geared toward unique needs of your particular region.

In any discussion about working with parents and families, two stereotypes frequently come up in teachers' minds.

Absent Parents

First, there is the "absent parent," who never appears at meetings, nor do they respond to calls, emails, or texts from school. We've already addressed research about the importance of involved parents. Still, it's worth noting variations exist depending on school location and family dynamics. While absent fathers are more common, an absent mother has a greater negative impact on student achievement, particularly with male children (Liu, Alvarado-Urbina, and Hannum 2019).

Regardless of which parent is present or absent, it's vital to consider why some are not as engaged as others. An uninvolved parent is not an uncaring parent. In discussing "why some parents don't come to school," Margaret Finders and Cynthia Lewis (1994) note that "educators must understand the barriers that hinder some parents from participating in their child's education" (p. 50). The authors go on to identify several factors parents share for impacting—and impeding—their school involvement: past experiences, work schedules and other time commitments, economic constraints, cultural and linguistic differences, and more. When planning family outreach programs and opportunities, schools should consider accommodations for parents who are as diverse as their students. In the words of Joyce Epstein, Founder and Director of the National Network of Partnership Schools: "The way schools care about children is reflected in the ways schools care about children's families" (2009, p. 7).

Helicopter Parents

On the other end of the spectrum is the "helicopter parent." This parent seems to constantly hover over their child's education and bombard teachers with questions, concerns, or critiques. Research has found that college students who grew up under helicopter parents wind up struggling with school burnout, self-efficacy, and self-control (Darlow, Norvilitis, and Schuetze 2017; Love et al. 2020). While parental involvement is important for student success, *over*-involvement can be detrimental to children's development. It can also perpetuate inequalities by influencing schools' treatment of students from privileged families, a common source of helicopter parents (Calarco 2020).

So how do you deal with the droning buzz of helicopter parents? First, it's important to consider the motivation behind such behavior, just like with our students. Helicopter parents come in different models—protective, involved, outspoken, or a combination thereof (Hiltz 2015). Overprotective parents who enable their children may need reminders of school policies or classroom procedures regarding student accountability. This includes any paperwork parents have signed to acknowledge their awareness and agreement. If a parent wants to be more involved, teachers could share a list of opportunities needing sponsors or services (e.g., chaperoning events; providing snacks, decorating or cleaning school grounds, distributing flyers, etc.). Teachers can harness a vocal parent to advocate for the school and students, emphasizing positive news via word of mouth or social media. No matter the case, parents should still be held accountable to established boundaries and appropriate actions that are also expected of students and school staff.

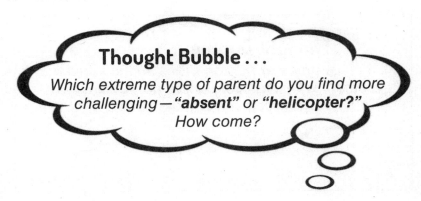

Thought Bubble . . .
*Which extreme type of parent do you find more challenging—"absent" or "helicopter?"
How come?*

Not the Enemy #3: Other Teachers

Maybe a better term is "fellow teachers," to remind everyone that you and your colleagues are on the same side. Still, how many of us have a fellow teacher in our building who really gets on our nerves? (And admit it: How many of us occasionally get on our coworkers' nerves?)

It's okay to concede that teachers don't always get along perfectly with other teachers. We're imperfect beings, after all, each with unique gifts and quirks. In ideal conditions, a team of teachers can build upon one another's strengths to create schoolwide synergy (see Chapter 9). In reality, we often butt heads and encounter frustration—and that's just with our colleague in the neighboring classroom.

We shouldn't be surprised by the occasional annoyance or disagreement. Heck, superheroes fight each other all the time. In fact, fighting is usually how they initially meet. Comic historian George Marston (2022) notes that the very first crossover between two Marvel heroes came in 1940, when the company still went by Timely Comics. It was a two-issue battle between Namor the Sub-Mariner and the original android Human Torch. Since then, we've seen "meet-and-beat" showdowns between Namor and the Fantastic Four, the Fantastic Four and the Hulk, the Hulk and the Avengers, the Avengers and the X-Men, and so on. (Detecting a pattern?) And that's just in the comic books. Think about your favorite movie featuring multiple superheroes. Chances are they introduced themselves to one another with a punch or laser blast.

There's no mystery in why these battles occur. Heroes duking it out is loads of fun to watch. It provides an action-packed scene between two or more fan-favorite characters. And most of the time, they eventually work out their differences to defeat the *real* villain.

Heroes versus heroes is dangerous and entertaining. The same is true for teachers versus teachers—but not in a good way. Given the pressures involved with teaching, disagreements are bound to happen. We don't always see eye to eye when it comes to assessments, curriculum, scheduling, resources, management, discipline, and more. And for whatever reason, some coworkers may just rub you the wrong way.

Thought Bubble . . .
*What **types of personalities** irritate you the most? What types of people do YOU irritate? How can you **alleviate** both?*

As teachers, we must not allow friction to fester. Moreover, we should never undermine our colleagues in front of students. Staff meetings and private conversations provide avenues for discussion and debate. A classroom full of kids, however, is off limits for bickering or complaining about fellow teachers. Resist the urge to blow off steam in front of impressionable minds. Avoid any gossip or rumormongering by students and staff alike. Dampen combustible situations with kindness and good-natured humor. Lie low when you need to. Speak highly of colleagues in front of others. No one is impeccable, but everyone has successes worth commending and strengths worth harnessing as a team (more on that in the next chapter).

Jane Bluestein, author of *The Win-Win Classroom* (2012), shares several recommendations for teachers interacting with difficult coworkers. Take a look at the following summary and consider how it compares to your work in the classroom:

- Don't take it personally.
- Consider the other person's perspective and experiences.
- Plan ahead with preventative measures.
- Pick your battles. (Is it something worth fighting?)
- Be direct and seek resolution.
- Maintain healthy boundaries.
- Get help from others.

Interestingly, a lot of these highlights align with effective management and discipline. Teachers, if you already practice such habits with students, you've got a head start when challenges arise with colleagues.

A teacher-teacher conflict that gets out of control can cause immense collateral damage. This probably doesn't mean property destruction—although it could happen—but rather results in hurt feelings, ruined reputations, and reduced classroom learning. In any disagreement, seek a win-win solution. Both parties will not get everything they want. But such an outcome embraces a more meaningful, longer-lasting peace.

In discussing hero-versus-hero battles, legendary Marvel creator Stan Lee acknowledges the need for a no-lose result:

> One of the most difficult things to do is to have two of our heroes fight each other, because in a fight usually one wins. Now whoever loses, that tends to deglamorize that hero in the eyes of the kids. Because they don't like their hero to lose (cited by Thomas 2006, p. 85).

I hope students recognize their teachers as heroes. And I hope each of us can be heroic in the toughest circumstances. Let's work through our differences and work together for their benefit.

Not the Enemy #4: Administration

For a while in the comic books, superhero Wolverine became headmaster of the X-Men's school for mutants. Founder Professor X gave his blessing and this advice to the fan-favorite hero: "Best accept the fact that you will never again seem even remotely 'cool' to any of your students. And you haven't even started losing your hair yet. Which you will, by the way" (Aaron and Bachalo 2012, p. 3). I don't know about the hair loss thing, but I would argue that school administrators lose their "coolness factor" not only with students, but with many teachers as well.

A lot of us get along well enough with our fellow classroom teachers. But when it comes to principals, superintendents, and other administrators, we view them in a vastly different light. This should not be so.

I cringe when colleagues refer to themselves (or a peer) as going "to the dark side" when they shift career paths from the classroom to building supervision or administration. Remember, nearly all principals and superintendents began their professional careers as full-time classroom teachers. As such, everything addressed about fellow teachers above pertains to our interactions with administration. They, too, are fellow educators. They just have a different role in the school system. And these roles are important. For example, principal leadership is second only to teacher quality in terms of a school's impact on student learning (Louis et al. 2010).

Don't assume a teacher goes into administration just for a higher income, either. They don't get paid that much better, if at all (Forsyth 2003). In most schools, veteran teachers still earn more than new principals. And principals have longer contracts that go into or entirely through the summer months.

Like teaching, administration can be a hard job. Instead of working with just one classroom, a principal must oversee the entire school. Superintendents have an entire district, and they often get hired with the goal of spearheading a successful school bond election. Those are always fun, right?

Other administrative positions may be responsible for specific duties in the building or district—curriculum planning, budget and facilities, assessment and data analysis, or particular groups of students. And a lot of times, administrators deal mostly with more challenging constituents. As one principal told me, the thing he missed most about no longer teaching in the classroom was being able to interact with all the students, not just the ones who got suspended or expelled.

Sure, there are subpar administrators. Just like there are less-than-stellar teachers. But most are doing their best to serve multiple stakeholders under a wider web of scrutiny. When Wolverine was mutant school headmaster, he had to deal with murderous aliens and a giant monster living underneath campus, along with state department inspections and funding woes. On some days, your school leaders may prefer the former threats over the latter. Cut them some slack.

Make your supervisors' lives easier by doing the best you can do. Speak honestly and respectfully when issues emerge. Ask for guidance and provide feedback. Share authentic appreciation for their leadership, including the times when they have to make tough decisions. (*Especially* during those tough times.)

Not all disagreements among school faculty and staff are bad. Reviews of school-based conflict found several productive outcomes: new and creative ideas, informed decisions, self-evaluation and development, and more open lines of communication (Adeyemi 2009; Tshabalala and Mapolisa 2013). Still, plenty of negative consequences can occur if things go south: closing off communication, perpetuating rivalries and hostility, wasting resources and energy. Even in the thick of things, effective school leaders (including teachers) must emphasize the positives, a common ground and focus toward improvement and understanding. Again, these strategies align with what we know works best in classroom management and discipline. Apply your pedagogical skills not only to establish rapport with students, but to maintain cooperation among educational peers.

Remember, we're all on the same side.

So, Who Is the Enemy?

We started this chapter discussing how any superhero is only as good as their archenemy is bad. And so far, we've looked at different people who are *not* our enemies—students, parents and families, fellow teachers, and school leaders. Conflict and consternation may appear, but we can all still work together with the same central aim of educating children.

Nevertheless, teachers do have a singular archenemy, waiting and ready to strike and subvert our efforts. So, who is this mysterious menace?

Check the mirror. Our worst enemy is ourselves. (Gasp!) To be more accurate, our enemy is ourselves at our worst.

You've heard this already, but it bears repeating: We're all human. No one in your school is perfect. Not the students. Not the staff. Not you.

> "Perfection . . . sometimes it's our worst enemy. I tried to be perfect once. Decided to just try to be better. Found a good way to start that . . . is by accepting who you are."
>
> – Wonder Woman,
> *Wonder Woman* #22 (2013)

Don't be too hard on yourself. We each have amazing strengths and classroom "superpowers." We care about kids and our content. We enjoy learning and helping others. But sometimes each of us has a bad day. Or a tough season in life. We get down, discouraged, or just plain grouchy. The glass is not only half empty, but cracked and leaking.

Don't give in. Find a way to renew your passion. Keep the hope. Fight the good fight.

Fight off inclinations of that "evil" version of yourself. Such *mano a mano* battles occur in comic books, where the hero must defeat a demented clone or alternate reality doppelganger. And they happen on screen, too. In *Superman III* (1983), mild-mannered Clark Kent must defeat his own Superman persona, corrupted from kryptonite home-brewed by comedian Richard Pryor. (It was the 1980s; just go with it.) More recently in movies and TV, Doctor Strange has sparred with deranged versions of himself from different multiverses (2021; 2022).

Logistically, these on-screen duels require tricky special effects. And story-wise, they are often painful to watch. It's rather unpleasant seeing the hero get the crap beat out of them—especially by their own hands. But a just victory makes the outcome that much more triumphant. The hero has conquered their own faults—for the moment, at least.

Teachers don't need to worry about punching themselves. But we should consider reflecting on our work and intentions. Are we still on the right track? Are we stuck in a rut? Have we settled for "good enough" too often, so that it's become the enemy of great (Collins 2001)? Are we hurting our own chances at reaching students by adhering to bad habits?

The notion that teachers are their own worst enemies is not necessarily the result of ill intentions. In fact, we may not even be aware of this counterproductive dynamic. Often, we just slip into poor customs or routines. Perhaps we grow too rigid, holding tight to perfectionist tendencies. Or maybe we get too comfortable, a little lackadaisical.

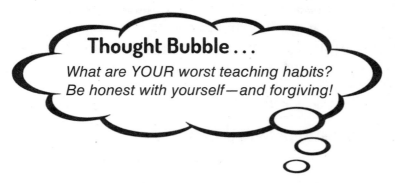

Thought Bubble . . .
What are YOUR worst teaching habits?
Be honest with yourself—and forgiving!

For me, it wasn't until my third year teaching when I finally felt like I was fairly competent. Maybe even pretty good. I'm sure I was better than my first year. But I had developed some bad habits, too.

For example, I used poor questioning as an easy escape. My favorite prompts were "Does that make sense?" and "Does anyone have any questions?" I cannot remember a single time when a brave student actually spoke up and said, "No, Mr. Bergman. Please elaborate on that again, this time with better examples," or, "Yes, Mr. Bergman. I do have a question perfectly formed in my mind and ready to pose that will cultivate further discussion and deliberation." Usually, my lazy questions were met with silence. In blissful ignorance, I quickly pressed on with the lesson before any problems became evident.

Only later in my career did I learn about the power of purposeful open-ended prompts for student engagement and authentic assessment. I'm still working to use better questions, in conjunction with other strategies and devices in my educational utility belt (see Chapter 6).

Check Yourself!

One of the most powerful tools is recording my classroom instruction for review and reflection. As with heroes fighting themselves, it's not particularly fun to watch yourself teaching. And it's a well-known fact—supported by science—that people do not like the sound of their own voice (Samuelson 2017). But hearing and viewing how you actually behave and interact with students can be revelatory and revolutionary for your teaching. If you haven't viewed yourself in the act of teaching since it was required for a college class or internship, give it a try.

Most phones have more than sufficient memory and camera technology to capture your classroom. And they're small enough you can set your device off to the side where no one will notice. Nobody but you needs to see the evidence, which you can promptly delete if that makes you feel better. But before you trash that video, take a moment to review at least part of it. If you're too busy to watch, let it play and listen to the recording while you clean your classroom or commute home.

Even five minutes of footage will give you enough data for honest self-evaluation and earnest self-improvement. You may ask yourself, "Did I actually say that?" or "Do I really look that way?"

Yes, it can be painful at times. But not as bad as punching yourself in the face.

Avoid Villainous Traps (and Labels)

In writing about the search for equity and access in education, Cornelius Minor (2019) notes, "When things hurt, it feels logical to look for the person or thing doing the hurting. In hero terms, we need a bad guy or a supervillain. . . . The true masterminds—the *real* enemies—in this dystopia are the business-as-usual attitudes, binary thinking, and *inflexibility* with which we have been conditioned to approach these problems" (p. 10, emphases in original). All three mindsets are villainous traps we must avoid.

Things can change for the better, as we work on growing and changing ourselves. A lot of educational topics are more complex than simple matters of "either/or." In most cases, opposing views about a school issue are not exclusively good or bad. Furthermore, Minor (2019) recommends we de-emphasize dichotomous labels (e.g., new/veteran, rural/urban, poor/wealthy) that limit our students and ourselves:

> To choose to live out the first few years of my profession as a new teacher ignores and silences all the parts of me that are not new to children, to cities, to youth culture, or to literacy. Yes, someone new to the profession has lots to learn about teaching, but that person has skills and knowledge that we would be foolish to ignore. Similarly, to subscribe to the falsehood that my years in the system make me a veteran ignores and silences all the parts of me that still need mentoring and community and new insights and feedback and love. (p. 10)

Openness to change and acceptance of our multifaceted nature result in more flexibility. Teachers must be malleable—ready to adjust, yet sturdy and solid even under extreme conditions.

Conflicts will always exist in education, much like they do in literature. There are different types of "foes," even as there are different levels of danger and potential damage.

Hero vs. Villain. Hero vs. Society. Hero vs. Nature. Hero vs. Self.

Teachers should seek positive outcomes with every possible conflict. And be careful labeling a "villain" when the real threat is miscommunication, misunderstanding, or unmatched motivations. Pursue resolution and reconciliation. This includes holding ourselves accountable to the same standards as our students and peers.

But don't be too tough.

Everyone could use some grace, including you and me.

 ## To Be Continued!

Further Reading

Aaron, J., Bachalo, C., and Bradshaw, N. (2013). *Wolverine and the X-Men, Volume 1*. New York: Marvel Comics.

Johns, G. and Porter, H. (2005/2006). *The Flash, Vol. 7: Rogue War*. New York: DC Comics.

Loeb, J. and Lee, J. (2002/2019). *Batman: Hush*. New York: DC Comics.

Marston, G. (2022). The extensive history of Marvel superheroes fighting each other. Newsarama (7 April). https://www.gamesradar.com/why-marvel-superheroes-fight-each-other/.

Further Viewing

Bradley, A.C. (writer) and Andrews, B. (director). (2021). What if … Doctor Strange lost his heart instead of his hands? [Television series episode]. In: *What If…?* (producer C. Wassenaar). Marvel Studios.

Feige, K. (producer) and Herron, K. (director). (2021). *Loki* [Television series]. Marvel Studios.

Feige, K. (producer) and Raimi, S. (director). (2022). *Doctor Strange in the Multiverse of Madness* [Motion picture]. Marvel Studios.

Feige, K. (producer) and Russo, A. and Russo, J. (directors). (2016). *Captain America: Civil War* [Motion picture]. Marvel Studios.

Spengler, P. (producer) and Lester, R. (director). (1983). *Superman III* [Motion picture]. Warner Bros.

Questions for Reflection and Discussion

1. Reflect on various superheroes and identify the greatest villain for each. What patterns or relationships do you notice between heroes and their archenemies?

2. Think of the students you currently teach. What "challenging" students come to mind? (These are the ones who make us earn our paychecks! ☺) What unmet motivations, unclear communication, or other barriers might be challenging these students? How can you help them? Which colleagues can you visit with to help you?

3. What are potential dangers of mistakenly regarding the following groups as your "enemies" in education?

   • Students
   • Parents
   • Fellow teachers
   • Administration

4. What are other groups or people commonly considered "enemies" to teachers or schools? Why might this be a mistake?

5. For those individuals/groups listed in Questions 3 and 4, how can you practice and promote the notion that "we're all on the same side"?

6. No two people get along perfectly all the time. (Just ask any married couple.) Knowing that moments of conflict are inevitable, how can you maintain healthy partnerships with other school stakeholders?

7. What do you think about the expression "You are your own worst enemy"? How have you encountered this notion in the realm of teaching and learning?

8. How can a teacher remain vigilant and reflective of their professional practice without becoming overly self-critical?

9. In addition to recording and reviewing your teaching, what are other ways to hold yourself accountable and improve?

10. Reflect on Cornelius Minor's comments (*We Got This*, 2019) about the three "real enemies" teachers face when solving problems:

    • Business-as-usual attitudes
    • Binary thinking
    • Inflexibility

    a. Which of these three "enemies" do you find most troubling or do you struggle with the most?

    b. How can you overcome them to find successful solutions and positive outcomes?

References

Aaron, J., Bachalo, C., and Bradshaw, N. (2013). *Wolverine and the X-Men, Volume 1*. New York: Marvel Comics.

Adeyemi, O. (2009). Principals' management of conflicts in public secondary schools in Ondo State, Nigeria: a critical survey. *Educational Research & Review* 4 (9): 418–426.

Albert, L. (1996). *Cooperative Discipline*. Detroit, MI: Ags Pub.

Bluestein, J. (2012). Dealing with difficult colleagues. Education World. https://www.educationworld.com/a_curr/bluestein-dealing-with-difficult-colleagues-part1.shtml.

Bradley, A.C. (writer) and Andrews, B. (director). (2021). What if . . . Doctor Strange lost his heart instead of his hands? [Television series episode]. In: *What If . . .?* (producer C. Wassenaar). Marvel Studios.

Calarco, J.M. (2020). Avoiding us versus them: how schools' dependence on privileged "helicopter" parents influences enforcement of rules. *American Sociological Review* 85 (2): 223–246.

Canter, L. (2010). *Assertive Discipline: Positive Behavior Management for Today's Classroom, Fourth Edition*. Bloomington, IN: Solution Tree Press.

Center on School, Family, and Community Partnerships. (2022). Engaging families for high school success. Johns Hopkins University. https://www.sfcp.jhucsos.com/efhss/.

Charles, C.M. (2014). *Building Classroom Discipline, Eleventh Edition*. New York: Pearson.

Collins, J.C. (2001). *Good to Great: Why Some Companies Make the Leap . . . and Others Don't*. New York: HarperBusiness.

Constantino, S.M. (2008). *101 Ways to Create Real Family Engagement*. Galax, VA: ENGAGE! Press.

Curwin, R.L., Mendler, A.N., and Mendler, B.D. (2018). *Discipline with Dignity: How to Build Responsibility, Relationships, and Respect in Your Classroom, Fourth Edition*. ASCD.

Darlow, V., Norvilitis, J., and Schuetze, P. (2017). The relationship between helicopter parenting and adjustment to college. *Journal of Child & Family Studies* 26 (8): 2291–2298.

Dreikurs, R. (1968). *Psychology in the Classroom, Second Edition*. New York: Harper & Row.

Epstein, J.L. (2009). School, family, and community partnerships: caring for the children we share. In: *School, Family, and Community Partnerships: Your Handbook for Action, Third Edition* (eds. J.L. Epstein, M. Sanders, B. Simon et al.), 7–29. Thousand Oaks, CA: Corwin Press.

Feige, K. (producer) and Raimi, S. (director). (2022). *Doctor Strange in the Multiverse of Madness* [Motion picture]. Marvel Studios.

Finders, M. and Lewis, C. (1994). Why some parents don't come to school. *Educational Leadership* 51 (8): 50–54. https://www.ascd.org/el/articles/why-some-parents-dont-come-to-school.

Forsyth, J. (2003). Administrator pay vs. teacher pay. *The School Administrator* 60 (11): 6.

Ginnott, H.G. (1972). *Teacher & Child: A Book for Parents and Teachers, Third Edition*. New York: Avon Books.

Glasser, W. (1998). *Choice Theory in the Classroom*. New York: HarperCollins.

Global Family Research Project. (2022). Resources. https://globalfrp.org/Articles.

Gray, S.F. (2001). A compilation of state mandates for home–school partnership education in pre-service teacher training programs. Unpublished manuscript, Pepperdine University.

Hill, N.E. and Tyson, D.F. (2009). Parental involvement in middle school: a metanalytic assessment of the strategies that promote achievement. *Developmental Psychology* 45 (3): 740–763.

Hiltz, J. (2015). Helicopter parents can be a good thing. *Phi Delta Kappan* 96 (7): 26–29.

Jones, F. (2007). *Tools for Teaching, Second Edition*. Santa Cruz, CA: Fredric H. Jones & Associates, Inc.

Liu, R., Alvarado-Urbina, A., and Hannum, E. (2019). Parental absence and student academic performance in cross-national perspective. Paper presented at the Annual Meeting of the Population Association of America. Austin, TX (10–13 April). http://paa2019.populationassociation.org/abstracts/191312.

Louis, K.S., Leithwood, K., Wahlstrom, K.L. and Anderson, S.E. (2010). Investigating the links to improved student learning: final report of research findings. University of Minnesota, University of Toronto, and Wallace Foundation. https://conservancy.umn.edu/handle/11299/140885.

Love, H., May, R. ., Cui, M., and Fincham, F.D. (2020). Helicopter parenting, self-control, and school burnout among emerging adults. *Journal of Child and Family Studies* 29 (2): 327–337.

Marston, G. (2022). The extensive history of Marvel superheroes fighting each other. Newsarama (7 April). https://www.gamesradar.com/why-marvel-superheroes-fight-each-other/.

Metropolitan Life. (2002). The MetLife survey of the American teacher 2002–student life: school, home, and community.

Metropolitan Life. (2013). The MetLife survey of the American teacher 2012–challenges for school leadership. https://www.metlife.com/content/dam/microsites/about/corporate-profile/MetLife-Teacher-Survey-2012.pdf.

Minor, C. (2019). *We Got This: Equity, Access, and the Quest to Be Who Our Students Need Us to Be*. Portsmouth, NH: Heinemann.

National Association for Family, School, and Community Engagement. (2010). Family engagement defined. https://nafsce.org/page/definition.

Parent Teacher Association. (2010). National standards for family-school partnerships. https://www.pta.org/home/run-your-pta/National-Standards-for-Family-School-Partnerships.

Rogers, B. (2015). *Classroom Behaviour: A Practical Guide to Effective Teaching, Behaviour Management and Colleague Support*. London: SAGE Publications Ltd.

Rudney, G.L. (2005). *Every Teacher's Guide to Working with Parents*. Thousand Oaks, CA: Corwin Press.

Samuelson, K. (2017). Why do I hate the sound of my own voice? *Time* (19 June). https://time.com/4820247/voice-vocal-cords/.

Spengler, P. (producer) and Lester, R. (director). (1983). *Superman III* [Motion picture]. Warner Bros.

Thomas, R. (2006). *Stan Lee's Amazing Marvel Universe*. New York: Sterling Publishing Co., Inc.

Tshabalala, T. and, Mapolisa, T. (2013). An investigation into the causes of conflict in Zimbabwean schools: a case study of Nkayi south circuit. *Journal of Humanities and Social Sciences* 1 (1): 13–22.

Wong, H.K. and Wong, R. (2018). *The First Days of School: How to Be an Effective Teacher, Fifth Edition*. Mountain View, CA: Harry K. Wong Publications.

> "There was an idea . . .
> to bring together a group of
> remarkable people,
> see if they could become
> something more."

– Nick Fury,
The Avengers (2012)

 ## 9 Teammates

I have a geeky confession to make: *Iron Man 2* (2010) is one of my favorite movies in the Marvel Cinematic Universe.

This may not seem like a controversial stance, but the second Iron Man film (and third overall in the MCU) is not universally beloved. *Iron Man 2* sits in the bottom half of Marvel films in terms of global box office earnings (Clark 2022). More incriminating evidence is that this early MCU sequel is one of the lowest reviewed and ranked by critics (A.V. Club 2022; Miller and Langmann 2022; Vo 2022).

Still, there are so many reasons to enjoy *Iron Man 2*. Of course, you have more quips from Robert Downey Jr. as the title character, and the film has its own take on one of the most famous Iron Man comic book stories ever, "Demon in a Bottle" (*The Invincible Iron Man* #120-128, 1979). Plus, we see more growth for the supporting cast, along with a growing cast in general. The biggest reason I like *Iron Man 2* is witnessing the MCU's first on-screen superhero team-up. In the movie's climax, Iron Man and War Machine fight side by side (after first fighting each other, natch). At the same time, Black Widow gets to shine doing her super spy/hand-to-hand combat stuff. Heck, even Happy Hogan helps out in his own bumbling way.

The Marvel movies feature all kinds of teams and mingling among heroes. This includes multiple Avengers iterations and the growing roster of Guardians of the Galaxy. But I encourage you to go back and watch the earliest example in *Iron Man 2*. It's not a perfect collaboration; yet consider how diverse the characters are in terms of professions, backgrounds, talents, and dreams. It's all the more amazing when they work together for a common goal. And the same is true for the Avengers, Guardians, and other superhero team-ups.

Iron Sharpens Iron (Man)

As a younger comic book reader and cartoon viewer, I always gravitated toward the team titles: *X-Men, Justice League, Teen Titans, Teenage Mutant Ninja Turtles,* and others. Simply put, these stories show more heroes. More bang for your buck. Whether it is witty dialogue or innovative combinations of superpowers, teams and team-ups let heroes bounce off each other in unique ways.

I wish the same were true for teachers. But it's a common lament that teaching is an isolated profession. This long-held belief is backed up by decades of research into the lives of teachers (e.g., Andrews, Sherman, and Webb 1983; Cookson 2005; Goodlad 1984; Lortie 1975; Ostovar-Nameghi and Sheikhahmadi 2016). Sure, a teacher is surrounded by students all day. And there are regular staff meetings and constant emails. Yet many teachers still struggle to maintain meaningful relationships with colleagues.

Isolation to Collaboration

In one nationwide survey conducted by Scholastic and the Gates Foundation (2012), teachers reported spending only 3% of their day collaborating with professional peers. In a typical *week*, this totals up to about 1 hour and 15 minutes for teacher teamwork.

Thought Bubble . . .
*How much time do YOU **collaborate** directly with colleagues during a given day? Week?*

A common form of weekly collaboration is a single sit-down session for formal conversation and coordination. Such team meetings and staff gatherings quickly fill up with announcements and logistical plans, occurring at the expense of engaged dialogue and creativity. Collegial deficiency is evident in a subsequent Scholastic/Gates nationwide survey (2014), in which teachers rate "not enough time collaborating with colleagues" as the second highest challenge they face. Outranked only by "constantly changing demands," lack of collaboration time was voted higher than common educational concerns such as management, finances, overcrowded classes, and more.

Teacher isolation has strong ties to occupational stress (Dussault et al. 1999), and is particularly damaging to new teachers, who are more prone to leave the profession (Sleppin 2009). While isolation is multifaceted with many possible interventions, one important step is improving teacher teamwork.

> "It's kinda nice not being the only Spider-person around."
>
> – Gwen Stacy,
> *Spider-Man: Into the Spider-Verse* (2018)

Schools with strong teacher collaboration have higher student achievement scores (Goddard and Goddard 2007; Supovitz, Sirinides, and May 2010). The better the collaboration, the greater the gains in students' scores (Ronfeldt et al. 2015). While some of these effects may be correlative as opposed to causation, we do know that professional collaborations do impact teachers as well as their students. In the research field of "school social capital," studies have found that teachers' relationships far outweigh their individual abilities in terms of overall effect (Leana and Pil 2006; Pil and Leana 2009). For example, a below-average teacher can produce average results when they participate in robust peer collaborations (Leana 2011).

Caption Capture: In what ways have you seen **strong teacher collaboration** benefit your students? Your professional peers? Yourself?

Get to Know Your Teammates (and Yourself)

Clearly, teamwork is a key element for teachers, much like it is for superheroes. But before we discuss *how* we collaborate, let's examine *who* is collaborating. It's vital to get to know your teammates. The following sections discuss some common hero types found in superteams. As you review these roles, reflect on your colleagues. What faces come to mind? Also consider yourself—where do you fit in?

The Leader

This is an obvious role in any group. Someone has to lead the charge, steer the ship, direct traffic, conduct the orchestra, and other motivational metaphors. You can find tons of books about leadership; just look for thick tomes stamped with bold-font titles and author portraits featuring crisp suits and stoic stares. But the quickest way to learn about leadership is to follow good leaders, and eventually grab the reins and drive your team forward (that was another metaphor). Leadership is both task-oriented—getting the job done—and relationship-focused—cultivating camaraderie among the team.

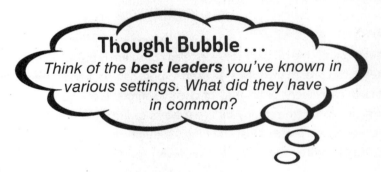

Thought Bubble...
*Think of the **best leaders** you've known in various settings. What did they have in common?*

A good leader doesn't bark orders or boss people around. They lead through example. You've probably heard of the term "servant leader," made popular in the late twentieth century from writings by Robert Greenleaf (1970/2015; 1977/2002) and others. *Entrepreneur* magazine (Hayzlett 2019) highlights four signs of servant leadership:

- Diversity of thought
- Culture of trust
- Unselfishness
- Producing more leaders

A leader will step into the spotlight, but not for the glory. They seek to serve others and strive for the greater good, sometimes at great sacrifice. And at the right moment, they step aside and let someone else take the lead.

The Brain

Sure, we each have a brain, but we all know people we consider "brainy." Maybe they have advanced degrees and are experts in a specialized field. Other folks are simply blessed with astute intellect. They could possess an off-the-charts IQ, innately born with above average intelligence. Many smart people I know, however, got that way through hard work and thoughtful humility. They pay attention. They ask questions. They are the first to admit they don't know everything, and are eager to learn more. To me, this demeanor of lifelong learning is the root of wisdom.

The "wise sage" is one type of brainy teammate. They are older, more experienced, and can provide insight from a veteran's perspective. But even though they've "been around the block" a few times, they don't have to blab about it. That's another sign of wisdom: knowing how much to share, and when to share it.

Seek out smart people, who may be some of the quietest people in your group. Observe and tune into those with more expertise, experience, or extraordinary genius. They won't have all the answers. No one does. But if they are truly wise, they'll admit their limits, provide perspective, and join the search for solutions.

The Brawn

For some teammates, the primary solution to any problem is brute force. The brawn role in a superteam can take many forms—big and strong, compact and potent—powered by muscles, magic, machinery, or an array of energy sources. Likewise, the "brawn" in your school team can come from many different walks of life. This strength may rise from personal experience, professional training, cultural upbringing, even birth order (Leman 2009). No matter the case, they are driven and direct.

Brawns may be blunt to a fault, but at least you know where they stand. And when something needs to get done, they are ready to go. Every team needs at least one brawn. They break down barriers. They won't take "No" for an answer. They're not afraid to get dirty and do the heavy lifting. This could be figurative or literal. There are moments when a brawn needs healthy restraint, but on occasion it's necessary to unleash their power. (Remember the Hulk at the end of the first *Avengers* movie?)

If you struggle with assertiveness, learn from your brawny colleagues. This may be especially helpful with classroom management. A brawn can model the "no fear" approach required when addressing unruly classrooms and maintaining order. Many brawns are also intensely loyal. When things get tough, they've got your back.

The Techie

Think about your coworkers. Who has the newest phone? Smartwatch? Other wearable tech? Who is constantly sharing the latest, greatest app or website? Who keeps assorted devices and power strips plugged in their classroom? Chances are that person is your team's techie. (Maybe it's you. Are you reading these words on a glowing screen right now? Or downloading them directly into your mind?)

There are different types of tech users, just like there are all kinds of technology. We're referring to electronic varieties here, which people apply in multiple ways and degrees. On any team, the techie is an "early adopter," perhaps even an inventor or inno-vator (Rogers 2003). According to the Pew Research Center (Kennedy and Funk 2016), more than one-fourth of all Americans (28%) are early technology adopters. These are individuals eager to try new products. They enjoy tinkering with cutting-edge tools and testing their limits.

In a school, the techie may or may not have an official Information Technology (IT) title. They might just like their toys, and are happy to help others with troubleshooting. Things may not work as intended, but a techie is comfortable with snags and unexpected outcomes. A teammate with this attitude is an asset—as long as their contraptions don't turn evil and take over the world. (Or school.)

We've talked before (in Chapter 6) about how technology can be both helpful and hurtful to learning. The best techies know the difference. They have technological liter-acy in the truest sense of the word (Shume 2013). If you are literate, you know much more than how to read and write. You can also perceive and articulate patterns, refer-ences, themes, irony, and other literary devices. The same principle applies to an indi-vidual literate in technology. They understand not only how to use a tool, but also where and when (and when not to). Furthermore, a trusted techie is aware of wider impact and potential consequences. And most importantly for a team, they help others with these decisions, not just their devices.

The Sneaker

I'm not talking about shoes here, although this type of teammate is also quiet, flexible, and durable. The opposite of a team's brawn, the sneaker still gets things done. They may seem underpowered, but that lets them fly under the radar. By nature, a sneaker is unas-suming. They are clever, accessing resources and reaching audiences that others cannot. The sneaker knows the path of least resistance. And if you're lucky, they'll let you in on their secrets.

Deft maneuvers are critical in schools, which often operate like organizational mazes. How do you get classroom materials? Who decides the lunch schedule? When's the best time to make copies? Who is the contact for approving summer school? Where is the cleanest staff restroom? Need a new office chair or pencil sharpener? What other questions have you always wanted to ask?

Check with the team sneaker. They can help you out.

Beyond immediate concerns, the sneaker can also demonstrate ways to deal with bigger barriers. Such "institutional constraints" may be external or internal influences, limited resources and time, regulations and restrictions, or other obstacles teachers encounter that hinder effective instruction (Berliner 2000; Brickhouse and Bodner 1992; Ihrig 2014; Wilcox 2017). These walls may not crumble under a brawn's direct attack. Instead, there are ways to navigate and negotiate amid a complex system. Sneakers understand their school community and climate, and they can help others through the labyrinth.

The Speedster

People work at different paces. The speedster gets stuff done fast. Grading. Writing reports. Planning lessons. These tasks and more can be time consuming, so it's nice to know someone who does their part quickly. While everyone on a team has their own responsibilities, having a speedster means fewer tight deadlines and less stress at crunch time. They also keep things moving forward, sidestepping distractions or traps that bog down progress.

A speedster can zoom ahead and report on their progress, providing insight for rest of the team. Even so, you do need to be wary of teammates who are too impatient. Speedy work can result in a sloppy job that needs redoing. Unfortunately, an overeager speedster can serve as an example for others, showing what pitfalls to avoid and reinforcing the adage, "Look before you leap." Marvel at a speedster's pioneering spirit, but be ready to catch them and provide course correction, when necessary.

The Jokester

Although we've already addressed using humor with your students (Chapter 5), it can have similar effects with your colleagues, too. The jokester's role is to provide levity and cut tension. Poor timing and lame jokes, however, only make things worse. On many superteams, the jokester character is either loved or loathed by the audience. This is partly due to the subjective nature of comedy.

Some individuals are simply gifted with a quick wit or quirky sensibility. Actor Paul Rudd plays Ant-Man in the Marvel movies, often serving a comedic role in action-packed scenes. His humor, however, seems to rise with relative ease. Reflecting on his work, Rudd says, "I don't consider myself a comedian because I don't really concern myself too much with jokes" (IMDB 2022). Humorous asides or unassuming antics are healthy to everyday conversations. They provide relief during lengthy meetings or after a difficult conference.

A jokester can fall out of favor when they try too hard. Sure, one snarky comment may get a few laughs. But it's not so funny after the tenth zinger, or when someone has to say "Get it?" following every punchline. And as with classroom humor, jokes shouldn't be crass or hurtful. (In my experience, whenever someone says, "No offense, but . . ." they are going to say something offensive. If you think a joke might offend someone, don't say it.)

Timing is everything. For those prone to jest, be careful to offer your joke at appropriate moments. If you have a teammate playing the jokester role, kindly let them know when humor is welcome. Sometimes no reaction is the best way to respond. This works with many student comedians, and the same is true for colleagues. They'll get the hint. And if they don't, you can politely say, "Not now. Let's get this work done first," or "Sounds funny. Tell me later, okay?" Or maybe they need some redirection and encouragement: "Have you ever considered stand-up? Or performing in theater?" Then help your jokester find the nearest open mic event or improv group. They can try out their stuff on stage for a more deserving audience.

The Rebel

Obviously, an entire team won't have 100% agreement on any particular matter. But there's always at least one member in the group who seems to disagree on everything. The rebel zigs when everyone else wants to zag. They go against the grain, and don't mind ruffling a few feathers along the way. Such is the *modus operandi* of the classic antihero.

Don't be too quick to dismiss rebel-type individuals in your group. A team can still be cohesive, strengthened by different viewpoints. In fact, I'd be suspicious of any collective that claims complete union among its members. Such a notion gives off vibes of a creepy "hivemind." That's a danger to democracy and synergy. If everybody is exactly the same, then someone (or two or three or more) is redundant.

Rebels can be dangerous, too, especially if they go off the deep end in terms of professionalism and ethics. There are appropriate channels to express dissent. But in matters that allow flexibility, give people the freedom to do their own thing. Nonconformists are a breath of fresh air, and they can provide counterarguments and counterintuitive solutions to common problems.

The Loner

Like a rebel, loners often do their own thing—they just don't tell anyone about it. In fact, at times it might feel like the loner is not really on the team at all. Maybe they show up to meetings because it's required, but good luck getting a word out of them. And during informal gatherings, they always remain on the periphery.

Sadly, some loners simply check out and refuse to participate. It could be laziness. Or it could be they are in a season of life with other priorities. Or they could simply be die-hard introverts. Like a withdrawn student, a loner may not know what's expected of them. Or they don't know how to contribute. Other loners are reluctant to join in because of trust issues. They've been burned before and don't want to risk it. And, as mentioned in Chapter 2, burnout is a particular danger to introverted teachers (Godsey 2016; Walker 2016).

Whatever the case, watch for those in your group who linger on the fringes. Invite them to share at safe moments. Don't scare them off. And give them some space. Some loners may appear disinterested, but make major contributions behind the scenes. In their research of teacher collegiality, Ostovar-Nameghi and Sheikhahmadi (2016) note, "What one teacher considers as isolation may be seen as individual autonomy by others" (p. 198). Such solo work can be an essential part of the greater team effort.

If any of these possibilities describe you, that's okay. As an introvert myself, I admit that we each have moments when we want to be left alone to do our work. Still, there are times when we loner types have to come out of our shells and shine. On many superhero teams, the loner has a habit of disappearing during pivotal fights, showing up later when things are truly hopeless. Thanks to unseen efforts, the loner helps save the day with a new discovery or device.

Teammate Role	Potential Positives (+)	Potential Negatives (-)
Leader	+ Provide direction + Servant leader	- Too bossy - Glory hog
Brain	+ Astute intelligence + Additional experience	- Know-it-all - All think, no action
Brawn	+ Assertive + Hard worker	- Blunt - Collateral damage
Techie	+ Early adopter + Troubleshooter	- Tech > Teach - Robot uprising
Sneaker	+ Shrewd maneuvers + Alternate solutions	- Manipulative - Unethical solutions
Speedster	+ Fast finisher + Pioneering spirit	- Impatient - Potential pitfalls
Jokester	+ Provide levity + Funny	- Inappropriate - Annoying
Rebel	+ New ideas + Counterintuitive	- Abrasive - Counterproductive
Loner	+ Independent + Behind-the-scenes	- Aloof - Absent

Chart of teammate roles.
What other types of teammates are there? What types are you?

Complex Characters

Not every team has each of these separate individuals. Depending on the situation, not every role is essential. Often, there are duplicates and members with similar skills or dispositions. Moreover, many of us possess several of these talents and fill multiple roles. We wear different hats for different occasions. Or, as poet Walt Whitman eloquently declares in Song of Myself: "I am large, I contain multitudes."

Like any fully formed character, fan-favorite superheroes are multidimensional. In addition to their personality and past, they possess an array of skills. On the Avengers, Iron Man is both techie and jokester. He is also smart and has a rebellious streak. The X-Men's Beast is brilliant and quippy, an interesting juxtaposition to his brawny appearance. Wonder Woman is a central figure of the Justice League, as both a leader and one of its strongest members. Batman has occasionally served the League as team leader, but is a loner just as often. (Plus, he's really sneaky.)

Caption Capture: List a few **"teams"** you currently are a part of. Then add the main **"role"** you play for each (use the superhero types).

Team/Group   *Your Role*

We must be careful not to pigeonhole someone into a permanent category. As with our students, it's important to avoid labeling and limiting individuals (DeWitt 2018; Gold and Richards 2012). Still, no one can be everything at all times. It helps to know your strengths and weaknesses–see previous chapters on powers and vulnerabilities–as well as your tendencies in different group settings. How do you work best in large groups? Small groups? General discussions? Specialized tasks? Also, how do you respond to other personalities and positions? When do you need to adjust your role?

For superheroes, shifting team duties can result in unique stories and interesting character studies. Similarly, teachers must occasionally realign team dynamics to produce innovative solutions. Everybody still contributes, and can gain a greater appreciation for one another. Depending on the context, individuals may need to step up or step back in favor of a colleague. But as a team, they stand together for positive change.

Thought Bubble . . .
*What **Team Role(s)** do YOU prefer?*
*Why might your role **change** for different teams?*

Get Together (and Get Along)

So, now that you know more about yourself and your teammates, *how* do you actually work together? Teaching may be an isolated profession, but there are still ways to collaborate and socialize. Yes, it requires work. And yes, it competes with other important tasks for your time and energy. But professional relationships can be worthwhile. Teacher collegiality is complex, with varying aspects of communication, independence, and interdependence, entrenched in both emotional and cultural nuances (Löfgren and Karlsson 2016).

After reviewing research on the impact of teacher collaboration, Shah (2012) concludes, "The process of collegiality is likely to work only when a significant number of teaching personnel at a specific school becomes convinced that it will actually lead to improved teaching and learning" (p. 1244). So perhaps the most important criterion for teacher teamwork is buy-in to the benefits for self and others. This applies to all kinds of collaborative contexts—formal meetings, daily interactions, online communication, document sharing, and more.

> **Caption Capture:** What is your **preferred format(s)** or structure for teacher collaboration? What do you like about it?

Let's look closer at in-person collaborations, found in numerous school committees, workgroups, and assorted "teams" organized by grade level, department, building, or other categories. You could also lump big group meetings into this category, but these staff assemblies often deal with announcements and reminders. While it's important to distribute information, a lot of times an email or handout works just as well. We want to focus on team gatherings oriented toward instructional actions and educational outcomes.

A popular term in recent decades is "professional learning community," described as "an environment that fosters mutual cooperation, emotional support, and personal growth as [educators] work together what they cannot accomplish alone" (DuFour and Eaker 1998, p. xii). A professional learning community (PLC) can be schoolwide or span across a district, but frequently functions in smaller units. In my experience, the fewer the people at a meeting, the more work actually gets done. So, in the case of large PLCs or other whole-group gatherings facing a monumental task (e.g., school improvement, curriculum mapping, strategic plans, etc.), consider how to split the crowd into serviceable teams with specific tasks.

How often should a team meet? It depends. Bigger groups tend to meet less often—maybe once a month, maybe just once a semester. Small groups with a precise purpose may meet more often. Maybe a team meeting is part of your regular schedule, part of that weekly 1 hour and 15 minutes teachers report as collaboration time with their peers (Scholastic/Gates 2012). For an ad hoc committee (or "task force," which sounds much more heroic), there may be a condensed timeline and defined due date, after which they're done. And again, teamwork involves electronic correspondence and shared documents as well as traditional meetings.

When you meet as a team, what do you talk about? What do you do? Hopefully more than just announcements. Schools that boast a strong professional learning community keep student learning as a primary focus (Louis, Kruse, and Marks 1996). Teamwork oriented around assessment analysis, curriculum decisions, and instructional strategies is associated most closely with student learning gains (Ronfeldt et al. 2015; Strahan 2003; Vescio, Ross, and Adams 2008; Supovitz 2002). Further research has found that along with evidence-based decision-making, effective collaboration occurs in "high-depth meetings" described as dialogical, conversational, reflective, and attentive to implementing future actions (Horn et al. 2020).

What follows are two collaborative approaches, or "teamwork tactics," commonly found in schools. While many other programs or strategies exist, reflect on how the features described in the following examples relate to your specific teaching context. Consider similar actions you and your teammates can try.

Teamwork Tactic #1: Lesson Study

In college, I had a choir director who would mark off time on his posted weekly schedule for "Score Study." At first, I found this task rather odd, especially compared to other duties listed such as classes, vocal lessons, meetings, and so on. But during choir rehearsals, our director often described to us the insight he gained after musing over a certain score, or musical arrangement. Maybe it was a unique harmonization, a recurring rhythm, or a lyrical flair. After pointing out the noteworthy features, the director guided our singing to accentuate these elements. If he hadn't paused to scrutinize each composition, these beautiful details would have remained hidden and unheard, resulting in a lackluster performance. In the same way a musician should "study the scores" they perform, teachers also must study the lessons they teach.

Lesson study is one way teachers can collaborate and function as a professional learning community (Kanellopoulou and Darra 2018; Penteri, Karadimitriou, and Reka-lidou 2013). Typically, a lesson study group contains three to six teachers, with a recommended time commitment of 10 to 15 hours over three to four weeks (Fernandez 2002). That's far more than the hour(ish) per week most teachers have available for collaboration, so lesson study may require a schoolwide commitment or district initiative for supporting staff and providing necessary time.

Or if you lack any formal system for lesson study, find a few colleagues to join your quest. You don't need a full-fledged program as outlined in the resources shared here. With creativity and flexibility, your team can find ways to enact lesson study components. This includes co-planning and setting research goals, observing lessons and collecting data, and reflecting on your results (Stepanek et al. 2007).

Maybe you and your "study buddies" take turns covering or combining classes so others can observe a featured lesson. Or instead of in-person visits during the day, you record classes and review them later. Handwritten notes could replace lengthier meetings or documentation. Come up with a quick fill-in template. These efforts may require time you normally allot for other duties; but it's worthwhile if it leads to enhanced teaching and learning. And after sharing your findings with others, your team may be able to secure additional resources and assistance from the powers that be.

Teamwork Tactic #2: Curriculum Integration

While lesson study usually involves teachers from the same grade and subject, curriculum integration offers opportunities for interdisciplinary teamwork. Simply put, an interdisciplinary unit "integrates" and applies knowledge and skills traditionally associated with different subjects or disciplines (Jacobs 1989). Often, these units focus on a central topic, theme, or problem (Shriner, Schlee, and Libler 2010), or even an issue or question from students (Campbell and Henning 2010).

Curriculum integration examples are as obvious as using a science experiment to practice algebra and graphing skills, and as unique as the instructors' imaginations. At my first teaching job, the neighboring middle school incorporated a building-wide interdisciplinary unit about the Greek Olympic Games. Every class studied some aspect of the ancient athletes—math, history, language arts, visual arts, science, P.E. and more—and applied content from their particular subject.

As a formal educational strategy, curriculum integration frequently appears in middle level education (Wall and Leckie 2017). But it's not limited to any specific age or grade. Historically in the United States, interdisciplinary projects gained prominence in the progressive movement of the early twentieth century (Vars 1991). At John Dewey's Laboratory School in the University of Chicago (described in Chapter 4), students used all sorts of subjects to research, design, and operate a small farm—just one example of their daily contributions to the school's "micro-society." Even though interdisciplinary ideas are not new, teachers can still find new ways to collaborate and combine content for meaningful learning.

Brophy and Alleman (1991) observe that "Curriculum integration is sometimes necessary to teach about topics that *cut across or transcend* school subjects," but they also provide a cautionary note: "However, curriculum integration is *not* an end in itself but a *means* for accomplishing basic educational goals" (p. 66, emphases added). Done poorly, curriculum integration is pointless or counterproductive. I liken "forced" interdisciplinary units to the urge of creators to cram all the superheroes they can into a crossover story. There are so many people on the page or on screen that the audience can't follow what's going on. Multiple protagonists become superfluous and often get in each other's way. Others are forgotten. Or worse, one (or more) hero behaves out of character just to be noticed. They're memorable, but for the wrong reasons.

Keeping this caveat in mind, teachers should aim for curriculum integration projects that enrich and elevate content, while avoiding unintended dilution, inaccurate distortions, or unnecessary distractions. One model for developing interdisciplinary units emphasizes two main steps:

1. Identify a standards-based theme involving multiple subjects.
2. Choose and refine specific activities that provide a balanced integration of the involved subjects (Lonning, DeFranco, and Weinland 1998).

Both of these phases require collaboration among teachers from various subjects. And overall, curriculum integration encourages students to strengthen and share diverse thoughts and talents. That's true teamwork, and, ultimately good citizenship. Or put another way, "Curriculum integration centers the curriculum on life itself. . . . It is rooted in a view of learning as the continuous integration of new knowledge and experience so as to deepen and broaden our understanding of ourselves and our world" (Beane 1995, p. 622).

Educators Assemble!

In the same way teachers shouldn't force illogical curriculum integration, we must be careful to avoid forcing untenable collaboration. Ideally, professional partnerships would arise naturally and effortlessly. And sometimes it feels that way. Have you ever just "clicked" with a colleague or department? More realistically, however, effective teamwork entails both structured parameters and perceptive nuance.

If you wait for spontaneous rap- port, it may never happen. But if you impose required partnerships with stringent restrictions, the response will be resentment, resistance, and possibly rebellion. Citing Hargreaves' research on teacher relationships (1994), Ostovar-

Nameghi and Sheikhahmadi (2016) summarize, "Demanding teachers to collaborate disturbs their right as professionals to work in isolation and can result only in 'contrived congeniality' rather than a true collaborative culture" (p. 199). Remember, some of your teaching colleagues are introverted loner types. And all of us prefer "alone time" every now and then. But a hermit's life is not healthy for teachers. This is why a little bit of structure helps in cultivating collegiality.

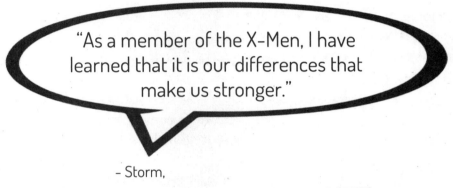

"As a member of the X-Men, I have learned that it is our differences that make us stronger."

- Storm,

X-Men '92 Infinite Comic #6 (2015)

Both of the "teamwork tactics" discussed here provide avenues to strengthen teacher alliances. Teachers participating in lesson study workgroups report improved communication and relationships, along with overall efficacy (Chong and Kong 2012). Curriculum integration projects promote a sense of community among teachers (Drake and Reid 2010; MacIver 1990). Moreover, after participating in an interdisciplinary unit, most teachers show interest in continuing this type of cooperative work (Edgerton 1990).

Besides teamwork, a common feature of these two approaches is support. A school or district that wants staff to collaborate and invigorate curriculum must provide time and resources to do so. Teachers can enact such projects themselves, but sustainability requires formal programming. And for any team effort to truly work, there still needs to be room for choice and creativity.

As with every lesson you teach, a healthy balance exists between structure and spontaneity. The same applies to teacher collaboration and goes beyond co-planning and committees. No matter how formal or informal, teacher teamwork occurs through co-teaching and mentoring (see Chapter 10), as well as with colleagues beyond buildings and borders (see Chapter 11).

To Be Continued!

Further Reading

Defilippis, N., Weir, C., and Green, R. (2005). *New X-Men: Academy X, Vol. 1–Choosing Sides*. New York: Marvel Comics.

Goyer, D.S., Johns, G., and Pacheco, C. (2002). *JLA/JSA: Virtue and Vice*. New York: DC Comics.

Simone, G. and Benes, E. (2004). *Birds of Prey, Vol. 1–Of Like Minds*. New York: DC Comics.

Waid, M. and Kitson, B. (2017). *Avengers: Four*. New York: Marvel Comics.

Further Viewing

Berkowitz, S. (writer) and Riba, D. (director). (2003). Secret Society [Television series episode]. In: *Justice League* (producer B. Timm). Warner Bros.

Feige, K. (producer) and Favreau, J. (director). (2010). *Iron Man 2* [Motion picture]. Marvel Studios/Paramount Pictures.

Feige, K. (producer) and Gunn, J. (director). (2014). *Guardians of the Galaxy* [Motion picture]. Marvel Studios.

Feige, K. (producer) and Whedon, J. (director). (2012). *The Avengers* [Motion picture]. Marvel Studios.

Simone, J. (U.S. producer) and Satō, K. (director). (2013). *Tiger & Bunny, Set 1* [Television series]. Sunrise/Viz Media/Warner Bros.

Questions for Reflection and Discussion

1. What do you think about the notion "teaching is an isolated profession"? How well does it match your experience(s)? What do feel about working alone or with other teachers?

2. You probably have some idea about your relative introvert/extrovert personality. Here are two online quizzes (both free) you can take to reflect on your tendencies.

   • Longer (25 minutes): https://www.psychologytoday.com/us/tests/personality/extroversion-introversion-test.

   • Shorter (5 minutes): https://ideas.ted.com/quiz-are-you-an-extrovert-introvert-or-ambivert/.

   a. How do the questions or results inform your choices and actions?

   b. How much do your tendencies change in different situations—classroom teaching, school meetings, professional versus personal life, and so on?

3. Which of the different teammate roles presented in this chapter are you most likely to have? How does your specific role change depending on circumstances? Which role(s) do you admire and desire to have more often? Which role(s) do you find annoying or unnecessary? Why?

4. Review the article "What type of educator are you?" (Hill and Berardelli 2019), available for free at the ASCD website: https://www.ascd.org/blogs/what-kind-of-educator-are-you. Which of these types do you most closely match: Gate-Keeper, Coach, Advocate, Empowerer, Passionate, Relentless, Cheerleader, or Houdini? When are you like other types?

5. What are other types of teammates not addressed in this chapter (ASCD, Question 4)? How do they function in a group?

6. Reflect on Nick Fury's comment from the first *Avengers* movie (2012): "There was an idea . . . to bring together a group of remarkable people, see if they could become something more. See if they could work together when we needed them to fight the battles we never could."

   a. When have you experienced a similar need for such a group to form and work together?

   b. Describe a time when you participated on a team to accomplish something impossible for any single individual. What were the circumstances? Outcomes? Lessons learned?

7. Lesson study and curriculum integration are just two types of "teamwork tactics," examples of formal teacher collaboration in schools. What are some other programs, projects, or ways to encourage and support teacher collaboration?

8. How do you feel about formal (structured) collaboration compared with informal (spontaneous) collaboration? In what ways can schools and teachers encourage cooperation and communication without forcing "contrived collegiality" (Hargreaves 1994)?

References

Andrews, S.D., Sherman, R.R., and Webb, R.B. (1983). Teaching: The isolated profession. *Journal of Thought* 18 (4): 49–57.

A.V. Club. (2022). The Marvel Cinematic Universe movies, ranked from worst to best. https://www.avclub.com/the-marvel-cinematic-universe-ranked-from-worst-to-best-1834158288.

Beane, J.A. (1995). Curriculum integration and the disciplines of knowledge. *Phi Delta Kappan* 76 (8): 616–622.

Berliner, D.C. (2000). A personal response to those who bash teacher education. *Journal of Teacher Education* 51 (5): 358–371.

Brickhouse, N.W. and Bodner, G.M. (1992). The beginning science teacher: classroom narratives of convictions and constraints. *Journal of Research in Science Teaching* 29: 471–485.

Brophy, J. and Alleman, J. (1991). A caveat: Curriculum integration isn't always a good idea. *Educational Leadership* 49 (2): 66.

Campbell, C. and Henning, M. (2010). Planning, teaching, and assessing elementary education interdisciplinary curriculum. *International Journal of Teaching and Learning in Higher Education* 22 (2): 179–186.

Chong, W. and Kong, C. (2012). Teacher collaborative learning and teacher self-efficacy: the case of lesson study. *The Journal of Experimental Education* 80 (3): 263–283.

Cookson, W. (2005). The challenge of isolation and professional development. *Teaching Pre K-8* 36 (2): 14–16.

DeWitt, P. (2018). Are labels preventing students from succeeding? *Education Week* (13 May). https://www.edweek.org/education/opinion-are-labels-preventing-students-from-succeeding/2018/05.

Drake, S. and Reid, J. (2010). *Research Monograph #28: Integrated Curriculum-Increasing Relevance While Maintaining Accountability*. The Literacy and Numeracy Secretariat and the Ontario Association of Deans of Education.

DuFour, R. and Eaker, R. (1998). Professional learning Communities at work: best practices for enhancing student achievement. National Educational Service/Association for Supervision and Curriculum Development.

Dussault, M., Deaudelin, C., Royer, N., and Loiselle, J. (1999). Professional isolation and occupational stress in teachers. *Psychological Reports* 84: 943–946.

Edgerton, R. (1990). Survey feedback from secondary school teachers that are finishing their first year teaching from an integrated mathematics curriculum. Institution of Education Sciences (ED328419).

Feige, K. (producer) and Favreau, J. (director). (2010). *Iron Man 2* [Motion picture]. Paramount Pictures.

Fernandez, C. (2002). Learning from Japanese approaches to professional development: the case of lesson study. *Journal of Teachers Education* 53 (5), 393–405.

Goddard, L. and Goddard, D. (2007). A theoretical and empirical investigation of teacher collaboration for school improvement and student achievement in public elementary schools. *Teachers College Record* 109: 877–896.

Godsey, M. (2016). Why introverted teachers are burning out. *The Atlantic* (25 January). https://www.theatlantic.com/education/archive/2016/01/why-introverted-teachers-are-burning-out/425151/.

Gold, M.E. and Richards, H. (2012). To label or not to label: the special education question for African Americans. *Educational Foundations* Winter-Spring: 143–156.

Goodlad, J.I. (1984). *A Place Called School*. New York: McGraw-Hill.

Graham, P. (2007). Improving teacher effectiveness through structured collaboration: a case study of a professional learning community. *RMLE Online* 31 (1): 1–17. doi:10.1080/19404476.2007.11462044.

Greenleaf, R.K. (1970/2015). *The Servant as Leader*. South Orange, NJ: Greenleaf Center for Servant Leadership.

Greenleaf, R.K. (1977/2002). *Servant Leadership: A Journey into the Nature of Legitimate Power and Greatness, 25th Anniversary Edition*. Mahwah, NJ: Paulist Press.

Hargreaves, A. (1994). *Changing Teachers, Changing Times: Teachers' Work and Culture in the Postmodern Age*. New York: Teachers College Press.

Hayzlett, J. (2019). 4 principles of servant leadership. *Entrepreneur* (16 October). https://www.entrepreneur.com/article/340791.

Horn, I., Garner, B., Chen, I-C., and Frank, K.A. (2020). Seeing colleagues as learning resources: The influence of mathematics teacher meetings on advice-seeking social networks. *AERA Open* 6 (2): 1–19.

Ihrig, L. (2014). The effects of socialization on beginning science teachers' pedagogical decision making and science instruction. Doctoral dissertation. Iowa State University.

Internet Movie Data Base. (2002). Paul Rudd quotes. https://m.imdb.com/name/nm0748620/quotes.

Jacobs, H.H. (ed.) (1989). Interdisciplinary curriculum: design and implementation. Association for Supervision and Curriculum Development.

Kanellopoulou, E-M. and Darra, M. (2018). The planning of teaching in the context of lesson study: research findings. *International Education Studies* 11 (2): 67–82.

Kennedy, B. and Funk, C. (2016). 28% of Americans are 'strong' early adopters of technology. Pew Research Center (12 July). https://www.pewresearch.org/fact-tank/2016/07/12/28-of-americans-are-strong-early-adopters-of-technology/.

Leana, C. (2011). The missing link in school reform. *Stanford Social Innovation Review* 9 (4): 30–35. doi:10.48558/t2gn-2980. https://ssir.org/articles/entry/the_missing_link_in_school_reform.

Leana, C.R. and Pil, F.K. (2006). Social capital and organizational performance: evidence from urban public schools. *Organization Science* 17 (3): 353–366.

Leman, K. (2009). *The Birth Order Book: Why You Are the Way You Are*. Grand Rapids, MI: Revell/Baker Publishing Group.

Löfgren, H. and Karlsson, M. (2016). Emotional aspects of teacher collegiality: a narrative approach. *Teaching and Teacher Education* 60: 270–280.

Lonning, R.A., DeFranco, T.C., and Weinland, T.P. (1998). Development of theme-based, interdisciplinary, integrated curriculum: A theoretical model. *School Science and Mathematics* 98 (6): 312–319.

Lortie, D.C. (1975). *Schoolteacher: A Sociological Study*. Chicago: University of Chicago Press.

Louis, K.S., Kruse, S., and Marks, H. (1996). Schoolwide professional community. In: *Authentic Achievement: Restructuring Schools for Intellectual Quality* (ed. Fred Newmann and Associates), 179–203. San Francisco: Jossey-Bass.

MacIver, D.J. (1990). Meeting the needs of young adolescents: advisory groups, interdisciplinary teaching teams, and school transition program. *Phi Delta Kappan* 71 (6): 458–464.

Micheline, D., Layton, B., Romita Jr., R., and Infantino, C. (1979/2006). *Iron Man: Demon in a Bottle*. New York: Marvel Comics.

Miller, M. and Langmann, B. (2002). Every Marvel Cinematic Universe movie, ranked from worst to best. *Esquire* (11 November). https://www.esquire.com/entertainment/movies/g13441903/all-marvel-cinematic-universe-movies-ranked/.

Ostovar-Nameghi, S.A. and Sheikhahmadi, M. (2016). From teacher isolation to teacher collaboration: Theoretical perspectives and empirical findings. *English Language Teaching* 9 (5): 197–205.

Penteri, E., Karadimitriou, K., and Rekalidou, G. (2013). Involvement of future and active teachers in an advanced model of teacher education. Conference of the Network of Practice Exercises in the Department of Early Childhood Education, on "Improving the Education of Future Teachers in Crisis of Institutions: Proposals, Applications." Alexandroupolis (26–28 September).

Pil, F.K. and Leana, C. (2009). Applying organizational research to public school reform: the effects of teacher human and social capital on student performance. *The Academy of Management Journal* 52 (6): 1101–1124.

Pomson, A.D.M. (2005). One classroom at a time? Teacher isolation and community viewed through the prism of the particular. *Teachers College Record* 107 (4): 783–802.

Rogers, E.M. (2003). *Diffusion of Innovations, Fifth Edition*. New York: Simon & Schuster.

Ronfeldt, M., Farmer, S.O., McQueen, K., and Grissom, J.A. (2015). Teacher collaboration in instructional teams and student achievement. *American Educational Research Journal* 52 (3): 475–514.

Scholastic/Bill & Melinda Gates Foundation. (2012). Primary sources: America's teachers on the teaching profession. New York: Scholastic, Inc. https://www.scholastic.com/primarysources/pdfs/Gates2012_full.pdf.

Scholastic/Bill & Melinda Gates Foundation. (2014). Primary sources: America's teachers on teaching in an era of change. New York: Scholastic, Inc. https://www.scholastic.com/primarysources/PrimarySources3rdEdition.pdf.

Shah, M. (2012). The importance and benefits of teacher collegiality in schools: a literature review. *Procedia – Social and Behavioral Sciences* 46: 1242–1246.

Shriner, M., Schlee, B., and Libler, R. (2010). Teachers' perceptions, attitudes and beliefs regarding curriculum integration. *The Australian Educational Researcher* 37 (1): 51–62.

Shume, T.J. (2013). Computer savvy but technologically illiterate: Rethinking technology literacy. In: *The Nature of Technology: Implications for Learning and Teaching* (eds. M.P. Clough, J.K. Olson, and D.S. Nederhauser), 85–100. Rotterdam, The Netherlands: Sense Publishers.

Sleppin, D. (2009). New teacher isolation and its relationship to teacher attrition. Doctoral dissertation. Walden University.

Stepanek, J., Appel, G., Leong, M. et al. (2007). *Leading Lesson Study: A Practical Guide for Teachers and Facilitators*. Thousand Oaks, CA: Corwin Press.

Strahan, D. (2003). Promoting a professional collaborative culture in three elementary schools that have beaten the odds. *The Elementary School Journal* 104 (2): 127–146.

Supovitz, J.A. (2002). Developing communities of instructional practice. *Teachers College Record* 104 (8): 1591–1626.

Supovitz, J., Sirinides, P., and May, H. (2010). How principals and peers influence teaching and learning. *Educational Administration Quarterly* 46 (1): 31–56.

Vars, G.F. (1991). Integrated curriculum in historical perspective. *Educational Leadership* 49 (2): 14–15.

Vescio, V., Ross, D., and Adams, A. (2008). A review of research on the impact of professional learning communities on teaching practice and student learning. *Teaching and Teacher Education* 24 (1): 80–91.

Vo, A. (2022). All Marvel Cinematic Universe movies, ranked by Tomatometer. Rotten Tomatoes. https://editorial.rottentomatoes.com/guide/all-marvel-cinematic-universe-movies-ranked/.

Walker, T. (2016). Schools need introverted teachers, but avoiding burnout a challenge. *NEA Today* (4 February). https://www.nea.org/advocating-for-change/new-from-nea/schools-need-introverted-teachers-avoiding-burnout-challenge.

Wall, A. and Leckie, A. (2017). Curriculum integration: an overview. *Current Issues in Middle Level Education* 22 (1): 36–40.

Whitman, W. (1891/1982). Song of Myself (Section 51), in *Leaves of Grass. Whitman: Poetry and Prose*. New York: Library of America/Penguin Random House Inc.

Wilcox, J. (2017). Exploring the relationship between beginning science teachers' practices, institutional constraints, and adult development. Doctoral dissertation. Iowa State University.

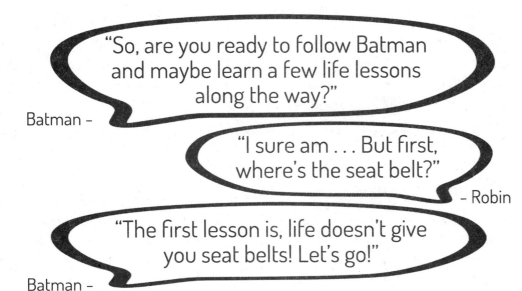

"So, are you ready to follow Batman and maybe learn a few life lessons along the way?"

Batman –

"I sure am . . . But first, where's the seat belt?"

– Robin

"The first lesson is, life doesn't give you seat belts! Let's go!"

Batman –

The LEGO Batman Movie (2017)

Sidekicks and Mentors

When Batman first appeared in *Detective Comics* #27 (May 1939), he acted as a lone vigilante in a gloomy, grim criminal world. This solitary status quo lasted less than a year. Eleven months later, in April 1940, the cover of issue #38 introduced readers to Batman's new sidekick–Dick Grayson, aka Robin, the Boy Wonder.

The impact was immediate. Robin's debut sold twice as many copies compared to the previous month's issue (Brooker 2001). Soon after, it seemed every hero had their own young sidekick–Captain America and Bucky, Green Arrow and Speedy, the Sandman and Sandy, Human Torch and Toro (Weldon 2016). Later on came Flash and Kid Flash, Aquaman and Aqualad, Wonder Woman and Wonder Girl, and more. Some pairs stuck around longer than others. Still, nothing outshines the original Dynamic Duo. It has endured for over 80 years, persevering through the occasional spat, split, or stand-in. "Even now in the cultural lexicon, Batman and Robin go together as naturally as peanut butter and jelly" (Geaman 2015, p. 1).

A Dynamic Duo

Robin's popularity and commercial success relate to the narrative advantages of having a sidekick. Sure, you get two characters for the price of one, an added bonus just like with any superhero team. But by bringing Robin into the mix, Batman doesn't have to do all the heavy lifting, story-wise. In an analysis of Robin's character, Bell (2015, p. 9) identifies three primary purposes of the sidekick's role:

- A point of identification for younger readers.
- A source of humor and emotional expression.
- A loyal partner and family member for Bruce Wayne.

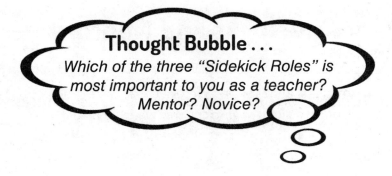

Thought Bubble . . .
Which of the three "Sidekick Roles" is most important to you as a teacher? Mentor? Novice?

Teachers also need sidekicks for these very same reasons—and more.

Depending on the situation, your sidekick may be any number of important individuals—a paraprofessional or paraeducator (or just plain "para"), a classroom aide or assistant, or even student helpers. For the purposes of this chapter, I focus on those sidekicks who are nearest to you as instructors and are up-and-coming as educators themselves. In other words, these sidekicks are pre-service teachers (PSTs), also known as "student teachers," "teacher candidates," or "teaching interns."

Pre-service teachers are college students—traditional or nontraditional, undergraduate or graduate—near the end of their preparation program. In addition to earning a degree, PSTs are seeking initial licensure or certification to get a job teaching in a school. As they approach program completion in their final few semesters, PSTs typically spend less time in college classes and more time in pre-K–12 schools. In the schools, the PST observes, assists, reflects, and eventually assumes regular classroom duties such as teaching and planning lessons. All the while, the host teacher—also called a *mentor* or *cooperating teacher*—models instruction and provides guidance and feedback. Essentially, the PST acts like a Robin to the host teacher's Batman. (Just replace shadowed alleyways or nighttime rooftops with a midday classroom and desks.)

While this present discussion deals mostly with PSTs, much of the content applies to all novice teachers or anyone new to your school, as well as the important classroom helper roles already mentioned. As you consider the ideas here, reflect on applications to your particular sidekick(s), as well as your own possible role as a sidekick to others.

First, however, let's get back to the importance of sidekicks. If you are a full-time teacher, you already have plenty of responsibilities. Why even consider adding more to your plate by hosting and mentoring a newbie PST in your classroom?

Of course, it's important to invest in the future generation of teachers. They need to learn how to teach. What better way than by working with experienced teachers and their students? But what's in it for you? Beyond altruism or the opportunity to share wisdom, there's got to be a more tangible reward. (And it's not money, either. Based on my experiences, mentor teachers may get a very small stipend for hosting PSTs—enough for a dinner out at a nice restaurant, but not *too* nice.)

For real motives to have a sidekick, look no further than Robin's role with Batman.

Sidekick Role #1: Point of Identification (and Accountability)

Batman earned his reputation as The World's Greatest Detective solving crimes through investigation and deductive reasoning. In early comic book adventures by himself, however, Batman would have to explain his ideas via lengthy monologues—talking to himself out loud, in thought bubbles, or captions. This proved monotonous for both the readers and writers. As cocreator Bill Finger noted, "Batman didn't have anyone to talk to, and it got a little tiresome always having him thinking" (cited in Bell 2015, p. 10). The solution was inspired by another famous detective, Sherlock Holmes, and his faithful companion Dr. Watson. Standing in for the audience, a sidekick will ask questions and serve as a sounding board. With Robin nearby, Batman could divulge insights and decisions with conversational ease.

When teachers work with a "sidekick" student teacher, they can verbalize the thought process about lesson plans, objectives, and reflections. Together, they draw out ideas that might otherwise remain unspoken or overlooked. Over the course of a semester, questions naturally arise such as "How did you know to do that?" "How much time should this take?" "Why did you respond that way?" or any number of "What ifs." A student teacher helps you consider possible "holes" in your lessons. Instead of letting your instruction switch to autopilot or cruise control, you can use a student teacher to hold yourself accountable and alert.

Furthermore, student teachers ask questions that encourage an orientation toward students' perspectives and learning. They are more apt to identify with your class—whether through less familiarity with the content, or by more familiarity with the students themselves. In most cases, a student teacher is younger than the mentor teacher. They are closer in maturity to the students in the classroom, whether by a few years or a few decades.

This was another way Robin complemented Batman. As Boy Wonder, he acted as a window into the Dark Knight's grown-up world. That role is especially important considering the original audience of young comic book readers. Artist Jerry Robinson observed how an additional sidekick "enlarged the readership identification. The younger kids could then identify with Robin, which they couldn't with Batman, and the older ones with Batman. It extended the appeal on a lot of levels" (cited in Bell 2015, p. 11).

Teachers should find work with a student teacher appealing on many levels. It fosters dialogue about your instructional craft. It helps keep you accountable and reflective. And it can help keep you young.

Sidekick Role #2: Source of Humor and Emotional Expression

Evidence of Robin's youthful spirit often appears through his sense of humor. Credit for the idea of a "wisecracking kid" goes to Batman cocreator Bob Kane, who believed comic relief would increase the sidekick's appeal to young readers (Weldon 2016). Corny jokes, puns, and a slew of "Holy [fill-in-the-blank]" comments followed, and soon became the Boy Wonder's call sign (along with his emerald green bloomers).

Working with a student teacher provides numerous opportunities for laughter. Together, you will find fun in the everyday struggles and successes of the classroom. I've talked before about humor as a type of superpower (Chapter 5), and even as an important role on any team (Chapter 9). An appreciation for good-natured wit begins early in one's career—such as student teaching—and can continue to thrive with ongoing mentorships.

I remember making multiple mistakes during my teaching internship experiences. Maybe I stumbled over a student's name, got stuck working an example problem, or was shaky in my content knowledge. (Thanks to one particular error, I'll never forget that 1 unit of horsepower equals 746 watts.) My mentors were quick to correct, but also quick to share a chuckle, then forget and move on. Such exchanges not only helped me in my development and confidence, but also modeled grace and humor for our students.

Miles Morales – "You got any Spider-Man tips you can tell me now?"

"Yeah, I got plenty. Disinfect the mask. You're gonna want to use baby powder in the suit, heavy on the joints. You don't want any chafing, right?" – Peter B. Parker

Miles – "Anything else?"

"Nope, that was everything." – Peter

Spider-Man: Into the Spider-Verse (2018)

In addition to humor, Robin's presence broadens the emotional stakes of any given Batman adventure. The sidekick's reactions "make the high points of each story higher, the low points lower" (Bell 2015, p. 12). Parallel peaks and valleys appear when working with a student teacher. They can help mentor teachers rediscover the thrill and joy of children learning concepts and mastering tasks. Student teachers experience similar highlights in their own successes.

And there will be moments of misery as well. (I remind my student teachers it's reasonable to feel like crying sometimes; that means you care enough to do it right.) Whether or not your student teacher cries, they will have days when nothing seems to work. This is when a mentor teacher can provide an even keel, rescuing their sidekicks from the depths of despair. Robin "can miss a clue or make another mistake because his youth means he is still growing and learning, capable of doing better next time" (Bell 2015, p. 13). As Batman to your student teacher's Robin, you can remind them about the natural trajectory of progress and pitfalls. And if you're brave, reassure them by sharing a few examples from your own experiences.

Sidekick Role #3: Loyal Partner and Family Member

Ultimately, a dependable sidekick develops into an indispensable partner. And sometimes it feels like you're inseparable. When you work with a student teacher, often you spend more daytime hours together than with your students, other colleagues, and your own family. And maybe you'll continue working with each other in the same building or district for the foreseeable future. Many times, however, student teachers graduate and get their credentials, then move on to another community.

Whatever the case, the two of you will share a bond that can continue in years to come. You might bump into each other at professional conferences and meetings. Or maybe you stay connected through social media. Each of you can be a treasured voice of encouragement and a listening ear to one another.

"As far as I'm concerned, we're in this together."

- Kate Bishop,
Hawkeye,
"Echoes" (2021)

No matter how much you keep in touch, a student teacher will keep memories of their moments with you. Your sage advice and supportive comments will come back to them at key moments. Your example of teaching and professionalism will echo in their own instruction and interactions. And you, too, will remember your conversations and collaborations. And you may rely on these experiences as you take another sidekick under your wings.

Serving as a mentor to new teachers provides further meaning to your career in education. You are not only reaching and relating to students in your immediate care, but impacting others who will do the same, along with their future classrooms. It is a unique combination of both instant and enduring influence. And it has direct dividends, as much as a superhero with a sidekick. Glen Weldon, author of *The Caped Crusade* (2016), notes how "The mere presence of Robin in a given story deepens its impact by supplying Batman with something to care about, over and above any abstract notion of justice" (p. 35). Likewise, deepen your impact in education by inviting others to join your classroom crusade.

Caption Capture: In addition to the three sidekick roles discussed here, list **other advantages** for teachers working with classroom "sidekicks."

Teaching (and Learning) with a Sidekick

Teacher sidekicks come in a variety of shapes and sizes, as do mentorships and school induction programs. Likewise, you can find a wide range of resources and materials for mentoring and supporting new teachers (e.g., Breaux and Wong 2003; New Teacher Center 2021; Rudney and Guillaume 2003; and others). Although we're focusing on preservice teachers (PSTs), many of these examples translate to other settings and alternative apprenticeships. Regardless of your sidekick's origins or circumstances, the following sections discuss some common elements and progressions toward an established teaching career.

Early and Engaged

Whatever the type of experience, I encourage PSTs to get involved with their placement school as early as possible. This can be challenging, since they have countless other responsibilities—family, work, college courses, extracurricular activities, and more—that compete for attention. Nevertheless, the time and energy they invest in their internship experiences will pay off.

This commitment starts prior to day one. Before the first day of classes when students arrive, the PST should visit the school and begin working with the mentor teacher. Together, they can get to know one another without the constant buzz of nearby children and typical school-day bustle. Also, the PST can participate with regular back-to-school in-service events or professional development activities for staff. Formal meetings, training sessions, and—perhaps most important—allotted worktime enable the newcomer to establish a firm foundation and familiarity with the school, and with their mentor.

When students show up on the first day of classes, having the PST present and participating makes a powerful statement. In the children's eyes, the classroom already has two teachers. One individual (the mentor) may be more outspoken and experienced, but the second (the PST) stands on equal footing as a fellow instructor. For all the kids know, both of you have been in that classroom since the dawn of time.

Consider the undesirable effects of a PST not appearing until after the semester begins. Already, the mentor teacher and students have developed a rapport. When the PST joins, they are at a disadvantage of catching up with procedures and personalities in the classroom (as well as the entire school building). This is true whether the delay is a month, a week, or even a few days. If that's not bad enough, the children tend to perceive this newbie as an unwelcome and uninformed intruder. Good luck getting students to listen and follow anything the PST has to share, whom they consider as "less than" their "regular" teacher.

Early exposure also affords the PST an opportunity to witness those crucial first days of the semester. Over and over, studies reaffirm this early time of year as a pivotal moment. Regardless of grade level, the first days are when a teacher establishes classroom climate and initiates management expectations (Bohn, Roehrig, and Pressley 2004; Brooks 1985; Cook et al. 2018; Duong et al. 2019; Emmer, Evertson, and Worsham 2003; Evertson, Emmer, and Worhsam 2003; Wong and Wong 2009). A PST who is present on the very first day has firsthand exposure and experience with setting up classroom culture. More than merely witnessing these procedures, they can get involved, providing assistance and building relationships.

Some PSTs may not join a school placement until the spring semester or midterm. In that case, the classroom they visit will have an established culture and system of routines. Nevertheless, starting on or before the very first day of classes in the second semester (or a trimester) can help solidify the PST's role. And even though it may be the middle of the academic year, a lot of classrooms resemble the back-to-school fall season. They resume with a fresh start, featuring new student groups and reteaching procedures.

Depending on where the PST is in their preparation program, the amount of participation may vary. If they are just beginning their teacher education coursework and field experiences, required tasks may be mostly observational. With more expertise in later semesters, the PST will be expected to play a more active role. Regardless of requirements, those with greater involvement and interactions with students will see beneficial results in the form of heightened awareness, composure, and abilities in the classroom.

Despite this recommendation for early immersion, mentors and PSTs should be cautious about doing too much, too soon. Don't let the PST dive in with more than they can handle. Overwhelmed, their interactions with students may backfire, alienating some in the classroom. The effects are similar to a sidekick that bursts onto the scene. Overexposure to a new character—especially a brash upstart—can lead to audience annoyance and rejection. (Or if taken to the extreme, it can lead to violence. Such was the case for the second Robin, Jason Todd, whom fans voted to kill off in 1988's "A Death in the Family" story, *Batman #426–429*. But don't worry; Jason came back to life years later, albeit as a grumpy antihero.)

A PST's preparation to teach requires both structured guidance and free experimentation. While there is give-and-take throughout the mentorship, a purposeful progression toward more responsibility is the best path. The first few steps are essential, establishing expectations and relationships from the start.

Introductions and Orientations

Early engagement requires more than classroom experiences with the students. Teaching is complicated work, and schools are complicated places. Many districts or buildings provide an orientation session to welcome interns and PSTs (as they often do for new teachers and staff). These events are helpful, and my university colleagues and I also provide a checklist for additional guidance. This is not an exhaustive "how-to," nor does it require strict step-by-step adherence. Instead, it is simply a resource for easing the PST into the school experience. Again, depending on your sidekick's situation, different items are more applicable than others.

Example Checklist for Mentor Teachers of Interns (Pre-Service Teachers)

- [ ] **Establish a rapport** with your intern. Remember your own feelings of anxiety, curiosity, and hope when you were just beginning.

- [ ] **Plan an introduction** for your intern that conveys a professional status to pupils, faculty, and staff.

- [ ] Acquaint your intern with **emergency procedures** (fire, tornado, intruder, etc.).

- [ ] Acquaint your intern with **classroom routines, procedures, and management** strategies.

  - In particular, share expectations regarding pupil behavior and the resulting consequences when those expectations are not met. This is an area about which interns tend to be most anxious. They don't want to overstep, but they do want to help and be seen as a co-teacher alongside you.

  - Communicate what role you want your intern to play in handling classroom management/discipline issues, noting if/how this role will change as the semester progresses.

- [ ] Assist your intern in **learning students' names** (e.g., provide a seating chart, or encourage them to create one, so they can use it to learn students' names).

- [ ] Enable your intern to **interact with the students** by distributing papers, taking attendance, teaching mini-lessons, and working with individual pupils and small groups.

- [ ] Acquaint the intern with your preferred **lesson-planning format**. Your intern may also have a required lesson plan format for their university, which they can share with you.

- [ ] Apprise your intern of class work that has been completed and that is currently underway. **Share texts, materials, tentative plans for upcoming units** so your intern can plan ahead and prepare to assist you as needed.

- [ ] **Guide** your intern in developing and teaching their own activities, lessons, and/or units, as appropriate for the curriculum scope and sequence and overall semester schedule. Earlier teaching experiences may include **co-teaching strategies** together.

- [ ] Set aside some time regularly to **confer with your intern**. Establishing email correspondence may be one solution.

- [ ] **Communicate concerns** or questions to the university supervisor.

Try using this example checklist as a jumping-off point for your interns or other classroom "sidekicks." What else would you add to the list?

Regardless of circumstances, mentors can get their mentees off to a good start with intentional introductions. In addition to students, consider other individuals and offices with whom the PST will work. Start with teachers in neighboring classrooms, who are critical lifelines in a pinch. Also introduce everyone in your department or team. Not all at once, necessarily, but within the first few days, if not before the start of school. In the same way that you may give your PST class rosters or seating charts with students' names and faces, provide a helpful staff directory—perhaps a printout from the school website. Have them meet guidance counselors, special education staff, and the librarian/media specialist. Principals and other administrators are important to know, along with office and custodial personnel (these last two groups are perhaps the *most* important to know for daily school life).

When you provide introductions, use it as an opportunity to practice professionalism. Refer to your PST as "Miss _____," "Mister _____," or whatever the appropriate honorific (see Chapter 2). Be careful not to get too casual and use first names only. This perpetuates any notions that the PST is not a "real" teacher. Definitely avoid condescending monikers like "Skippy, the Student Teacher." Use of formal titles is not only fitting in front of students, but also with colleagues. Many times, it will be the first season of life when your PST regularly goes by their official "teacher name," so help them get used to it.

Other items for orientation are school facilities and operations. Don't assume anyone has told your PST about these details. Do they check in with the front office every time they visit? What's the best building entrance? If the PST drives to school, where should they park? Do they need a code to use the copier machine? Can they access school email and enter online grades? Do they get an official school lanyard or ID card? And of course, where is the best bathroom?

Your PST will benefit from introductions outside the school, as well. If they are new to the community, help them make connections. This could be with individuals or groups who are key school partners or stakeholders. What local businesses or services are noteworthy, for either professional networking or personal interest? (For example, what are some healthy options to unwind after a stressful week?) Other resources are educational organizations and associations—either regional or national—which you can encourage your PST to join. All of these provide support and additional resources for their teaching and learning.

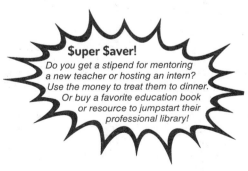

$uper $aver!
Do you get a stipend for mentoring a new teacher or hosting an intern? Use the money to treat them to dinner. Or buy a favorite education book or resource to jumpstart their professional library!

Classroom Cooperation

While a PST may spend more time observing at the start of the program or semester, eventually they must join as active participants in classroom instruction. They are your sidekick, after all, not a spectator. Avoid turning responsibility for each lesson into an "I do" versus "You do" demarcation. In most cases, one or the other should not do all of the work. Both the mentor and PST contribute as co-teachers. Cooperative instruction can appear in many different forms. The chart in the following image summarizes types of co-teaching, as outlined by researchers and teacher educators Bacharach, Heck, and Dahlberg (2010).

Co-Teaching Strategies

Summarized from Bacharach, Heck, and Dahlberg (2010)

One teach, one observe		One teacher has the primary instructional responsibility while the other gathers specific observational information on students or the (instructing) teacher.
One teach, one assist		One teacher has the primary instructional responsibility while the other assists students with their work and monitors behaviors, often lending a voice to students or groups who hesitate to participate or add comments.
Station teaching		Station teaching occurs when the co-teaching pair divides the instructional content into parts. Each teacher instructs one of the groups. The groups then rotate or spend a designated amount of time at each station. Independent stations are often used along with teacher-led stations.

Parallel teaching 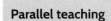	Parallel teaching occurs when the class is divided, with each teacher instructing half the students. However, both teachers are using similar strategies and addressing the same instructional material. The greatest benefit to this method is the reduction of the student-to-teacher ratio.
Supplemental teaching 	Supplemental teaching allows one teacher to work with students at their expected grade level while the other teacher works with those students who need the information or materials extended or remediated.
Alternative teaching (differentiated) 	This teaching strategy provides two approaches to teaching the same information. The learning outcome is the same for all students; however, the avenue for getting there is different.
Team teaching 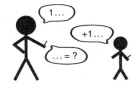	Team teaching incorporates an invisible flow of instruction with no prescribed division of authority. From the students' perspective, there is no clearly defined leader; both teachers share the instruction, are free to interject information, and are available to assist students and answer questions.

Summary of co-teaching strategies.
Which ones work best for you and your classroom "sidekicks"?

The type of co-teaching a mentor and PST employ for a particular lesson depends on the content and classroom context. It also may rely on each person's relative comfort level. Still, learning often includes a healthy dose of discomfort (Taylor and Baker 2019). Like a sidekick, PSTs will stumble and go through growing pains. But these are truly teachable moments. The novice should be aware and alert of their hard-earned progress throughout the entire process. Leadership coach Peter Bregman (2018, 2019) calls this "emotional courage," which entails honest conversations, reflection, and overall transparency.

That said, a PST shouldn't lay out all of their faults in front of a class of kids. There are already plenty of clumsy moments during lessons. The time for frank discussion and review can occur afterward, in the quiet safety of an empty classroom or teachers' lounge. As a mentor teacher, watch and record noteworthy aspects of your PST's teaching so you can share this data later, if they don't bring it up themselves. (During an early lesson in my PST experience, my university supervisor provided "color commentary" while he was videorecording my teaching, adding remarks throughout: "Be careful with . . ." "Watch out for . . ." "Here you can . . ." I still use this grainy footage, sharing it with my own PSTs so they can notice the wealth of instructional decisions and actions to consider—and critique.) No matter how you review a lesson, don't just focus on negative things. Every activity has some positive elements, too. This includes those "disasters" that feel like everything went wrong. If you dig deep enough, you'll find a jewel.

Embedded in some of the co-teaching strategies here are actions aligned with lesson study (Fernandez 2002; Kanellopoulou and Darra 2018). As a mentor, you work with your PST to plan goals, prepare lessons, observe and review each other's instruction, and more (Stepanek et al. 2007). Lesson study can serve as a sort of ongoing professional development for new teachers (Archer et al. 2013). You may not be able to complete a full-scale lesson study and research project. Still, the components can provide a framework for collaboration and mentoring. Review the "teamwork tactics" shared in Chapter 9 for more details. And while you're at it, consider how the co-teaching strategies discussed here apply not only to sidekicks, but to all of your teammates.

Caption Capture: In what ways is working with "sidekick" novice teachers **similar** to teaching younger students in the classroom? **Different**?

Similar	*Different*

A Delicate Dynamic

As with teacher collaborations in general, mentorships involve a delicate balancing act between structure and flexibility. Added to this complexity is a third individual present in most pre-service teaching experiences—the university supervisor. Typically, the supervisor is an official representative of the teacher preparation program at the university or college. They come from all walks of educational life—faculty professors or adjunct instructors; full-time or semi-retired; with experiences as teachers, administrators, graduate students, and more.

Beyond personal attributes, teacher preparation programs themselves use various models and materials for internship experiences. Whether individual or institution, you'll notice different levels of attention and communication. Some are more hands-on than others, and some partnerships are stronger or weaker depending on their history.

While we're speaking of pre-service teacher programs here, similar variations occur in new teacher induction programs. A supervisor may have close connections to your particular classroom and content, or they may come from other departments, buildings, or even districts. And although there may be a system in place for procedures and policies, each individual supervisor will bring their own perspectives and personalities.

When a supervisor joins the pair of mentor teacher and PST, they form what Rudney and Guillaume (2003) call the "supervision triad" (p. 46). This trio almost sounds like a superhero team, and in some ways it is. Notice that the PST is included in the group, since they also play an important role in planning, discussing, and reflecting on their growth. Even so, they may not feel they are on equal footing with their mentor and supervisor, considered to have the final say on the PST's qualifications.

Each member of this triad has different duties and perspectives, which has the potential to create tension and friction. The mentor is ultimately responsible for the students in their classroom and school. The supervisor answers to a university's teacher preparation program and accreditation. The PST has to navigate between priorities of these two individuals, as well as their own professional and personal development.

If that's not challenging enough, the PST is still technically a guest in the mentor teacher's classroom, even with early engagement and participation with students. Based on their experiences, the mentor has developed a pragmatic approach that may appear intuitive and natural. Sometimes, the PST has an alternative idea they'd like to try—or must implement for college credit—and need the mentor's approval. Consider the unease of a PST telling their mentor, "Thanks for showing me your plans, but I'm going to do something else. Okay?" How the conversation ends depends on many factors, including the idea's quality and the mentor's flexibility.

To this awkward mix, add an outside supervisor. Usually, they are less known by both mentor and PST. And they make fewer appearances—perhaps once or twice a month, compared to the daily interactions between mentor and PST. After visits, the supervisor offers suggestions or valuations, which may feel judgmental toward both PST and mentor.

I liken this interaction to when a third character swoops onto the scene to join the hero and sidekick. In the case of Batman and Robin, maybe it's Catwoman or Batgirl or even Alfred the butler. Having a rich history with the Dark Knight, they exchange inside jokes, playful jabs, or resentful asides. Or the third party could be another hero like Wonder Woman, Superman, or the Flash. While well-established, these heroes offer much different skill sets and personalities compared to Batman. As a result, the sidekick may grow confused or conflicted, dealing with mixed messages and ideas unlike their mentor's example. It can be a sticky situation.

The good news is that in a supervision triad, all three have the same overall objective—helping students learn. In their book, *Maximum Mentoring* (2003), Rudney and Guillaume identify universal threads of effective mentorships, and one major component is clear communication in all directions. Troubles arise from muddled messages and silent assumptions. Other necessary ingredients for a healthy triad are honesty, support, reflection, encouragement, and an emphasis on application. I've learned the same principles to be true through my own experiences as a PST, mentor, and supervisor across different schools and states.

No matter the system or program, PSTs and other novices in the classroom require support and clear communication regarding tasks and expectations. They need multiple mentors—official or unofficial, school- and university-based—that can model professionalism and practical application of educational theory. When PSTs do begin assuming more duties, mentors provide beneficial feedback that encourages future attempts and further reflection. As PSTs gain more independence in their teaching, they also should practice more independent thought. In the end, our young wards must spread their wings and fly—and occasionally flail or flutter—toward freedom.

Thought Bubble . . .
*At this point in your teaching, are you more like **Batman or Robin**? In what ways?*

Find Your Batman

Whether a novice or veteran, we can all serve as sidekicks to others. This may mean fulfilling a supportive role to assist others. It also means having a "mentee attitude" throughout your career. Lifelong learning means there's always more to learn. So who is your Batman? Whom do you consider a mentor and model for teaching excellence? It doesn't have to be anything official. But keep your eyes and ears alert for others you can emulate.

Pay attention to your colleagues during staff meetings and informal gatherings. Who shows a pattern of positive attitude and productive contributions? Maybe they don't talk much; but when they do, people listen. In the teachers' lounge at lunch, who has the integrity to respect privacy and students' personhood? As you walk the hallways, whose classrooms emanate a lively and learning-focused aura? These are the types of teachers you want as your mentor.

Your Batman doesn't have to be in your same field of study. They could teach a different subject or grade level, or possibly work in a different building. When I taught high school science, I learned about student jobs and group strategies by spending time in the classroom of a fourth grade teacher. Another colleague—who taught business and accounting—demonstrated classroom procedures akin to an office or company. Since his senior students were close to graduation, he allowed more flexibility and freedom to instill personal responsibility and professional judgment.

Caption Capture: Write down tips or tools shared by a mentor—ones that you **still use** today:

Maybe your best mentors are those you meet at conferences or through educational organizations. You can learn much from workshops, including useful nuggets that aren't even the main topic. In my time attending presentations, I've gained all kinds of classroom techniques such as attention-getters, call-and-response, recruiting volunteers, and more. Membership in associations also provides publications and online resources—an ongoing mentorship through the written word.

Or maybe your Batman is also your Robin. When I recruit teachers to act as mentors for interns and PSTs, a common response is "Sure, I'd love to learn from them!" This may sound backwards, as the mentor teacher is expected to serve as an example and provide wisdom. However, these mentors know a PST can offer fresh perspectives of the classroom. This could be due to college coursework and other endeavors, or a closer proximity to younger generations and pop culture trends. In my experience, the mentor teachers most eager to learn from PSTs are also the ones with the most to teach. These mentors have a lot to offer because they, too, are willing to learn and grow.

Sidekick Paragons

Do you work with paras? Paraeducators or paraprofessionals—also called instructional assistants or teachers' aides—play a pivotal role in schools. They often assist students with exceptionalities, but appear in all kinds of classrooms. Between 1990 and 2018, the total number of paras in U.S. public schools doubled (Bisht et al. 2021). Whereas the ratio of teacher-to-para was 6:1 in 1990, now it is closer to 4:1. The positive effects of paras on student achievement are noticeably stronger for students in historically underserved and underrepresented populations (Hemelt, Ladd, and Clifton 2021).

So how do you partner with paras? Your school should have a system in place for working with paras, and you can find resources for partnership strategies as well. One text—*Effective Strategies for Working with Paraeducators* (Styer and Fitzgerald 2015)—provides a helpful overview. Three overarching topics are cultivating teamwork, establishing protocol, and providing supervision and evaluation. This trio aligns with themes we've addressed in both this chapter on Sidekicks as well as Chapter 9. As with any working relationship, clear communication about expectations and feedback is essential.

When planning lessons, teachers can provide details about appropriate tasks for the para(s). Organize these guidelines in a manner similar to the notes you make for your own actions and interactions during the lesson (Yates et al. 2020). Specific instructional roles include one-on-one attention with an individual student (Hall et al. 2010), small group or station teaching (Chopra, Carroll, and Manjack 2018), and focused interventions (O'Keeffe, Slocum, and Magnusson 2011). Paras also help with general management and recordkeeping (Kerry 2005), as well as building connections with students' families (Chopra and French 2004; Lewis 2005).

You can find additional ideas from the co-teaching strategies provided in this chapter (Bacharach, Heck, and Dahlberg 2010). Check with your school or department on any particular requirements or guidelines for expected para duties. And, of course, check with your para(s). Like always, communication is a key step for productive collaboration.

To Be Continued!

Further Reading

David, P., Nauck, T., and Ramos, H. (2017). *Young Justice Book One*. New York: DC Comics.

Dixon, C. and Templeton, T. (2021). *Batman Adventures: Robin, The Boy Wonder*. New York: DC Comics.

Fraction, M. and Aja, D. (2021). *Hawkeye: The Saga of Barton and Bishop*. New York: Marvel Comics.

Lemire, J. and Nguyen, D. (2022). *Robin & Batman*. New York: DC Comics.

Slott, D., Gage, C., Ramos, H., and Camuncoli, G. (2012). *Spider-Man: Danger Zone*. New York: Marvel Comics.

Taylor, T. and Cabal, J. (2019). *Friendly Neighborhood Spider-Man, Vol. 1*. New York: Marvel Comics.

Further Viewing

Burton, T. and MacGregor-Scott, P. (producers) and Schumacher, J. (director). (1995). *Batman Forever* [Motion picture]. Warner Bros.

Feige, K. (producer) and Russo, A. and Russo, J. (directors). (2014). *Captain America: The Winter Soldier* [Motion picture]. Marvel Studios.

Igla, J. and Feige, K. (producers) and Thomas, R., Templemore-Finlayson, A., and Ellwood, K. (directors). (2021). *Hawkeye* [Television series]. Marvel Studios.

Lin, D., Lord, P., Miller, C., and Lee, R. (producers) and McKay, C. (director). (2017). *The LEGO Batman Movie* [Motion picture]. Warner Bros.

Questions for Reflection and Discussion

1. In addition to the advantages discussed in this chapter, what are other benefits to having a sidekick in the classroom? Drawbacks?

2. Complete the "Are You Batman or Robin" survey at https://brainfall.com/quizzes/ are-you-batman-or-robin/#rJSm6hDvz and review the results. How well does this

relate to your classroom teaching and mentoring? In what ways are your results similar? Different? Compare your results with your colleagues, students, family, or friends. What surprises you? What questions would you ask to determine relative roles as mentor or sidekick?

3. Marvel Comics architect Stan Lee was not a fan of youthful sidekicks. In an interview with National Public Radio, he stated, "I hated teenagers in comics because they were always sidekicks. And I always felt if I were a superhero, there's no way I'd pal around with some teenager, you know." (You can read the full interview transcript at https://www.npr.org/2006/12/27/6684820/ stan-lee-on-realism-in-the-world-of-comic-heroes.)

    a. What do you think about sidekicks for superheroes? How could they be beneficial (or detrimental) to the main character? The creators and their story? The readers?

    b. What about sidekicks in the classroom? How could they be beneficial (or detrimental) to the mentor teacher? The students? The lesson or activity?

4. Not all superhero sidekicks are teenagers (e.g., Happy Hogan in *Iron Man*, Wong in *Doctor Strange*, Foggy Nelson in *Daredevil*, etc.). Similarly, many novice teachers are experienced adults, older than their mentors. How might this change in age difference impact the relationship? In what ways does it not matter?

5. Think of other experiences when you've had a mentor or sidekick. These could be past or present, and could be a hobby, another occupation, other organizations, and so on. What insight or ideas have you gained from these mentorships? How well do they translate to educational settings like the classroom or school building?

6. What is the best piece of advice or wisdom you've gotten from a mentor? If you've worked with a lot of sidekicks before, what have you learned from them?

7. Paras (paraeducators/paraprofessionals/aides/etc.) play a unique role in the classroom, often focused on particular students or services. If you've worked with a para before, what advice or insight do you have on collaborating with them? What questions or concerns do you have about working with paras?

8. A common adage is "actions speak louder than words." To what extent is this applicable to mentoring new teachers? What else is necessary to support a new teacher's learning and teaching?

References

Archer, R., Pope, S., Onion, A., and Wake, G. (2013). Working group report: lesson study in research and CPD in mathematics education. http://www.bsrlm.org.uk/wp-content/uploads/2016/02/BSRLM-IP-33-2-01.pdf.

Bacharach, N., Heck, T.W., and Dahlberg, K. (2010). Changing the face of student teaching through coteaching. *Action in Teacher Education* 32 (1): 3–14.

Bell, J.L. (2015). Success in stasis: Dick Grayson's thirty years as Boy Wonder. In: *Dick Grayson, Boy Wonder: Scholars and Creators on 75 Years of Robin, Nightwing and Batman* (ed. K.L. Geaman), 8–27. Jefferson, NC: McFarland & Company, Inc., Publishers.

Bisht, B., LeClair, Z., Loeb, S., and Sun, M. (2021). Paraeducators: growth, diversity and a dearth of professional supports. Annenberg Institute at Brown University (EdWorkingPaper: 21–490). https://www.edworkingpapers.com/sites/default/files/ai21-490.pdf.

Bohn, C.M., Roehrig, A.D., and Pressley, M. (2004). The first days of school in the classrooms of two more effective and four less effective primary-grades teachers. *The Elementary School Journal* 104 (4): 269–287. http://www.jstor.org/stable/3202942.

Breaux, A. and Wong, H. (2003). *New Teacher Induction: How to Train, Support, and Retain New Teachers*. Mountain View, CA: Harry K. Wong Publications.

Bregman, P. (2018). *Leading with Emotional Courage: How to Have Hard Conversations, Create Accountability, and Inspire Action on Your Most Important Work*. Hoboken, NJ: John Wiley & Sons, Inc.

Bregman, P. (2019). Learning is supposed to feel uncomfortable. *Harvard Business Review* (21 August) https://hbr.org/2019/08/learning-is-supposed-to-feel-uncomfortable.

Brooker, W. (2001). *Batman Unmasked: Analyzing a Cultural Icon*. New York: Continuum Publishing.

Brooks, D.M. (1985). The first day of school. *Educational Leadership* 42 (8): 76–78.

Chopra, R.V., Carroll, D., and Manjack, S.K. (2018). Paraeducator issues and strategies for supporting students with disabilities in arts education. In: *Handbook of Arts Education and Special Education* (eds. J.B. Crockett and S.M. Malley), 105–128). New York: Routledge.

Chopra, R.V. and French, N.K. (2004). Paraeducator relationships with parents of students with significant disabilities. *Remedial and Special Education* 25 (4): 240–251.

Cook, C.R., Coco, S., Zhang, Y. et al. (2018). Cultivating positive teacher-student relationships: preliminary evaluation of the Establish-Maintain-Restore (EMR) Method. *School Psychology Review* 47 (3): 226–243.

Duong, M.T., Pullmann, M.D., Buntain-Ricklefs, J. et al. (2019). Brief teacher training improves student behavior and student-teacher relationships in middle school. *School Psychology* 34 (2): 212–221.

Emmer, E.T., Evertson, C.M., and Worsham, M.E. (2003). *Classroom Management for Secondary Teachers, Sixth Edition*. Boston: Allyn & Bacon.

Evertson, C.M., Emmer, E.T., and Worsham, M.E. (2003). *Classroom Management for Elementary Teachers, Sixth Edition*. Boston: Allyn & Bacon.

Fernandez, C. (2002). Learning from Japanese approaches to professional development: the case of lesson study. *Journal of Teachers Education* 53 (5): 393–405.

Geaman, K.L. (2015). Introduction: the sensational character find of 1940. In: *Dick Grayson, Boy Wonder: Scholars and Creators on 75 Years of Robin, Nightwing and Batman* (ed. K.L. Geaman) 1–5. Jefferson, NC: McFarland & Company, Inc., Publishers.

Hall, L.J., Grundon, G.S., Pope, C., and Romero, A.B. (2010). Training paraprofessionals to use behavioral strategies when educating learners with autism spectrum disorders across environments. *Behavioral Interventions* 25: 37–51.

Hemelt, S.W., Ladd, H.F., and Clifton, C.R. (2021). Do teacher assistants improve student outcomes? Evidence from school funding cutbacks in North Carolina. *Educational Evaluation and Policy Analysis* 43 (2): 280–304.

Kanellopoulou, E-M. and Darra, M. (2018). The planning of teaching in the context of lesson study: research findings. *International Education Studies* 11 (2): 67–82.

Kerry, T. (2005). Towards a typology for conceptualizing the roles of teaching. *Educational Review* 57 (3): 20–30.

Lewis, K.C. (2005). Chapter 6: Seen but not heard: ESEA and instructional aides in elementary education. *Review of Research in Education* 29 (1): 131–149.

New Teacher Center. (2021). Teacher induction program standards. https://newteachercenter .org/resources/teacher-induction-program-standards/.

O'Keeffe, B.V., Slocum, T.A., and Magnusson, R. (2011). The effects of a fluency training package on paraprofessionals' presentation of a reading intervention. *The Journal of Special Education* 47: 14–27.

Rudney, G.L. and Guillaume, A.M. (2003). *Maximum Mentoring: An Action Guide for Teacher Trainers and Cooperating Teachers*. Thousand Oaks, CA: Corwin Press, Inc.

Starlin, J. and Wolfman, M. (1998/2011). *Batman: A Death in the Family*. New York: DC Comics.

Stepanek, J., Appel, G., Leong, M. et al. (2007). *Leading Lesson Study: A Practical Guide for Teachers and Facilitators*. Thousand Oaks, CA: Corwin Press.

Styer, C. and Fitzgerald, S. (eds.) (2015). *Effective Strategies for Working with Paraeducators, Second Edition*. Kirkland, WA: Styer Fitzgerald Publishing.

Taylor, K.B. and Baker, A.R. (2019). Examining the Role of Discomfort in Collegiate Learning and Development. *Journal of College Student Development* 60 (2): 173–188.

Weldon, G. (2016). *The Caped Crusade: Batman and the Rise of Nerd Culture*. New York: Simon & Schuster.

Wong, H.K. and Wong, R. (2018). *The First Days of School: How to Be an Effective Teacher, Fifth Edition*. Mountain View, CA: Harry K. Wong Publications.

Yates, P.A., Chopra, R.V., Sobeck, E.E. et al. (2020). Working with paraeducators: tools and strategies for planning, performance feedback, and evaluation. *Intervention in School and Clinic* 56 (1): 43–50.

"My father had a saying,
one that I even teach my students today.
'Where's the future? Right here.
Who's life is this? Mine.
What are you gonna do with it?
Live it by any means necessary.'"

– Black Lightning,
The Flash,
"Armageddon, Part 3" (2021)

 # Legacy Heroes

With nearly a century of stories in all kinds of media, superheroes have created a unique legacy. In fact, many famous heroes are legacies themselves. A character may assume a heroic identity, but they are not the only one who has served as that particular superhero.

For instance, the Flash—the "fastest man alive"—has been several different people over the years: Jay Garrick, Barry Allen, Wally West, Bart Allen, and others. The title of Green Lantern started with Alan Scott, but changed hands between Hal Jordan, Guy Gardner, John Stewart, Kyle Rayner, Simon Baz, Jessica Cruz, and Sojourner Mullein—and that's just humans from Earth! Even Batman has loaned his costume to others. His former sidekick Dick Grayson—the first Robin—has already spent two lengthy stints as the Dark Knight in the comic books (Dixon 1994; Morrison and Quitely 2001).

Marvel's own superheroes have also shared their namesakes with others—Captain America, Captain Marvel, Iron Man, Thor, Black Panther, Black Widow, Hawkeye, and more. Sometimes the mantle switches back and forth; sometimes it changes permanently. If you are familiar with movies and shows of the Marvel Cinematic Universe, you've seen many of these heroes passing their legacy to supporting cast members or new characters entirely.

Legacy heroes offer the chance to consider new perspectives and personalities, while still giving honor and respect to the original. It also reinforces the notion that a superhero is more than a single individual. Their power extends beyond one person or time period.

Just like teachers.

Thought Bubble . . .
In what ways have you witnessed teachers as "legacy heroes"?

Touching the Future

Think back to the famous quote from teacher-astronaut Christa McAuliffe: "I touch the future. I teach." This is more than a catchphrase or motto. It's the truth. Teachers make a difference in the lives of others—today and tomorrow, near and far. That is our legacy.

Teachers can shape the trajectory of history through daily classroom interactions. I'm not just talking about curriculum and content. (Review your teaching purpose and visionary goals from Chapter 1.) For those of you who teach a specific subject, most of your students will not pursue careers in your field of study. But they can have a greater awareness of these endeavors and appreciate everyday applications. Most of your students will not become teachers, either. But they can glean a love of learning and joy to help others learn. And they can emulate your pedagogical prowess as they teach in other settings—from new employee orientations to family dinner conversations. Reverberating through all of these endeavors are echoes of your own instruction.

We teach more than children. We reach their families, our communities, and colleagues. Get involved in your school's neighborhood. Even if you don't live in the same town, become familiar with the culture and citizens. Participate in local events and celebrations. (As a bonus, it's always fun to see a student's astonished expression when they notice their teacher outside the school.)

Join your educational associations, not just for professional development but for opportunities to advocate and enrich others. Present at conferences, write for publications, and volunteer for committees that shape policy and programs. Certainly, there are different seasons in life when you can do more or less, but always do something.

Outreach is one antidote to burnout and another way to serve others. Remind yourself that your work goes beyond the classroom walls.

"A hero is someone who is concerned about other people's well-being and will go out of his or her way to help them, even if there is no chance of a reward. That person who helps others simply because it should or must be done, and because it is the right thing to do, is indeed without a doubt a real superhero."

- Stan Lee

Honoring Your Heroes

Why become a teacher?

There are countless other occupations to consider. But for most teachers, it's more than just a job. In their discussion of effective teaching, Harry and Rosemary Wong (2009) put it this way: "A job is something a person does to earn a living; a career is something a person does as a lifetime pursuit" (p. 305). I had another mentor explain it to me this way:

"As a job, teaching is a lousy choice. You can find much easier ways to earn a paycheck. Teaching is a calling. You teach because you care. It's a commitment." These wise words came from one of my heroes. Not Captain America or Mr. Incredible. His name is Mr. Mueller.

Leigh Mueller was my high school chemistry and physics teacher, and he's one reason why I became a science teacher. Sound familiar? I imagine many teachers pursued the call of teaching due to the influence of another. I've had many influential teachers (see this book's dedication), but Mr. Mueller is noteworthy on several accounts. I remember his kind demeanor and calm conversational tone—never provoked by the random antics of rambunctious teenagers.

Mr. Mueller knew his stuff, too, sharing science concepts with vivid life applications. Sample lessons include dropping pumpkins from a grain elevator to calculate impact velocity, riding inside an airplane to experience forces of flight, and comparing bites of real and mock apple pies to investigate flavor chemistry. But class was never just about fun and games. We spent much more time analyzing experiments and deriving equations. Mr. Mueller emphasized process and understanding over mere memorization. He wanted his students to know our stuff, too. And I can attest that thanks to this high school preparation, my college-level Chemistry I and Physics I classes both felt like review.

Mr. Mueller shared a lot of wisdom during my two years in his classroom. One word came up time after time: *integrity*. He would often use this single word as his response to a student question or comment. Or it even served in place of giving any other directions. All Mr. Mueller had to say was "integrity," and the class knew what to do (and not do). Through his model, I've learned the importance of preparing students for life.

Even after graduating and moving out of town, I've revisited Mr. Mueller's classroom a few times. Once was when I was in my early years of college. I had returned to my hometown for winter break. College classes had finished for the semester, but high schools were still in session. Mr. Mueller welcomed me to join his class and observe a lesson. During this visit, I informed him I was thinking of becoming a science teacher. That's when he offered his insights about the call and commitment of teaching.

On another visit about 10 years later, I was finishing my Ph.D. program in science education (after half a decade of teaching high school science), and I wanted to give Mr. Mueller an update on my career path. My future wife was with me at the time (I was giving her a tour of the school), and she snapped a photograph of Mr. Mueller and me. I still use a copy of that picture on my door sign at work. It's a useful reminder of the many reasons why I teach. The portrait is also a conversation starter with students and colleagues about the calling of our profession—and its enduring effects.

I hope this tribute rings true with your own school memories and teacher experiences. Everyone has a unique path and perspective. Not everything will resonate the same way with each of us. And a classroom full of students will have different responses to your teaching. As hard as you try, you won't be everybody's favorite teacher. (But you can still try.) We all have a variety of personalities and preferences. But we can each be kind and compassionate, creative and collaborative in our education adventures. Students will not remember every lesson, but they can learn many more messages from our teaching.

> **Caption Capture:** Think of your **favorite teachers.** What did they have in common? What made them unique?

Influential Teachers and the "Super Seven"

What makes an influential teacher?

In one of my own research projects (Bergman 2018), I surveyed nearly a hundred future science educators (pre-service teachers), asking them to share information about their most influential teacher. The following list highlights the "Super Seven"–the seven most common traits found in responses describing these influential teachers. I've also included example comments, along with how frequently each trait appeared in the total number of answers. In other words, the first two–passion and rapport–were both in 42% of all the survey responses about influential teachers.

1. Passion (42%)
   - "She was unfailing in her positivity."
   - "[G]ot so excited about the subjects he was teaching . . . the interest was infectious."

2. Rapport (42%)
   - "She cared about us and how much we learned."
   - "He personally acknowledged each student."

3. Pedagogy (30%)
   - "She knew how to break down the material so it was easy to understand."
   - "[K]new when students have problems and what to say to each student, if it is different words to different students."

4. Time (30%)

- "[T]ook the time out to explain stuff."
- "He gave lots of time to students after class. As much as they needed to get it."

5. High expectations (24%)

- "She pushed me to be a leader in school."
- "The way she never gave up on you and made you believe in yourself more than you could imagine. She always had high standards for us."

6. Fun (22%)

- "She always made teaching look fun."
- "[He] showed me that chemistry is fun."

7. Helpful (20%)

- "She was always very helpful and kind."
- "His door was always open to his students and he was willing to help any student with whatever problems they had."

These responses came from prospective science teachers in Kansas, so obviously the sample size is limited. But ask yourself which of these traits align with *your* most influential teachers. What other characteristics did they exhibit?

In my study, most survey responses (80%) included more than one of these seven traits in their "influential teacher" descriptions. That means the Super Seven characteristics are not isolated, but rather intertwined with one another, even *synergistic*. Also consider that almost two-thirds (63.8%) of the influential teachers described by these future science teachers did not teach science. And as evident in the example responses, the actual subject was often not even mentioned. There is more to influential teaching than the content you teach. Or to quote Muppets creator Jim Henson (2005), "[Kids] don't remember what you try to teach them. They remember what you are" (p. 113).

Ask yourself what sort of influence you want to have on your students. How can you make a lasting, positive difference in the lives of your students, starting right now?

Leaving a Legacy

In many ways, every teacher is a "legacy hero." The privilege is not receiving personal fame for our profession, but in inspiring and shaping the generations to come.

Our impact is both immediate and long-term. Your classroom influence can reach the greater community and cross borders. This includes relationships with students, families, and fellow champions in education.

As with any genuine legacy, every teacher eventually leaves the classroom, and another will take their place. But the effects of our work extend into the far future, in the lives of those we taught as well as others we will never know.

Now *that* is a superpower.

 ## To Be Continued!

Further Reading

Baron, M., Messner-Loebs, W., and Guice, J. (1987/2020). *The Flash: Savage Velocity*. New York: DC Comics.

Morrison, G. and Quitely, F. (2009/2011). *Batman and Robin: Batman Reborn*. New York: DC Comics.

Waid, M. and Ross, A. (1996/2019). *Kingdom Come*. New York: DC Comics.

Whitley, J. and Charretier, E. (2017). *The Unstoppable Wasp, Vol. 1: Unstoppable!* New York: Marvel Comics.

Wilson, G.W., Alphona, A., Wyatt, J., and Pichelli, S. (2014/2019). *Ms. Marvel, Vol. 1: No Normal*. New York: Marvel Comics.

Further Viewing

Blejer, A. and Kamoche, D. (producers) and Skogland, K. (director). (2021). *The Falcon and the Winter Soldier* [Television series]. Marvel Studios.

Cook, J. and Harcourt, M. (U.S. producers) and Nagasaki, K. (director). (2016). *My Hero Academia*: Season 1 [Television series]. Studio Bones/Funimation.

Feige, K. (producer) and Russo, A. and Russo, J. (directors). (2019). *Avengers: Endgame* [Motion picture]. Marvel Studios.

Feige, K. and Moore, N. (producers) and Coogler, R. (director). (2022). *Black Panther: Wakanda Forever* [Motion picture]. Marvel Studios.

Roven, C., Snyder, D., Snyder, Z., and Suckle, R. (producers) and Jenkins, P. (director). (2017). *Wonder Woman* [Motion picture]. Warner Bros.

Questions for Reflection and Discussion

1. In addition to impacting current and future generations, what other aspects of teaching make it like a superpower?

2. Review those influential and favorite teachers from your own learning and life. Are they still teaching? Reach out to them and share your appreciation and encouragement. Write a note, or send a card or an email. If you're comfortable, "friend" them on social media. If possible, visit them in person.

3. Think of people you know who may follow your footsteps as new or future educators. Maybe these individuals have never thought about pursuing teaching as a profession. Starting now, how can you help pass along a teaching legacy?

References

Bergman, D.J. (2018). Prospective teachers' perceptions of influential teacher qualities. *The Advocate* 23 (6). https://newprairiepress.org/advocate/vol23/iss6/6/.

Dixon, C. (1994/2019). *Batman: Prodigal*. New York: DC Comics.

Henson, J. (2005). *It's Not Easy Being Green: And Other Things to Consider*. Glendale, CA: Kingswell.

Morrison, G. and Quitely, F. (2009/2011). *Batman and Robin: Batman Reborn*. New York: DC Comics.

Wong, H.K. and Wong, R. (2009). *The First Days of School: How to Be an Effective Teacher, Fourth Edition*. Mountain View, CA: Harry K. Wong Publications.

Index